Older Than The Nation

John Bard McNulty

Older Than
The Nation

The Story of
The Hartford Courant

The PEQUOT PRESS, Inc.

Stonington   Connecticut

TO

MARJORIE, HENRY, AND SARAH

Table of Contents

Introduction

"It is, dear reader, one of the oldest institutions on the continent." So wrote Thomas M. Day one hundred years ago—on The Courant's one hundredth anniversary.

The evidence of The Courant's long career exists in bound volumes going back to Number 00, October 29, 1764. A year earlier, the French and Indian War had come to an end with the signing of the Treaty of Paris. George Washington, a 32-year-old officer who had won fame at Fort Duquesne, had moved to Mount Vernon to attend to his estates. Washington would one day advertise some of his land for sale in The Courant.

Today The Courant's editorial page carries the daily heading: "Established 1764—The Oldest Newspaper of Continuous Publication in America."

The priority of American newspapers often has been investigated. Among recent studies is one by the distinguished historian of American journalism, Frank Luther Mott, who published his conclusion in the winter edition of the 1963 *Journalism Quarterly:* "Everything considered, it looks to me as though the *Hartford Courant* has the best claim to priority at the present time."

The Courant's claim to being the oldest rests on at least four points:

1. *Since 1764 The Courant has always been The Courant.* It traces no ancestry. It is not the outgrowth of a *Ledger,* which was the outgrowth of a *Post,* which sprang from a *Sentinel,* and so on. Since the beginning, *Courant* has formed the principal part of the newspaper's name at every stage. The Courant is not, as Editor Charles Hopkins Clark once put it, like the elderly gentleman who celebrated his golden wedding anniversary because, although he had been married to three successive wives, the sum of his married life came to fifty years.

The name *Courant,* incidentally, came into English about the year 1600 from the same word in Dutch, meaning newspaper.

2. *Since 1764 The Courant has always been published in the city where it started.* It has never, like some early newspapers, moved from town to town.

3. *There are no unexplained gaps in The Courant's 200-year record.* The Courant missed a few early issues, as when the Stamp Act went into effect or when the colony's supply of paper gave out. But these were problems of supply such as face any longstanding business firm. The Courant has always soon resumed service, continuing the regular numbering of its issues, and publishing from the same office and under the same owners. The Courant, as a business, has an entirely unbroken record.

4. *In its 200 years The Courant has bought, but has never been bought by, other newspapers.* It has merged with younger newspapers, which have lost their names and their identities in The Courant. The title *Courant* covers, and always has covered, this continuously published newspaper.

Acknowledgments

The writing of this history of The Courant has extended over several summers as well as during a sabbatical leave granted by Trinity College.

My particular thanks go to the staff of the Connecticut Historical Society, where much of the basic reading was done, and to the staffs of the Trinity College Library, the Watkinson Library, the Connecticut State Library, and the Yale University Library. I am deeply grateful, too, to the many persons who have granted me interviews.

I am indebted to the previous work of many scholars, and particularly to the published research of Dr. F. L. Mott, Dr. J. E. Smith, and Dr. A. E. VanDusen.

The staff of The Courant has been most helpful in supplying information and expediting the work. I am particularly indebted to Mr. Bob Eddy, Assistant to the Publisher, for his constructive criticism. It should be added that the members of the newspaper staff have been most scrupulous in leaving the interpretation of the findings entirely to my judgment.

During the course of the writing, my wife and family have frequently helped by protecting me from interruptions. My wife's patient reading and rereading of the manuscript has resulted in many helpful suggestions.

J. Bard McNulty

Trinity College, Hartford, September, 1964

1764-1777
Getting Started

E VERY DAY, in the hours before dawn, a roar fills the press-room of The Hartford Courant as massive presses turn out the latest issue of a newspaper founded in 1764. From loading platforms nearby, a fleet of trucks stacked with bundles of newspapers takes off for points throughout the state. Soon, newspapers begin arriving in nearly every one of Connecticut's 169 towns, along highways and byways, on front porches and in red route boxes—copies of a journal that still bears at the top of its front page, as it has over the past 200 years, the name, Courant.

When subscribers unfold The Courant over breakfast coffee, they read a newspaper that was already in its twelfth year when it printed the Declaration of Independence as news. It is an historic newspaper—the oldest of continuous publication in America. As readers turn the pages, they find news gathered with the help of electronic devices and set in type by automated tape-fed machines.

It was a late October day in 1764 when draymen unloaded the heavy timbers of Thomas Green's printing press and carried them up to the rooms above Mooklar's barber shop. As Green helped the men unload, he could see the gambrel-roofed State House—Court House, it was called in those days—across the street. Almost opposite stood the venerable Flagg Tavern, favorite resort of politicians during sessions of the General Court. Small shops and comfortable clapboard homes stood along the rutted main street under arching elms and maples.

Hartford was a moderately prosperous Connecticut River town of 4,000 persons. Sea captains and farmers, merchants and craftsmen lived side by side along Queen Street, as the principal thoroughfare was called. The river to the east and the wooded hills to the west hemmed in the growing community, bringing untamed nature pretty close to everyone's back yard. In 1776 townsfolk chased a bear down the main street past the South Meeting House and out into the meadows, where they shot and roasted it for dinner.

When all parts of the heavy press had been hauled up to the second story—the whole contraption, assembled, weighed half a ton—Green and his assistant, Ebenezer Watson, began putting it together with wooden pegs and big iron bolts. The assembled press stood higher than a man, sturdy and dignified.

Two hundred years later a press believed to have been Green's stands in The Courant's building, after a long sojourn in Wethersfield where it was used by the Comstock-Ferre Company to print labels on seed packages. Operating the machine is man's work. It is also slow work. To put out a single issue with the same number of pages and for the same number of subscribers as The Courant has today would have taken Thomas Green well over a year and a half—that is, if he had worked his usual 70-hour week.

Although operating the press took good muscle there was plenty of light work around a colonial print shop. Women often helped by wetting down the paper before it was printed, hanging it up to dry afterwards, or distributing the type after the printing was done. Thomas Green's wife, Desire, probably planned to help in the new shop, but she already had her hands full as the mother of two-year-old Nancy and seven-month-old Lucy, and she was expecting a third child.

So, in 1766, Green hired a lad of nine, George Goodwin. It is a tradition in the Goodwin family that George was hired as soon as he could carry a pail of water up the stairway to the shop, which may have truth, as one of George's jobs was probably that of wetting the paper for the press.

Green's shop evidently had a young staff: Thomas Green, 29; his assistant, Ebenezer Watson, 20, whom Thomas had known in New Haven; and, a bit later, George Goodwin, 9, water boy and general printer's devil.

The young proprietor was not new at the printing game. Printing had been his father's trade, his grandfather's, and his great-grandfather's. Great-grandfather Samuel had arrived in Cambridge, Massachusetts, at the age of 16 at the same time as Governor Winthrop. He could recall living in an empty cask when there was no other shelter from the weather. In Cambridge he learned the printing trade, and 22 of his descendents became printers. By the time Thomas was ready to set up his press over Mooklar's barber shop, New England had learned to look to the Greens for printing.

Thomas himself had learned a good deal about type and editing in his grandfather Timothy's printshop in New London. Then, in 1760, he had been given charge of James Parker's press in New Haven, where he turned out more than 50 publications. While in New Haven, he must have come to realize what a large volume of printing is required by a legislature in session. In those days, Connecticut had two capitals, New Haven and Hartford. So when his employer sold out in 1764 to Benjamin Mecom, nephew of Benjamin Franklin, Thomas Green moved to Connecticut's other capital at Hartford, where there was no newspaper.

The Green shop in Hartford, like other colonial print shops, provided a wide variety of goods and services. Printing alone could not keep the proprietor solvent. Green did job printing—broadsides, pads, and whatever his patrons ordered for business or personal use —and some book and pamphlet publishing. One of his first productions in Hartford seems to have been Ellsworth's *Almanack.* His shop served as a bookstore and stationer's, where Hartford people could buy primers, spelling books, bibles, copies of Watts' psalms, catechisms, quill pens, inkstands, and so on. He also offered pewter ware,

"AT THE HEART AND CROWN"—THE COURANT'S FIRST
SIGNBOARD
Letter in the bird's mouth signifies fast news reporting

The Connecticut Courant.

MONDAY, October 29, 1764.   (Number 00.)

• *HARTFORD*: · Printed by T.homas Green, at the Heart and Crown, near the North-Meeting-House.

Hartford, October 29th, 1764.

OF all the Arts which have been introduc'd amongst Mankind, for the civilizing Human-Nature, and rendering Life agreeable and happy, none appear of greater Advantage than that of Printing: for hereby the greatest Genius's, of all Ages, and Nations, live and speak for the Benefit of future Generations.—

Was it not for the Press, we should be left almost intirely ignorant of all those noble Sentiments which the Antients were endow'd with.

By this Art, Men are brought acquainted with each other, though never so remote, as to Age or Situation; it lays open to View, the Manners, Genius and Policy of all Nations and Countries and faithfully transmits them to Posterity.—But not to insist upon the Usefulness of this Art in general, which must be obvious to every One, whose Thoughts are the least extensive.

The Benefit of a Weekly Paper, must in particular have its Advantages, as it is the Channel which conveys the History of the present Times to every Part of the World.

The Articles of News from the different Papers (which we shall receive every Saturday, from the neighbouring Provinces) that shall appear to us, to be most authentic and interesting shall always be carefully inserted; and great Care will be taken to collect from Time to Time all domestic Occurrences, that are worthy the Notice of the Publick; for which, we shall always be obliged to any of our Correspondents, within whose Knowledge they may happen.

The CONNECTICUT COURANT, (a Specimen of which, the Publick are now presented with) will, on due Encouragement be continued every Monday, beginning on Monday, the 19th of November, next: Which Encouragement we hope to deserve, by a costant Endeavour to render this Paper useful, and entertaining, not only as a Channel for News, but assisting to all Those who may have Occasion to make use of it as an Advertiser.

☞Subscriptions for this Paper, will be taken in at the Printing-Office, near the North-Meeting-House, in Hartford.

BOSTON, October 1

IT is now out of fashion to put on mourning at the funeral of the nearest relation, which will make a saving to this town of twenty thousand sterling per annum.—It is surprizing how suddenly, as well as how generally an old custom is abolished, it shows however, the good sense of the town, for it is certainly prudent to retrench our extravagant expences, while we have something left to subsist ourselves, rather than be driven to it by fatal necessity.

We hear that the laudable practice of frugality is now introducing itself in all the neighbouring towns, (and it were to be wished it might thro'out the government) an instance of which we have from Charlestown, at a funeral there the beginning of last week, which the relatives and others attended, without any other mourning than which is prescribed in a resent agreement.

October 8. There seems to be a disposition in many of the inhabitants of this and the neighbouring governments to cloath themselves with their own manufacture.—At Hampstead, on Long Island, in the Province of N. York, a company of gentlemen have set up a new woolen manufactory, and having given notice to gentlemen shopkeepers and others, of any of the provinces, that by sending proper patterns of any colour, they may be supplied with broad-cloths, equal in fineness, colour, and goodness, and cheaper than any imported: the proprie-

not be true in fact, that the severity of the new a—t of p——t is to be imputed to letters, representations, NARRATIVES, &c. transmitted to the m——y about two years ago by persons of eminence this side the water—And that some copies of letters are actually in this town, and others soon expected. —To whatever cause these severities are owing, it behooves the colonies to represent their grievances in the strongest point of light, and to unite in such measures as *will be effectual* to obtain redress.

The northern colonists have sense enough, at least the sense of *feeling*; and can tell where the *shoe pinches*—The delicate ladies begin to find by experience, that the Shoes made at Lyn are *much easier* than those of the make of Mr. Hose of London—What is become of the noted shoemaker of *Essex*?

It is fear'd by many who wish well to *Great Britain*, that the new A—t of P——t will greatly distress, if not totally ruin some of HER own manufactures—It is thought that by means of this A—t, less of her woolen cloths, to the amount of some thousands sterling, will be purchas'd in this cold climate the insuing winter.

We are told that all the Funerals of last Week were conducted upon the new Plan of Frugality.

Nothing but FRUGALITY can now save the *distress'd* northern colonies from impending ruin—It ought to be a consolation to the good people of a certain province, that the great-

FIRST ISSUE OF THE COURANT APPEARED ON OCTOBER 29, 1764
Each page was about the size of a standard typewriter sheet

PUBLISHER JOHN R. REITEMEYER AT PRESS BELIEVED TO HAVE
PRINTED FIRST COURANT
Wooden press stands in Courant's lobby today

HANNAH BUNCE WATSON

Widowed at 27, she took over Courant, saved it in its worst crisis, saw it lead all American newspapers in circulation, and become the Patriots' major organ during the Revolution

and other household items. Today one can buy stockings at drug stores; then, one could buy calico at the printer's.

At some time before the end of October, 1764, Green hung out a sign in front of his shop—the Heart and Crown. The device vaguely suggested a coat of arms, the center being a shield surrounded with curlicues intertwined with leaves and flowers, the whole surmounted by a bird of doubtful species with a folded letter in its beak. The shield bore a large crown, beneath which appeared a heart that looked like a big valentine. Green probably knew that the heart and crown were already in use as a device by the Fleets, printers of Boston. Perhaps he thought the heart would suggest Hartford, and the crown, his loyalty as a British subject. The new sign took its place among others long familiar to Hartford inhabitants: the Sheaf of Wheat, the Bunch of Grapes near the door of Bull's tavern, and many others.

On Monday, October 29, 1764, Green published the first issue, "Number OO," of a proposed newspaper. It was to be called The Connecticut Courant and would, he explained, "on due Encouragement be continued every Monday, beginning on Monday, the 19th of November, next: Which Encouragement we hope to deserve, by a constant Endeavor to render this Paper useful, and entertaining, not only as a Channel for News, but assisting to all Those who may have Occasion to make use of it as an Advertiser."

At the top of Page 1 he declared:

> Of all the Arts which have been introduc'd amongst Mankind, for the civilizing Human-Nature, and rendering Life agreeable and happy, none appear of greater Advantage than that of Printing: for hereby the greatest Genius's of all Ages, and Nations, live and speak for the Benefit of future Generations.—
>
> Was it not for the Press, we should be left almost intirely ignorant of all those noble Sentiments which the Antients were endow'd with.
>
> By this Art, Men are brought acquainted with each other, though never so remote, as to Age or Situation; it lays open to View, the Manners, Genius and Policy of all Nations and Countries and faithfully transmits them to Posterity . . .

Green promised that the news in his paper would be timely and accurate—timely, that is, as American readers of that day understood timeliness, and accurate as far as the uncertain news channels would allow. Green explained that he received "Articles of News . . . every Saturday, from the neighbouring Provinces." These he proposed to publish the following Monday, almost as soon as he could get the items into type. This was quick service—but many of the items were already weeks or months old when he received them. His first issue carried a few items more than three months old. The section headed "FOREIGN AFFAIRS" bore the dateline, "Naples, July 10"—news three months and nineteen days old.

Local Hartford news generally was given short shrift by Green, following the practice common among colonial newspaper proprietors. It was believed everyone in town knew the local news anyway. In Green's prospectus fewer than a dozen lines carried strictly Hartford news: a notice of the death of Mrs. Sarah Lord and the departure of Samuel Wyllys for England.

The prospectus also gave promise of "a constant Endeavor to render this Paper . . . entertaining." As a sample, Green ran some pretended news in his first issue under faked datelines, items undoubtedly recognized by his readers as impudent political satire. Like most of his fellow townsmen, Green regarded William Pitt as the ablest of England's statesmen, and Lord Bute as a bungling ass. These views disguised as maritime news appear under the heading

INTELLIGENCE EXTRAORDINARY.

Deal, July 25 . . . We hear the ships Pitt, Temple and Devonshire, (which for some time have been laid up) are immediately ordered into commission, as his M———y is now sensible how active and successful these ships have always been.—At which time its thought the Sloops Tyranny, Oppression and Slavery, will be taken off their stations in America.

An irreparable defect has been discovered on board the Bute . . . they have condemned her; she is ordered up to Tower wharf, and as her head is a very curious piece of workmanship, it is to be taken off and placed on Temple bar.

The obvious irreverence of this and other items—today they might appear as editorials or under the by-line of columnists—no doubt tickled the merchants of Hartford, who must have been delighted that a spokesman for colonial rights had set up his press in their town. In any event, Green seems to have found the encouragement he was looking for—and thus began the publication of the newspaper that was to become the oldest in the nation.

Green varied his news offerings with poetry and other material designed to be "instructive." The first poem, a satire on Spanish claims to timber rights in the new world, appeared on December 10, 1764. On March 25, 1765, The Courant carried on its front page the alphabet, in Roman and italic, with a suggestion for a new letter, and with a pronunciation key for each letter. In so doing, Green started a tradition. The Courant still prints poetry in its weekly column, "This Singing World," and it still stresses education, as in its sponsorship of the Junior Classical League for young people interested in Greek and Latin classics.

ITALIAN. ROMAN.

Capitals.	Small.	Capitals.	Small.	How pronounced & spelt.
A	a	A	a	a
B	b	B	b	bee
C	c	C	c	ke
D	d	D	d	de
E	e	E	e	ce
F	f	F	f	eff
G	g	G	g	ghee
H	h	H	h	ke
I	i	I	h	aitch
J	j	J	i	i
K	k	K	j	jee
L	l	L	k	ka
M	m	M	l	ell
N	n	N	m	em
O	o	O	n	en
P	p	P	o	o
Q	q	Q	p	pee
R	r	R	q	que
S	s	S	r	ar
T	t	T	s	ess
U	u	U	t	tee
V	v	V	u	cu
W	w	W	v	ev
X	x	X	w	wu
Y	y	Y	x	ecks
Z	z	Z	y	yi
&	&		z	ez
			&	and

ALPHABET MADE PAGE ONE IN 1765
Courant's interest in education started early

Green's Courant, in appearance at least, had about it something of catch-as-catch-can. The earliest issue carried two columns on each of the four pages. Later, Green switched to three columns, and on occasion to two and a half. Sometimes a half column was run horizontally, so that the paper had to be turned sideways to be read. The pages were about the size of standard typewriter sheets, varying from 11½ to 14 inches long and from 6¾ to 9 inches wide. Partly because the paper was thick and rough and the type small, the impressions varied and were sometimes blurred.

Newspaper historian Frank Luther Mott says that newspaper circulations at that period ranged between a few hundred and a thousand or more. The average circulation of Boston papers Mott reports as 600. If his estimate that five per cent of white families in the colonies received a weekly newspaper can be applied to Hartford in Green's time, the circulation of the early Courant may have been less than 100 copies per issue for the first year or so. At any rate, circulation was miniscule by modern standards; that is why newspaper proprietors had to diversify to stay in business. The Courant probably sold for 6 shillings a year. Advertising increased under Green's management until it took up nearly a third of the paper.

In the first half of May, 1765, Green moved to the second floor of James Church's shop across from the Court House and next to David Bull's tavern. Church's shop was conveniently located for legislators or anyone else with business at the Court House across the street, and Green may have thought it advantageous to associate his own shop with that of another retailer.

However, a small but ominous cloud was forming on the horizon. In May, 1765, The Courant reported George Grenville's proposed Stamp Act, and June brought news that Jared Ingersoll of New Haven had been appointed stamp officer for the colony. Printers especially hated the levy because it taxed imported paper and paper goods. By September, 1765, feeling against the Stamp Act ran high. Organizations of Sons of Liberty had been formed in many towns. Jared Ingersoll had been hanged in effigy in New London and elsewhere. As the effective date for the Act, November 1, drew nearer, Green printed many columns of news and comment on the agitation sweeping the Colony.

Hartford heard in mid-September that Jared Ingersoll was on his way to the city to petition the General Assembly for protection. In one of its infrequent exclusive stories, The Courant reported the events that followed:

On Thursday morning, the whole Body (including a considerable Number from this Town) set off, on their intended Expedition, and in about an Hour met Mr. Ingersoll, at the Lower End of Wethersfield, and let him know their Business,—he at first refused to comply, but it was insisted upon, that he should resign his Office of Stamp Master, so disagreeable to his Countrymen,—After many Proposals, he delivered the Resignation . . ., which he read himself in the Hearing of the whole Company; he was then desired to pronounce the Words, *Liberty and Property,* three Times, which, having done, the whole Body gave three Huzzas.

It was one thing to deal with Mr. Ingersoll; it was quite another to cope with the Stamp Act itself, which went into effect as scheduled. No one knew for certain what to do. Nobody dared distribute the stamped paper that had arrived from overseas. Not one newspaper appeared on stamped sheets. Some newspaper proprietors simply broke the law. They published as usual on unstamped paper. Others, like the *Pennsylvania Journal,* temporarily suspended publication "in order to deliberate whether any methods can be found to elude this chain forged for us." Still others got around the law by resorting to technicalities, for instance by issuing papers without serial numbers so that they might pass as broadsides or handbills, which required no stamp. Green continued to conduct his business and gather news but withheld publication during November and the first week of December. On December 9 he issued his Courant on unstamped paper, evidently without molestation.

The colonies' anger over the Stamp Act brought about its repeal the following March. News of repeal, reaching Hartford on May 19, 1766, caused a celebration that provided Green with a local story of joy and sudden tragedy:

The morning was ushered in by the ringing of bells; the shipping in the river displayed their colors; at 12 o'clock 21 cannon were discharged and the greatest preparations making for a general illumination. But sudden was the transition from the height of joy to extreme sorrow. A number of young gentlemen were preparing fireworks for the evening in the chamber of the large brick school house, under which a quantity of powder granted by the Assembly for the purposes of the day, was deposited. Two companies of militia had just received a pound a man, by the delivery of which a train was scattered from the powder cask to the distance of three rods from the house where a number of boys were collected who, undesignedly and unnoticed, set fire to the scattered powder which soon communicated to that within doors and in an instant reduced the building to a heap of rubbish . . .

There follows the names of the six men killed and more than 20 injured.

One lesson the colonists learned from the Stamp Act was that if they wanted an uninterrupted supply of paper they had better get into the business of papermaking themselves. Christopher Leffingwell built the first paper mill in Connecticut, at Norwich, in 1766, and The Courant promptly began advertising for linen rags to make the paper.

Ten years later The Courant owned its own paper mill.

During 1767 Green began to think of returning to New Haven to join his younger brother, Samuel, who had started a press there in competition with Mecom. Thomas Green saw the possibilities of associating himself with two printing houses, one in each of the colony's capitals. Accordingly, with his assistant, Watson, he formed the partnership of Green and Watson in Hartford, probably in Decem-

A STONE HORSE, belonging to *Niel McLean, jun.* He goes by the Name of

Handsome Harry.

He is about 14 Hands and half high, a Dun Colour, with a Lift down his Back, a fine Blaze in his Face, trots all, and is three Quarters blooded. A very smart Horse, runs a swift Race, is five Years old, and was bred at Naraganset, by one John Easton.

COURANT'S FIRST ADVERTISING PICTURE
Prancing horse appeared in 1769

ber, 1767; and then, during the same winter, he moved back to New Haven as a partner in the printing establishment of Messrs. Thomas and Samuel Green.

In Hartford, Watson took charge of The Courant, Green's interest in it being solely financial. Watson spruced up the paper in several ways. He stated the policy, which is still the policy of The Courant, that no letters would be published unless the writers made their names known to the printer. Letters of a merely provoking nature he would reject. He livened up the advertising column by running The Courant's first advertising picture—of a prancing horse.

Before a year was out he moved his printing shop to new, more spacious quarters "near the Great Bridge"—that is, the bridge on the main street over the Little River, later known as the Park River. It was a two-story building with entrances on the ground floor and rooms for the press and printing materials upstairs. The ground-floor retail shop offered for sale sugar, chocolate, spices, coffee and tea, hats and pocketbooks, as well as stationer's goods.

One problem for Watson was collecting from subscribers. Less than a year after moving his shop he threatened delinquent subscribers with stoppage of the paper. When this failed, he actually withheld publication for a single issue to show he meant what he said. He wrote in his issue for November 6, 1769, that "by reason of the unexpected and persevering negligence of far the greater part of our customers . . . we are obliged to think of discontinuing the publication of our weekly paper . . . on the 11th of December next . . . We assure our customers that . . . we have not received from them upon an average so much as two shillings out of six, of what has been due from them . . ."

Watson's advertised rate for The Courant was six shillings a year, eight shillings for delivery by special post rider. Advertisements cost three shillings for ten lines for three weeks, and sixpence for each insertion thereafter. Such were the quoted rates. But a subscriber or advertiser, delinquent for many months, might appear with a load of cordwood or a basket of eggs in payment for what he owed. Barter was common and cash scarce. For many years The Courant gave subscribers the alternatives of paying in wheat, rye, flour, wood or cash. It may have been the cumbersomeness of barter and the difficulty of conveying cash that finally led Green to give up his financial interest in The Courant in 1770.

By 1771, post riders were calling for payment from Courant subscribers as far north of Hartford as Northfield, Massachusetts, and as far south as Durham; as far east as Coventry and Andover, and as far west as Poughkeepsie, New York. Watson, like The Courant's proprietors today, took much of Connecticut and a little beyond to be the newspaper's circulation area.

For out-of-town news—that is, for most of the news he printed—Watson depended upon the government "posts" and a local post rider. Every Saturday, with luck, the New York and Boston posts met

at Hartford. To notify the community, the post riders were instructed
to "wind their Horns" upon arrival and to wind them again half an
hour before leaving town. All too frequently, no horn was to be
heard on Saturday because the riders had been delayed by storms or
bad roads.

Watson reported the Boston Tea Party of 1773 in a single mock-
ing sentence:

We hear from B ston that laſt
Thurſday Evening, between 300 and
400 Boxes of the celebrated Eaſt-In-
dia TEA, by ſome ACCIDENT! which
happened in an attempt to get it on
Shore, fell overboard—That the Boxes burſt open and the Tea was ſwal-
lowed up the vaſt Abyſs !

But when the heavy-handed Coercive Acts of 1774 closed the port
of Boston, Watson's mockery vanished. Here was a threat to every
colony's charter rights, and it was not for an editor in the City of the
Charter Oak to laugh it off. As one of The Courant's correspondents
put it, "Let us contribute something to relieve the Sufferers in Boston.
Let us break off all Trade with Great-Britain . . . I hope there is none
in America . . . that value Liberty at so small a Price as tamely to sub-
mit to the cruel Insults of a tyrannical Ministry."

From that time on, things went from bad to worse until the fateful
19th of April, 1775. About 10 a.m. that day, a Wednesday, the crude
information network of the American colonies carried one of the
great news stories of modern times, the account of the clashes at Lexington and Concord, of the "shot heard 'round the world." It would
be hard to say whether the "Flash" that heralds a major news break
today in hundreds of newspaper offices at once is any more dramatic
than the lonely figure of Israel Bissell, riding post haste from Water-
town, Massachusetts, carrying the news of the battle of Lexington
and a letter in his mail pouch charging him "to alarm the Country
quite to Connecticut."

Bissell's horse fell dead of exhaustion at Worcester, Massachusetts. Getting a fresh mount, he headed south and reached Norwich,
in eastern Connecticut, by 4 p.m. the next day. The route before him
swung in a wide arc some thirty miles around Hartford. He reached

Long Island Sound at New London at 7 p.m. Riding through the
night, he spread the news down the coast from Lyme, to Saybrook,
and thence to Guilford and Branford, which he reached at noon. He
made New Haven by evening, and Fairfield by 4 p.m. Saturday after
a 78-hour trip.

Bissell's ride served its purpose of alarming the country. From
Watson's point of view in far-away Hartford it was sheer frustra-
tion. Rumors spread rapidly inland, probably reaching Hartford in
a day or so. On April 24, five days after the battle, Watson printed
a general account of the fighting based on "the latest accounts from
Boston." Courant readers learned: "Last Tuesday night the Gren-
adiers and Light Companies . . . in Boston were ferried in long-boats
from the bottom of the Common over to Phip's farm in Cambridge,
from whence they proceeded on their expedition to Concord." At
Lexington, early the next morning "they gave a specimen of their
savage designs, by firing several times on a number of innocent
men." In the Lexington and Concord encounters, the Courant reported 32 to 33 lost on our side as against upwards of 200 Regulars.

In a day when news stories often appeared even months late, Watson's report on Lexington and Concord must have seemed prompt,
even though readers had to wait until May 8 for their first eye-witness
account of the battles. Watson got this account, not from any of the
Connecticut towns visited by the hard-riding Bissell, but from
Worcester, Massachusetts, where Isaiah Thomas, after escaping from
Boston, had just set up his *Massachusetts Spy.* Watson printed
Thomas's famous account word for word. Since the story was ad-
dressed to readers who had already learned something of the battle,
it began, not with the news, but with a patriotic exhortation:

> W O R C E S T E R, *May* 3.
>
> A MERICANS! forever bear in mind the BAT-
> TLE of LEXINGTON ?—where Britiſh
> troops, unmoleſted and unprovoked, wantonly, and
> in a moſt inhuman manner fired upon and killed a
> number of our countrymen, then robbed them of
> their proviſions, ranſacked, plundered and burnt their
> houſes ! nor could the tears of defenceleſs women,
> ſome of whom were in the pains of childbirth, the
> cries of helpleſs babes, nor the prayers of old age,
> confined to beds of ſickneſs, appeaſe their thirſt for
> blood !---or divert them from the DESIGN of MUR-
> DER and ROBBERY !

Watson printed all the story, most of it in a long paragraph extending more than a column.

Connecticut residents opened their homes to refugees from Boston. On June 30 Gen. George Washington passed through Hartford on his way to Cambridge, where, Watson reported, Connecticut's Israel Putnam unfurled his standard bearing the motto *qui transtulit sustinet*—"He who hath brought us hither sustains us yet"—the motto later adopted for the Great Seal of the State. July 3 brought news of the battle of Bunker Hill, again by way of the post from Worcester. Soon Connecticut's Ethan Allan began making history at Crown Point and Ticonderoga. In August The Courant brought news of British men of war raiding Fisher's, Gardiner's and Plum Islands off the Connecticut coast.

As a patriotic gesture, Watson removed the Kings Arms from the head of his paper, put there after the stamp tax difficulty ended, and ran the emblem that Israel Putnam had displayed at Cambridge with its Latin motto. He was ahead of his time in recognizing its appeal for the people of Connecticut. Not until 1931 did the General Assembly adopt it as the official motto and state seal.

The exciting war news boomed The Courant's circulation. Watson was reduced to printing The Courant on the only stock he could get—wrapping paper. He appealed to the Daughters of Liberty to save their linen and cotton rags "coarse as well as fine. As rags are the only material of which that most necessary article, paper, can be made, if they are not saved the streams of intelligence will very soon fail."

Watson soon realized he had better get into the papermaking business himself. In partnership with Austin Ledyard he built a mill on the banks of the Hockanum River at "Five Miles," now in the town of Manchester. This was Connecticut's second paper mill. Since Watson had been collecting rags for Christopher Leffingwell's mill at Norwich, he might as well be collecting rags for a mill of his own nearer home. He told his readers about the mill project in August, 1775, but construction lagged. The issues for December 4 and 11, 1775, came out on wrapping paper. But even that gave out, and the next issue to come from his press was dated January 12, 1776, printed on spongy paper of decidedly poor grade. Not until March was the mill turning out stock of good quality.

Watson now also had to manage his papermaking business. He advertised for calves' pates, from which to make sizing to coat the paper, and for rags at three pennies a pound, and engaged rag collectors on commission. He informed his readers that "A little bag or basket, hung up in some convenient place will receive the rags with the same trouble that will be necessary to sweep them into the fire."

In July, 1776, The Courant carried the words now familiar to all Americans:

P H I L A D E L P H I A.
In CONGRESS, July 4, 1776.
A D E C L A R A T I O N
By the REPRESENTATIVES of the
UNITED STATES OF AMERICA,
In GENERAL CONGRESS assembled.

WHEN in the Courfe of human Events, it be-comes neceffary for one People to diffolve the political Bands which have connected them with ano-ther, and to affume among the Powers of the Earth, the feparate and equal Station to which the Laws of Nature and of Nature's God entitle them, a decent Refpect to the Opinion of Mankind requires that they fhould declare the Caufe which impel them to the Separation.

We hold thefe Truths to be felf-evident, that all

The Declaration of Independence appeared on Page Two, in keeping with the printing custom of the times that arranged the news in approximately the order in which it arrived at the printing office.

And then, in 1777, with circulation soaring and with overwhelming news to report from every colony, disaster struck The Courant, precipitating the worst crisis in its entire career.

1777-1779
The Darkest Days

IN THE FALL OF 1777, while the British at Brandywine were routing Washington's troops, Ebenezer Watson, the proprietor of the newspaper with the largest circulation on the continent, died after catching the smallpox.

In the next six months The Courant went through its darkest days. Watson's 27-year-old widow Hannah, left with five children (the oldest was 7), an estate to settle, and the largest journal of the patriot cause to publish, reported her husband's death in The Courant for September 22:

> On Tuesday last departed this life after a distressing sickness, Mr. Ebenezer Watson, Printer, in the 34th year of his age. A gentleman of a most humane heart, and susceptible of the tenderest feelings for distress, in whatever manner discovered—Jealous of the rights of human nature, and anxious for the safety of his country, his press hath been devoted to the vindication of rational liberty. The Governor's company of Cadets, of which he was an Ensign, in token of respect for the deceased, attended the funeral in their uniforms. He has left a melancholy widow, with five young children, and a numerous circle of friends to lament his death.

Fortunately for The Courant and for the information system of the patriots, the Widow Watson proved herself a highly competent young woman who knew how to keep her head in a crisis. Her picture shows frank dark eyes, straight dark hair, a determined mouth.

Demand for The Courant soared as Cornwallis took Philadelphia, Burgoyne surrendered at Saratoga, and Washington settled in for the cruel winter of Valley Forge. Less than three years earlier, before the Battle of Lexington, The Courant's circulation had stood at a meager 700. Watson had given thanks in print to 300 of his subscribers who had paid their accounts punctually and had threatened 400 with stoppage of their paper if they did not pay up. But by December of the same year he was writing of the great increase in circulation. And a few months later he asked readers who called for their Courants at the shop to come on Tuesdays because he could no longer print an entire edition on Monday. Watson was, in fact, printing what was evidently the newspaper with the largest circulation in the colonies. According to Isaiah Thomas, noted journalist-historian of the times:

> After the British troops gained possession of New York, as they did in September 1776, the newspapers on the side of the country in that place were discontinued, and the printers of them dispersed, The Courant became of much consequence; its circulation rapidly increased; and, for some time, the number of copies printed weekly was equal to, if not greater, than that of any other paper then printed in the Continent.

But increased circulation was wearing out Watson's type—a serious problem. Even after Abel Buell began casting type in Connecticut in 1769, and after others, notably in Pennsylvania, began making it from their own punches, most of the best types came across the Atlantic. It was slow and uncertain delivery. Printers often had to use a font or set of type until it was hardly legible. Late in 1772 Watson's subscribers began to complain. At first he pleaded poverty; then, through "unexpected assistance" from local friends, he sent off for new English types which did not arrive until June, 1774. By 1777, almost desperate, he planned to visit a distant state, probably Pennsylvania, to buy type. Such a journey, in wartime, was hazardous for the patriotic editor. As it turned out, he died before he could make the trip. But he had managed to get the type somehow, because in his estate is an item for £161 for "New Types Lately Imported from Philadelphia." This one item accounted for nearly half the total value of his printing office. The appraisers' inventory shows:

1 Printing press	20- 0-0
II Pair Printing Cases 15/	8- 5-0
2 Large frame for D 20/ 7 Small D 35/	2-15-0
Half the Shop Belonging to Green and Watson	30- 0-0
The Printing Room Over Mr. Doolittle's Shop	30- 0-0
Lye Trough 24/ Iron for Sign 10/	1-14-0
Large Iron Kettle 7/ Iron Pot 7/6	0-14-6
Iron Pounder 8/ Small Iron Kettle 2/	0-10-0
Blanks 3/10 Accompt Book 30/	5- 0-0
Old Wrighting Desk 8/ Iron Skillet 1/6	0- 9-6
37 Ream Printing Paper @ 10/	18-10-0
Saw 2/ 6 Small Gallies 9/0 2 Folio D 6/	0-17-0
1 Long D 2/ Salmons Gazetteer 4/	0- 6-0
3 Chairs 7/ 4 Composing sticks 48/	2-15-0
Twine 4/ Bank 4/ old Slice / Hand irons 2/6	0-10-6
All the Old Printing Types Belonging to the Office	50- 0-0
New Types Lately Imported from Philadelphia	161- 0-0

333- 6-6

The Courant had provided Watson a good living. His whole estate was appraised at £872 in silver money, not bad for a young man of 33 in those times.

January 1, 1778, Hannah Watson admitted young George Goodwin, the youth who had joined The Courant at the age of 9, to partnership. Though Goodwin was only 20 he knew printing thoroughly —better than Watson, according to Isaiah Thomas.

Almost at once, the young widow and her partner were plunged into a new disaster. January 27, 1778, the paper mill burned down, with the loss of all its machinery, about 100 reams of printing paper, and a great stock of writing paper, rags, and other supplies. Hannah Watson, her husband only four months dead, now faced a loss estimated at £5,000. According to Mrs. Watson, the mill "wholly supplied the press of Hartford from whence issue weekly more than 8000 news papers" and "a great part of the writing paper used in this state" as well as large quantities of paper "for the use of the Continental Army."

This was not a crisis for The Courant only; it was a blow to the patriot cause. The British had closed down every patriotic press they could lay hand on and had cut off all imports of paper. If The Courant went, Americans would lose their largest remaining patriotic

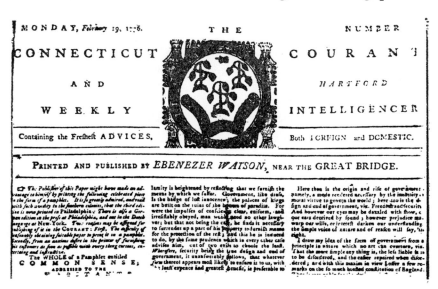

PATRIOTISM CROWDED THE NEWS IN 1776
Watson devoted most of four issues to Paine's Common Sense

journal—a newspaper that had published Tom Paine's *Common Sense* and was printing his *The Crisis* in installments, that ardently supported the American cause; one that circulated news of the highest importance to the embittered colonists. Hannah Watson and George Goodwin, in a poignant note, announced in The Courant for February 3, 1778, that they were obliged "to present their readers with a half sheet and at the same time assure them it is a prelude to none . . ."

Hannah Watson and Sarah Ledyard, widow of Watson's partner in the paper mill, appealed to the Connecticut Assembly for help. They asked for a "loan of a sufficient sum . . . without interest" to rebuild the mill at an estimated cost of "not less than 300 pounds." The Legislators knew very well what the loss of The Courant could mean to the American cause. The General Assembly acted the same day it received the petition, and did even better than the widows asked. It voted a State lottery of 6,000 tickets at $6 each—$5,000 to rebuild the mill, $31,000 in prizes.

At once The Courant began advertising the lottery and apparently most effectively, soon reporting that the "sale of tickets exceeds the managers' most sanguine expectations." The mill was rebuilt and turning out newsprint for The Courant that spring.

Somehow Hannah Watson and George Goodwin got the paper they needed until the rebuilt mill was in production, even resorting to wrapping paper as a substitute. The Courant never missed an issue in its worst crisis.

The cause of the paper mill fire was never discovered. Goodwin suspected Tory sabotage, especially since an attempt had also been made to burn the south schoolhouse by someone "purely devilish" who had thrown a shovelful of coal on the shelf where the children kept their books. He wrote:

> Thronged as this town is with British and Tory prisoners, rambling with impunity at all hours of the night and open to the secret malice of every hardened villain, would it not be proper that a suitable guard should nightly patrol the streets . . .?

When the spunky Hannah Watson inherited The Courant, women printers were rare but not unheard of in the colonies. At least ten women before her had conducted print shops. Among them were Dinah Nuthead, who managed a shop at Annapolis in 1696, although she did not publish a newspaper, and Elizabeth Timothy, who published the *South Carolina Gazette* as early as 1739.

On February 11, 1779, the Widow Watson married her next-door neighbor, Barzillai Hudson, 37 years old, who thereupon became a partner in The Courant. The partnership of Hudson and Goodwin was destined to last 36 years and to make a significant mark in American publishing. Goodwin's chief interest lay in printing—books as well as newspapers—while Hudson, a mason by trade, had talent for business management. They made a good pair. Under their guidance The Courant attained a financial stability that was the envy of other newspapers of the era.

Moreover, they went on to new fields of national importance after their gamble to publish the book of a frustrated young writer named Noah Webster. The firm name of Hudson & Goodwin came to be familiar wherever books were sold in America.

1779-1800
Establishing the Firm

THE PARTNERSHIP of Hudson & Goodwin flourished 36 years. The firm's imprint on Noah Webster's spelling book and on the Bible made its name familiar to Americans from the East coast to the frontier. In and about Hartford the company's retail store, printing shop, and paper manufacturing all prospered.

This prosperity gave The Courant an enviable stability in the rickety world of American journalism. And American journalism after the Revolution was indeed rickety. Newspapers appeared and disappeared like blinking lights on a theater marquee. More than 400 journals started during the period between the Revolution and the turn of the century. Among all the leading papers before the Revolution, barely a dozen survived to 1800.

The Courant was one of the survivors. It stood because of the tremendous circulation it built up during and after the Revolution and because it had the backing of the other Hudson & Goodwin enterprises. Few papers of the day had anything like the financial stability of The Courant.

The Courant's circulation was a national wonder. Back in 1778, when the Widow Watson petitioned the General Assembly for relief after the burning of the paper mill, she and her fellow petitioner, the Widow Ledyard, claimed a circulation of more than 8000. As this figure appeared in a formal presentation before the legislature, it probably came somewhere near the truth—nearer, that is, than the figures quoted by other newspapers of the period. Even London editors would have envied The Courant. Most newspapers in colonial America could count only a few hundred subscribers. The egregious Tory editor, James Rivington of New York, whom most patriotic Americans regarded as a notorious liar, claimed only 3600 subscribers, while the relatively reliable Isaiah Thomas claimed at one point a circulation of 3500 for his *Massachusetts Spy*.

If the Courant's circulation claim of 8000 can be taken at face value, Hudson & Goodwin may have had an income of £12,000 a year from subscriptions alone after they raised annual rates to 30 shillings in June, 1779. In 1780 the price went to ten silver shillings. These successive price increases were caused by the wartime inflation. In addition, advertising brought in a considerable sum, impossible to determine today and probably unknown even to the proprietors, who continued to accept barter for their advertising.

The Revolutionary War was still going on, and The Courant's war stories started to carry datelines uncomfortably near home. In 1781, Connecticut privateers and English shipmasters kept up a desperate game of hide and seek on Long Island Sound. American boats fitted out at New London, Norwich, Wethersfield, Rocky Hill, Stonington and Mystic, armed with guns made in Salisbury and manned by young Connecticut patriots from Lyme to Pawcatuck, scoured the coastal waters and brought prizes into New London. In April, The Courant reported that a British crew from Long Island had landed three miles west of Guilford, but the coast guard killed one of the Tories and routed the others. Another boatload of Tories attacked at New Haven harbor, killed the sentry, captured 11 men, and escaped.

The arrival of distinguished military visitors, such as Washington, Lafayette and John Paul Jones, in Hartford was reported. Rochambeau's army marched through in June. Said The Courant:

A finer body of men were never in arms. The exact discipline of the troops and the attention of the officers to prevent any injury to individuals have made the march of this army through the country very agreeable to the inhabitants . . .

Then, September 13, 1781, The Courant reported one of the most vicious attacks of the war—the traitor Benedict Arnold's raid on New London and the massacre at Fort Griswold, where 85 militiamen and all male members of many families were killed. As far as Connecticut was concerned, this bloodbath marked the climax of the war. On October 30, The Courant reported the surrender of Cornwallis at Yorktown.

Any printer could see with half an eye that peace would decrease the public's eagerness for news. It was clear, too, that as supplies became more plentiful, rival printers would move in. In Hartford, Nathaniel Patten had begun printing late in 1776 and Bavil Webster about 1778.

Hudson & Goodwin prepared for competition by expanding their paper-making and book publishing. Advertisements in The Courant late in 1781 show that the firm had acquired an interest in two more nearby paper mills. Hudson & Goodwin went for the book trade with such vigor that, by 1800, they had established the firm as a leader in the lucrative fields of religious, educational, and governmental publication, and had helped to start Hartford on the way to becoming a leading papermaking center.

They put up a new building, probably in 1782, on Main Street. It must have been a somewhat awkward structure, as its lot measured only 19 feet across the front.

Late in the summer of 1782 Hudson & Goodwin produced a sample of successes to come when they brought out a best seller, John Trumbull's *M'Fingal*. It is not the stuff of which today's best sellers are made. In that day's parched climate of American letters the poem impressed readers. Not to have read this mock epic marked a man as semi-literate—perhaps even unpatriotic. Trumbull seems to have been encouraged to write the poem by several eminent men including Silas Deane, John Adams, and possibly George Washington himself, who knew a young fellow of talent when he saw one. Trumbull had learned to read at the age of two, had read the entire Bible by four, and had passed the entrance examinations to Yale at seven, though he delayed entering the College until he was thirteen.

Readers of *M'Fingal* needed little but a strong anti-English bias and a stomach for jogtrotting in iambic verse:

> . . . once Egyptians [the American colonists] at the Nile
> Ador'd their guardian Crocodile [the English government]
> Who heard them first with kindest ear,
> And ate them to reward their pray'r;
> And could he talk, as kings can do,
> Had made them gracious speeches too.

To quote "macfingalisms" became a mark of the educated man.

M'Fingal was quickly pirated. The author and his publishers, unprotected by copyright, bitterly contemplated the wide sale of the best seller in unauthorized editions. Trumbull wrote: "Among more than 30 different impressions, one only, at any subsequent time, was published with the permission, or even the knowledge, of the writer."

Hudson & Goodwin's success with *M'Fingal* was soon topped by a more spectacular triumph—a gamble that produced perhaps the world's best seller, apart from the Bible. A year after they published Trumbull's poem, they began advertising the first volume of Noah Webster's three-part *A Grammatical Institute of the English Lan-*

guage, better known as "Webster's *Blue-Backed Speller."* Webster's biographer, Harry R. Warfel, says that a grand total of 100 million copies appears to be a reasonable estimate of sale over the decades. Hudson & Goodwin did not print anywhere near this many themselves—rights were granted several publishers, and pirates brought out their own editions—but the *Blue-Backed Speller* helped to keep Hudson & Goodwin busy and prosperous for years.

It was to the credit of the partners that they had risked publishing the Speller in the first place. Webster had tried hard to get a publisher: all turned him down. No printer wanted to gamble on an American speller in competition with Dilworth's well established English spelling book, then standard in schools along the Atlantic seaboard. Webster had not been able to find anyone, not even a friend, who would underwrite the enterprise.

In June, 1783, he approached Hudson & Goodwin. They would

·A
Grammatical Inſtitute,

OF THE
ENGLISH LANGUAGE,

COMPRISING,

An eaſy, conciſe, and ſyſtematic Method of

EDUCATION,

Deſigned for the Uſe of *Engliſh* Schools

IN *AMERICA.*

IN THREE PARTS.

PART I.

CONTAINING,

A new and accurate Standard of Pronunciation.

_____

BY NOAH WEBSTER, A. M.

_____

Uſus eſt Norma Loquendi.   CICERO.

_____

HARTFORD:
PRINTED BY HUDSON & GOODWIN,
FOR THE AUTHOR.

FABLE I. *Of the Boy that ſtole Apples.*

AN old Man found a rude Boy upon one of his trees ſtealing Apples, and deſired him to come down ; but the young Sauce-box told him plainly he would not. Won't you ? ſaid the old Man, then I will fetch you down ; ſo he pulled up ſome Tufts of Graſs, and threw at him ; but this only made the youngſter laugh, to think the old Man ſhould pretend to beat him out of the tree with graſs only.

Well, well, ſaid the old Man, if neither words nor graſs, will do, I muſt try what virtue there is in ſtones ; ſo the old Man pelted him heartily with ſtones ; which ſoon made the young chap haſten down from the tree and beg the old Man's pardon.

MORAL.

If good words and gentle means will not reclaim the wicked; they muſt be dealt with in a more ſevere manner.

FIRST EDITION OF WEBSTER'S
SPELLER
*Courant was initial publisher of this
100-million-copy best seller*

SPELLING LESSONS WITH A
MORAL
Later editions of Speller *had
illustrated dictation exercises*

accept the author's note for printing costs in exchange for exclusive printing rights to succeeding editions. It proved a fantastically impossible agreement, so great was the demand for the little book. The printers soon found that in hitching their wagon to Webster's star they had snagged a comet by the tail.

Hudson and Goodwin struck off a first edition of 5,000 copies. All were gone in nine months. In 1784, second and third editions appeared. It then became clear that printing and distributing the speller were more than any firm could manage. Printing rights were granted to other publishers. In Boston, Edes brought out an impression; in New York, Samuel Campbell; in Philadelphia, William Young; in Providence, John Carter. A million and a half copies had been sold by 1801, 20 million by 1829, and 75 million by 1885. Appleton took over the Speller in 1855 and set one of the largest presses in its plant running year after year on this book alone.

Hudson & Goodwin, recognizing their limitations, agreed in November, 1786, to exclusive rights to print and sell the Speller only in Connecticut, Rhode Island, Massachusetts, and New Hampshire. Even this proved too much. In 1788 they sold to Webster their rights outside Connecticut, retaining only certain rights to compete elsewhere if they chose. Webster received a cent for each copy they sold, until he made a lump sum settlement for the duration of the copyright in Connecticut.

The run-away best seller invited imitation. The first of many, Robert Ross's *The New American Spelling Book,* appeared, ironically, with the imprint of Thomas and Samuel Green, of New Haven. In Hartford, Nathaniel Patten bought up hundreds of Spellers, throwing them on the market at reduced prices. Patten accused Hudson & Goodwin of monopoly and profiteering, only to have them bring a charge that he had tried to conspire in a price-fixing deal. Webster supported his publishers in these and other entanglements, and Hudson & Goodwin received more than £100 in damages. The Speller proved to be profitable, if sticky, business.

Webster himself in the summer of 1783 began to write a series of essays for The Courant. Signing himself "Honorius," he explained the necessity for a United States. "The dignity, safety, and happiness of America," he wrote, "are inseparably connected with a union of all the states." The Courant was destined to publish thousands of words advocating the Union, becoming a leading proponent of Federalism. Increasingly, Hudson & Goodwin devoted space to the great political debates of their time.

In October, 1783, The Courant treated its readers to what some regarded as a dangerous novelty. The paper began publishing synopses of the discussions in the Connecticut State House of Representatives. To Hudson & Goodwin, this seemed a logical development. The pre-Revolutionary practice had been to publish only the titles of acts. Later, starting in 1776, the texts of some of the acts had been published, while the day-to-day business of the Assembly remained closed to the press. Hudson & Goodwin's synopses were a further step toward freedom of information. Three years later, in the fall of 1786, they began reporting actual debates in the House of Representatives. Said Hudson & Goodwin:

> The Editors of this paper propose to give their readers a concise history of the business and debates which shall come before the present session of the Assembly. They are no party, and wish to be considered simply as the narrators of facts . . . Should these sketches . . . enlighten or inform it will be an ample compensation for the extraordinary trouble . . ."

It took a long time to establish the right to report on legislative goings-on in America. As late as 1846 the U. S. Senate restricted reporters to those representing Washington papers. The Courant's successful storming of the Connecticut State House constitutes a significant early step in the fight for freedom of information.

On October 1, 1787, The Courant published the long-awaited text of a proposed Constitution for the United States of America. Interest in Connecticut had run high ever since the General Assembly sent three of the State's ablest public leaders to the Philadelphia Convention—Oliver Ellsworth, William Samuel Johnson, and Roger Sherman. And The Courant had helped to keep the interest alive with almost weekly articles on the need for a stronger union of the states.

Printing of the text brought political discussion in the state to fever pitch. Hudson & Goodwin gave columns of space to the advocates of the new Constitution and printed not a single letter opposing it. The paper carried Oliver Ellsworth's able and persuasive letters from "A LANDHOLDER" between November 5, 1787, and March 24 of the following year.

The General Assembly voted that a special assembly of delegates elected from each town should consider the proposed new government. The delegates met January 4, 1788, at the State House, but were soon driven by the cold to the First Society Meeting House, which could be heated.

The editors of The Courant clearly sensed the greatness of the occasion. Feelingly they reported the speeches that followed, such as Governor Huntington's:

> This is a new event in the history of mankind.—Heretofore, most governments have been formed by tyrants, and imposed on mankind by force. Never before did a people, in time of peace and tranquility, meet together by their representatives, and with calm deliberation frame for themselves a system of government . . .

The pressure of news about Connecticut's ratification of the Constitution squeezed a good many items off the pages. A number of advertisements went by the board, a circumstance that seems not to have caused Hudson or Goodwin much concern. There were historic doings to be reported, and if the advertisers didn't like it, they could console themselves with the crisp notice that: "Advertisements, &c., omitted for want of room, will appear in our next."

But in spite of pressure for space, Hudson & Goodwin did find room for the following advertisement, probably as a filler:

WRITING PAPER,
For Sale, by the Ream or lefs quantity, by HUDSON and GOODWIN.

Hartford began to grow: from 4,090 in 1790 to 5,347 in 1800. Business firms, including Hudson & Goodwin, prospered. The city's first commercial bank opened; the insurance business struck down firm roots; a theater opened; a new State House was built. The Courant's proprietors claimed a circulation unrivalled in the State.

There were growing pains too. Letters to The Courant complained of mud in Hartford's public square, of the miserable service of the Connecticut River Ferry to East Hartford, of the inadequacy of fire protection.

Hudson & Goodwin had just rejoiced over the ratification of the Constitution when, December 2, 1788, one of their paper mills in East Hartford burned with a loss of more than £700. For three months, The Courant appeared in reduced size. No doubt the fire strained the financial resources of the partners—they advertised two "slays to be sold, one of them very neat—pay made easy; a milch cow would be preferred and wood for the other if applied for soon."

Scarcity of coin hampered everyone. A postrider's account book that has survived in The Courant's files from the 1790's reports that he carried The Courant and its rival, *The Mercury,* to East Hartford, East Windsor, Enfield, Somers, Suffield, Ellington, and Long Meadow, Massachusetts. Whenever a subscriber paid, the rider carefully noted in his own kind of spelling the amount and type of payment. Some of his transactions raise interesting questions:

Subscriber:	How He paid	In shillings & pence
John Bancroft		
East Windsor	Barn Door Hook & Hinges	19/2
Nathaniel Burt		
Long Meadow, Mass.	Mulberry Trees	2/-
Levi Starns,	Window frames & Sash	
Enfield	& Seting Glass	20/6
William Chaffee,	190 ft of plank for	
Enfield	Stable floors, Some Rotten	10/-
Edward Kibbe,		
Somers	Mink skins	8/-
Thoder Smith,	Making Great Coat	
East Windsor	& over halls	11/-
Ebenezer Prier &		
Phinehas Hale,	By taking Care of	
Enfield	Thief	3/-

Such entries fill 190 tightly packed pages in the account book, from 1790 to past 1800. Subscribers commonly left accounts unpaid for a year or two. Phineas Moody of Somers made only one payment from 1796 to 1802: "1 pair womans Slips 5/-."

Scarcity of paper hampered all American printers during the 1790's. Hudson & Goodwin, in 1792, issued a moving appeal:

A P R O M P T E R.
Rags ! Rags !

How the best things grow out of the worst!—Even the bible is made out of rags! And yet people will not save their rags! Authors, printers, arts and sciences, and records all depend on rags for support, and yet rags are thrown away. *Great* people, that is, people *really* great, save rags.

Why? Because the saving rags is a very *little thing,* yet it is a little thing that has great effects . . .

It was in part Hudson & Goodwin's publication of religious and legal works that put a strain on their paper mill and prompted their intense interest in the American rag-bag. They published Barlow's third edition of Watt's *Psalms* in 1791 and Dwight's edition, both widely used in Congregational churches. They also sold bibles in their store, though the handsome Hudson & Goodwin Bible did not appear until 1809.

A list of important publications bearing the Hudson & Goodwin imprint also includes pamphlets by Ethan Allen, Joel Barlow's *Vision of Columbus,* Nathan Strong's poems, Benjamin Trumbull's *History of Connecticut,* and many works from the indefatigable Noah Webster, including his grammar, reader, and *The Prompter, or a Commentary on Common Sayings and Subjects,* these last three selling thousands of copies. Webster's *Essay on Slavery, History of Epidemic Diseases,* and *Sketches of American Policy* were also published by Hudson & Goodwin.

One intriguing gambit by the partners, the first American attempt at a magazine for children, did not succeed. *The Children's Magazine,* a periodical started in 1789, failed after a short life. Later, from 1800 to 1807, Hudson & Goodwin published the *Connecticut Evangelical Magazine* for the Connecticut Missionary Society.

In addition to books and magazines, of course, The Courant's advertising also was bringing in revenue. Some of the ads carry the flavor of the day.

In 1792 Joseph Hartford lost a "pied black and white Milch cow." He promised a reward for her return, requesting whoever had her to milk her twice a day. A few years later, when a 14-year-old indentured boy, Rufus Spalding, ran away from John Norris of Tolland, the indignant John characterized the fugitive as a lad who "talks much, but little truth," and offered two cents for his return. Before 1800, not many issues of The Courant appeared without some notice of an errant wife, a runaway slave or apprentice, or a strayed animal. Although The Courant, like other American papers, largely neglected local events in its news columns, much of the day-to-day news of the town turned up among these paid notices.

Another financial help came along in 1792 with the Federal Post-office Act fixing postage on newspapers at one cent and providing that all newspapers exchanged between printers be carried without charge. Up to that time, the carrying of newspapers had been legal (Ben Franklin had seen to that back in 1758), but editors had continued to have their troubles with mail deliveries, particularly when rival newspaper publishers also happened to be postmasters. Under these circumstances, editors sometimes had to pay to get their papers carried. By providing for the free carriage of "exchanges" and by binding postmasters by law to forward them, the Act guaranteed the lifeline of newspapers. In those day few papers could have survived without the regular practice of reprinting news from the papers exchanged with other journals.

The already highly diversified enterprises of Hudson & Goodwin took on a new dimension in 1794 when The Courant announced:

T H E A T R E.

BY PERMISSION.

On THURSDAY next, will be presented by a part of the Old
AMERICAN COMPANY,

A COMEDY, written by Mrs. INCHBALD, called the

CHILD of NATURE.

After which will be added a favorite FARCE, called

LOVE A-LA-MODE.

*** TICKETS, without which no person can be admit-
ted—to be had at Messrs. Hudson and Goodwins Office.

Doors would open at 6 o'clock and the play would begin promptly at 7.

The Courant proprietors even might have felt a glow of civic pride—soon one could speak of the "theater season" in Hartford. Clearly the city had come of age culturally. Or had it? The troupe had put on only a few performances, when the following plaintive notice appeared:

> It is the request of the company that their friends and patrons will not remove from the several parts of the house but by the doors, as it is a bad example to be followed, and, at the same time, disturbing in some measure, the tranquility of the house.

The same year, in the prospering city, The Courant carried other evidence of new growth—a small advertisement for Sanford and Wadsworth, who had gone into the fire insurance business:

> Hartford Fire Insurance-Office. The subscribers have this day opened an Office for the purpose of insuring Houses, Household Furniture, Goods, Wares, Merchandise, &c. against Fire. SANFORD & WADS-WORTH, March 10.

The oldest known printed insurance policy in the United States was drawn up by this firm, insuring the house of William Imlay of Hartford for £800 against fire.

Hudson & Goodwin's thriving business prompted a move to new quarters in April, 1796. The masthead read "NEAR THE BRIDGE" for the last time on April 18. The proprietors respectfully informed "their friends and customers that their office will be removed the present week to the new brick building nearly opposite the North Meeting House." The Courant was growing with the city. The paper's masthead on April 25 bore the legend: "OPPOSITE THE NORTH MEETING HOUSE." Here business continued to prosper. By 1799 Hudson & Goodwin were claiming a circulation of 5000, down from its wartime peak, of course, but on the gain.

Though Hartford and The Courant prospered, the turn of the century brought grief to Hudson & Goodwin—indeed, to all Federalists. The Courant's last issue for 1799 carried the mournful news of George Washington's death; and the last issue of 1800, the disturb-

NEWS OF WASHINGTON'S DEATH ENCLOSED IN HEAVY BLACK BORDER

ing and distasteful intelligence that Thomas Jefferson had been elected President of the United States. The proprietors published both stories with heavy hearts. These were sad times in the brick newspaper office opposite the North Meeting-House.

On December 23, 1799, a small notice on Page Three reported the first news of George Washington's death: "A letter from a member of Congress dated 18th of December, to his friend in New Haven, says, 'The illustrious GENERAL WASHINGTON, is no more.' The time of his death is not mentioned."

A week later the sad details had reached Hartford and The Courant reported them on the front page with heavy black borders on all pages. An account of Hartford's reception of the news appeared inside:

> The town never exhibited a more solemn and interesting appearance . . . The stores and shops were shut through the day, all business suspended; the bells were muffled and tolled at intervals from 9 in the morning until the services commenced. The meeting house was greatly crowded, and still a large proportion of the people could not get in at the doors . . .

Washington's death on December 14 had already been known three or four days in Hartford when The Courant printed it December 23. Such, of course, is the lot of weekly newspapers; news breaks seldom come just right for them. Furthermore, Hartford lay a little to the north of what was then the main travel route along the Eastern seaboard. The schedule below, showing the time-lag in reporting Washington's death, suggests how important news spread over the north-east in those days. Washington died at Mount Vernon.

Date of Report	Place and Journal	Lag after Event
Mon., Dec. 16	Alexandria (Va.) *Times*	2 days
Wed., Dec. 18	Winchester (Va.) *Centinel*	4 days
Thurs., Dec. 19	Philadelphia *Aurora*	5 days
Sat., Dec. 21	New York *Argus*	7 days
Mon., Dec. 23	The *Courant*	9 days
Wed., Dec. 25	Boston *Columbian Centinel*	
	Worcester, *Mass. Spy*	11 days
Mon., Dec. 30	Walpole (N. H.) *Farmer's Weekly Museum*	16 days

If the 18th Century closed with mournful news, the 19th began with still more dispiriting tidings. The year 1800 brought news of the presidential candidacy, and at length, the election of Thomas Jefferson. Jefferson's election, Hudson & Goodwin believed, could only be attributed to human perversity. How else, they reasoned, could one account for the election to the highest office in the land of an anti-Federalist, an anti-Christian, a dupe and cat's paw of the French?

Jefferson's anti-Federalism was beyond question. He had opposed every measure for a strong national government, arguing against the sound financial policies of Hamilton and against the creation of a strong American navy. His religious skepticism was equally plain. Had he not written, "It does me no injury for my neighbor to say there are *twenty gods,* or *no god?*" Clearly he had forsaken Christ to follow Tom Paine. Then, too, Jefferson took a complacent view of France—not the France that had come to the succor of the American

Colonies—but the France of Napoleon, a nation that, having forgotten every ornament of rational and civilized life, was "rapidly retreating toward a savageness and barbarity."

From late June, 1800, and through Jefferson's campaign for the presidency, The Courant ran a series of letters signed "Burleigh," detailing exactly what the nation would be in for if America should elect the miscreant Jefferson as chief executive. "Burleigh" found Jefferson somewhat lacking in the qualities of leadership. In fact, he gloomily predicted, if Jefferson became President:

> Neighbours will become the enemies of neighbors, brother of brother, fathers of their sons, and sons of their fathers. Murder, robbery, rape, adultery, and incest, will openly be taught and practised, the air will be rent with the cries of distress, the soil soaked with blood, and the nation black with crimes.

"Burleigh" reeled off this kind of propaganda with great facility and Hudson & Goodwin printed it by the yard. Evidently, some of The Courant's readers were impressed. One correspondent wrote the editors: "Perhaps before you are aware, you will find the nation stretched and racked on the ever rolling wheel of anarchy and torture."

On this note the partnership of Hudson & Goodwin made its debut on the 19th Century. Jefferson's administration was to provoke Hudson & Goodwin into so great an anger that they were to take on the United States government in a legal contest.

WASHINGTON ADVERTISED LAND FOR SALE IN COURANT: 1796
George Washington was President when he ran in The Courant the two ads shown in part above. One offers four farms around his beloved Mount Vernon estate for lease "to real farmers of good reputation and none others need apply." The other advertises for sale lands in present-day Ohio.

GEORGE GOODWIN
Urged adoption of U. S. Constitution

BARZILLAI HUDSON
Winner in historic U. S. Court case

NOAH WEBSTER
Courant printed his Speller

THOMAS JEFFERSON
He, Congress sued Courant

1800-1815

Supporting the Old Guard

WITH THE TURN of the century, Hudson & Goodwin dedicated themselves to the fight against Jeffersonianism. So bitter was their battle that it came before the United States Supreme Court in a highly unusual and significant case.

It started with a story in The Courant of April 16, 1806:

> The United States brig Hornet, Capt. Dent, sailed from the port of New York, for France, on Saturday morning, the 29th of March . . .
>
> Now, reader, mark—we are informed, and we believe the information correct, and therefore inform thee that this vessel carried *Two Millions of Dollars in SPECIE* ☞ *One Hundred and Twenty Thousand Pounds weight,* or SIXTY TONS of precious SILVER ☜ part of it borrowed by government, to purchase the Floridas, *it is said* . . .
>
> Reader, bear in mind, that this vessel is bound not for Spain, to whom the Floridas *belong,* but for France . . .

The editors were beside themselves with rage. As if the Louisiana Purchase had not been bad enough! That miserable French-loving, dictator-condoning, U. S. Constitution-hating, slave-holding Jefferson and his rabble of democrats had secretly shipped off sixty tons of silver to a government that didn't even own the territory the President wanted to buy! If there was ever a clear pay-off to France, this was it. Devoted Courant readers learned, presumably to their horror, that the obvious intent of the money was to pay Napoleon to stop seizing American ships at sea. In a word—though The Courant did not actually use the word—this was bribery. America was bribing France.

The Jeffersonian administration was outraged in turn by The Courant's outburst. In September, 1806, a Federal grand jury indicted the proprietors of The Courant for criminal libel under common law. It was a serious charge—libeling the President and Congress of the United States.

Although Hudson & Goodwin appeared to take their precedent-making bout with the courts calmly, it may be that the experience flustered them a little. At any rate, the issue of the paper that told of their indictment for libel carried the unusual date "September *31, 1806.*"

The case went to Circuit Court in 1807 and 1808, and at length came before the United States Supreme Court, which handed down its decision in February, 1812. The decision dismissed the suit on the grounds that, in the absence of statutory provisions, English criminal common law did not apply in the United States. *United States* v. *Hudson & Goodwin* proved to be a most important legal landmark.

The Courant's bare-knuckled fight with the Administration was of a piece with journalistic practices of the time. Before 1800, the American press had played its vital role in the struggle for independence and in the founding of a new nation. But after 1800— until the early 1830's—it descended to a level of vitriolic personal abuse and character assassination of public figures seldom, if ever, paralleled in the press. Where invective had once issued only from occasional hot-headed newspaper proprietors, it now became a staple.

Isaiah Thomas, whose *History of Printing* appeared in 1810, lamented the low state of American papers "which have been pronounced by travellers, the most profligate and scurrilous public prints in the civilized world." And Frank Luther Mott has said of American journalism's Dark Ages that, "Few papers were ably edited; they reflected the crassness of the American society of the times. Scurrility, assaults, corruption, blatancy were commonplace. Journalism had grown too fast." In the midst of all this murk, The Courant neither threw abroad a beacon of sweetness and light nor did it descend into the darker reaches of the pit. Like most American newspapers, it abandoned all semblance of neutrality, became fiercely partisan, gloated over the successes of its political friends and the alleged failures of its enemies.

Hudson & Goodwin's stated policy in 1786 had been that they were of "no party" and that they wished "to be considered simply as narrators of facts." Nine years later they publicly recognized the danger "of becoming the instruments of parties," and said any partisanship they might display would result from no other cause than love of country. But, by 1804, they were saying that Jefferson and his democratic minions were out to wreck America.

Samuel G. Goodrich in a book of recollections published in 1856 called Hudson & Goodwin a firm "then known all over this hemisphere, as publishers of the Bible, Webster's Spelling-book, and the

Connecticut Courant. They were, in the popular mind, regarded as the bulwarks of religion, education, and federalism—three pretty staunch supporters of the New England platform, in that epoch of the world. It is very seldom does plodding industry rise so high. Mr. Hudson was a homespun old respectability, of plain, strong sense, sturdy principles, and rather dry, harsh manners, having also a limp in the leg. He took charge of the financial department of the concern. Mr. Goodwin was a large, hale, comely gentleman, of lively mind and cheerful manners. There was always sunshine in his bosom and wit upon his lip. He turned his hand to various things, though chiefly to the newspaper, which was his pet. His heaven was the upper loft in the composing room."

Hudson & Goodwin proved themselves indefatigable swimmers against the tide of social and political change. They entered the 19th Century opposing the people's choice for President. In 1803, when the United States purchased the Louisiana Territory, Hudson & Goodwin denounced the purchase. They fought against a strong movement in Connecticut for the separation of Church and State. In an era when the right to vote was rigidly limited to males who owned property, Hudson & Goodwin resisted all attempts to extend suffrage. When the moribund Federalists called the notorious Hartford Convention in 1814, Hudson & Goodwin loyally backed that fiasco. In conservative Connecticut, The Courant's name led all the rest.

The Courant summed up its arguments against Jefferson on June 20, 1800, and for many years thereafter the paper's political statements were to ring changes on the same themes:

> I. Mr. Jefferson has long felt a spirit of deadly hostility against the Federal Constitution. . .
> II. If he should be elected President, the Constitution will inevitably fall a sacrifice to Jacobinism.
> III. The result will be dreadful to the people of the United States.

In the early 1800's, the emotional overtones of the word *Jacobinism* were something like those of the word *Communism* today. To call a man a Jacobin meant that, as the tool of a foreign power—France—he was trying to undermine the American government. The Courant waxed wonderfully indignant and marvelously foggy. The editors, alternately—and without any apparent sense of inconsistency —charged Jefferson and his democratic friends with ambition to destroy all government and with the exactly opposite ambition of setting up a government by dictatorship. For The Courant, it was open season on democrats.

Hudson & Goodwin began to recognize their need for a regular editorial writer. They wanted a man of correct principles and of learning, a facile writer, preferably with some newspaper experience. Such a man they found in Ezra Sampson, whom they engaged in 1804 at $600 a year. Sampson had been graduated from Yale, then Connecticut's only college and a bulwark of Federalism and church establishment. For 20 years, until his voice failed, he had served as minister to a congregation in Plympton, Massachusetts. He had then turned to writing.

A note of quiet pride is detectable in Hudson & Goodwin's announcement of the appointment of Sampson:

> We take the liberty to inform the public, that we have engaged an Assistant in Editing our Paper, a Gentleman distinguished for his literary talents and character. As his time will be wholly devoted to the business, we trust The Courant will become highly interesting in its future commentaries.

The appointment of an even more imposing gentleman was announced in the same issue—none other than a former Chief Justice of the U. S. Supreme Court, who would write an agricultural column, "Farmer's Repository." The writer was the distinguished Oliver Ellsworth, who did not think it beneath his dignity to dig into questions of fertilizers or the proper treatment of cattle. Jonathan Swift's familiar words appeared at the head of the column: "Whoever can make two Ears of Corn, or two Blades of Grass grow upon a spot of ground where only one grew before, deserves better of mankind and does a more essential service to his Country, than the whole race of Politicians put together."

Up to a point, The Courant's conservatism on almost all contemporary issues proved a decided asset. The upstart democrats of the cities might laugh at Hudson & Goodwin as the aging curators of a crumbling fortress, but to the vast majority of their subscribers, The Courant was a mighty bulwark against the tyranny of politicians and rabble rousers.

Hudson & Goodwin wrote in 1804:

> The *Connecticut Courant* is among the oldest establishments of this nature in our country. It has been publishing nearly forty years; and for the greater part of the time has had, and now probably has, a more extensive circulation than any news-paper in the United States. A support so uniform and respectable, affords satisfying evidence that it has been conducted on principles accordant with the public feelings and sentiments . . .

Clearly the partners believed the continuing prosperity of their paper to stem from a great tradition and from a consistent advocacy of what, to use their own expressions, were "respectable" and in "the interests of morals, religion, science . . . and our republican government."

While Hudson & Goodwin were grappling with great national issues, they were also struggling with small but pressing problems in their own printing plant. Between 1806 and 1810 compositors had to struggle with type faces in which the old form of lower case *s* no longer appeared. As one observer put it, "No longer was it announced that 'the floop, Nabby, was funk in Long Ifland found,' for the letter 's' had at last taken on its legitimate work." In The Courant during December, 1806, both the old-style and the new-style *s* appeared in the news columns. New type had been purchased, much neater than the old. Gradually, between 1807-1809, the new type began to take over the news columns while the old style lingered in advertisements, finally disappearing in 1810. For a couple of years the advertisers simply had to take what was left after the news had been set in up-to-date type. This arrangement no doubt seemed entirely reasonable to the proprietors. After all, The Courant was primarily a *news*paper.

A fresh difficulty arose in March, 1807, when one of The Courant's paper mills was ruined by a spring freshet. Furthermore, the dam was broken and, adding insult to injury, a good many subscribers simply did not pay for their newspapers.

The proprietors issued a plaintive plea, referring to readers "whose accounts are more than a year old," and to the "many . . . whose accounts are . . . four or five years old."

Collecting was hard when cash was scarce and transportation difficult. Dunning delinquents, always a miserable chore, was rendered still more miserable because the amounts were relatively small and the delinquents scattered.

The weekly Courant cost $1.50 a year in 1803, $1.75 in 1805, and $2.00 in 1813, then remained unchanged for many years. Advertising rates in 1815 stood at a dollar a square for three weeks and 20 cents a square per insertion thereafter. The square, the unit of measurement of newspaper advertising until well after the Civil War, was 12 lines in one column. Later, the size of the square varied with economic conditions.

Adding to the problems of the proprietors was a circulation probably topping that of any other paper in the nation. In October, 1808,

The Courant claimed a circulation of 4,600 a week. Only a few American papers claimed half that figure. Until the 1830's, average circulation, even of the big-city dailies, seems to have hovered around 1000. The Courant's page size was increased in 1809 to 13x19½ inches, adding a total of 186 square inches to the whole paper.

Still further pressures were brought to bear on the Hudson & Goodwin print shop in 1809, when the firm imported the type for the first Bible printed in Connecticut. Set in England, the type for each page arrived locked in its iron chase and ready to go on the press. The handsome published books carried the H&G monogram on the title page. H&G Bibles quickly became a staple of the firm's output.

In 1812 Hudson & Goodwin began dabbling in a novelty of journalism that was to have a great future. In the issue for January 8 they tried their hand at headlines. These included "A DOUBLE MURDER" over one story, "HIGH-HANDED VILLANY" over another, and "INTERESTING DEBATE."

The use of headlines was a departure for The Courant. Back in 1775, the heading for the Battle of Lexington had read simply "WORCESTER, *May 3*." As time passed, some American papers began adding labels at the head of their stories. On January 8, 1812, The Courant ran a story from the Richmond *Enquirer* that gives a sample of news style in those days. It starts out:

OVERWHELMING CALAMITY.

In the whole course of our existence, we have never taken our pen under a deeper gloom than we feel at this moment. It falls to our lot to record one of the most distressing scenes which can happen in the whole circle of human affairs. The reader must excuse the incoherence of the narrative; there is scarce a dry eye in this distracted city. Weep, my fellow citizens; for we have seen a sight of woe, which scarce any eye had seen, or ear hath heard, and no tongue can adequately tell.

How can we describe the scene? No pen can point it; no imagination can conceive it. A whole theatre wrapt in flames—a gay and animated assembly suddenly thrown on the very verge of the grave—many of them, oh! how many! precipitated in a moment into eternity.

June, 1812, brought the declaration of what the Federalist press was pleased to call "Mr. Madison's War." New England voiced its almost uniform opposition. In 1814 Connecticut's Federalists met with delegates from Massachusetts and Rhode Island, and unofficial observers from Vermont and New Hampshire, in the deplorable Hartford Convention. The Courant, while not exactly egging the delegates on, nevertheless printed letters calling for a New England declaration of neutrality and for withholding Federal taxes. The paper pointed out that the names of many distinguished men appeared among the delegates.

On January 6, 1815, The Courant published an "Extra" carrying the Convention's official report, which turned out to be milder than some had anticipated. It blasted Madison's administration in proper partisan spirit, called for state control of defense, and proposed several amendments to the U. S. Constitution, including the limitation of the President to one term.

Unfortunately for the delegates, while they had been making big medicine in Hartford, other events were taking shape that quickly put their efforts in the shade. Two days after the publication of their official report, Jackson fought the battle of New Orleans, and on February 14 The Courant carried the joyful news of peace. The citizens of Hartford, who had had enough of the unpopular war, promptly staged a massive celebration.

In October, 1815, Hudson & Goodwin announced the coming dissolution of their partnership. Readers were told that after November 15, the paper would be published by George Goodwin and his sons Richard, George, Jr., and Henry, under the firm name of George Goodwin & Sons.

The printers amicably divided their assets—substantial for those days—of $120,000. The Goodwins took The Courant to the upper floors of the Sheldon and Goodwin building, opening a bookstore on the ground floor. They also kept the rights to the Testaments, to the mills at the upper falls in East Hartford, and to an undisclosed sum of money. The Hudsons kept those all-time best sellers, the Bible and Webster's Speller. They also kept one of the paper mills and the bookstore, including its stock of goods.

So ended the successful partnership of a printer's devil and a mason's apprentice. Both the trades of printing and of masonry have produced their immortals—a Ben Franklin and a Ben Jonson. No one—least of all Hudson and Goodwin themselves—ever claimed that the partners in Hudson & Goodwin Co. were men of genius. But the two did show that the American dream can come true. Starting with little more than native intelligence and an honest willingness to work, they established themselves as the respected proprietors of a widely respected firm, as pillars of church, law and order, and as patrons of education and right living. As publishers of famous books and a famous newspaper, they hobnobbed with the great and near great of their day—governors, senators, signers of the Declaration of Independence, and framers of the Constitution, with Noah Webster, Timothy Dwight, and a host of others. Though neither partner had much formal education, both helped to shape public opinion throughout the State and far beyond its borders. In many households, the teachings of religion were learned from Hudson & Goodwin bibles, thousands of children all over the country and for years to come were taught from Hudson & Goodwin spellers and textbooks, and the windows that opened on the world of affairs for many years were the four weekly pages of Hudson & Goodwin's newspaper. Reflecting on these things, the former printer's devil and mason's apprentice must have felt a deep sense of pride and accomplishment.

1815-1836
The People's Paper

GEORGE GOODWIN believed that an important difference between this Country and the rest of the world was that we had a large, vigorous, and intelligent middle class. As a successful self-made man, he proudly identified himself with this class, and under George Goodwin & Sons, The Courant became an advocate of middle class principles:

> *The People* are that respectable and all-important middle class that stands between the great ones and the rabble, and checks the ambition of the one, and the licentiousness of the other . . . They are to be found nowhere among the thousands of millions in Africa, and Asia. . . . even throughout the whole continent of Christianized Europe, the order of men called *The People,* has scarcely a shadow of existence.
>
> *We the People!* What body of men upon earth can say it with so lofty a tone as ourselves?

Subscribers to The Courant felt secure in the knowledge that their newpaper was the product of a respectable, God-fearing father and his sons, who believed in the sanctity of family ties, in the principles of George Washington, in the Congregational Church Establishment, and in a bright future for the State of Connecticut.

George Goodwin's substantial house stood on State Street across from the State House. There his twelve children were born, and his gracious wife, Mary, maintained a cheerful, bustling haven for children and grandchildren, friends and visiting dignitaries. The spicy smell of gingerbread and nutcakes hung in the air. At the proper seasons, "election cake" was produced by the oven-full. The usual number of mince pies produced for Thanksgiving was 60.

George cut a striking figure walking to the office. Six feet tall, he usually wore a broad-brimmed hat, a continental coat and waistcoat, and low shoes with silver buckles. His portrait shows a roundish head, a ruddy complexion and shrewd, good-humored eyes crinkled at the corners into deep crow's feet. Wisps of hair near the ears emphasize the round baldness of the top of his head. Small, tufted eyebrows high above the eyes give the face an expression of amused wonder at the goings on in a sometimes crazy world. The mouth is a firm and determined straight line.

Richard, the eldest of George's sons, had worked with Hudson & Goodwin for nine years. A Master of Arts from Yale, he had a sound classical background and probably wrote many of The Courant's editorials. He was almost 33 years old when Goodwin & Sons was organized in 1815.

George, Jr., 29, was a graduate of Yale in the class of 1806. He had gained business experience as a partner in a grocery and hardware business. As the son with the most merchandising experience, he took charge of the paper-manufacturing in East Hartford. According to his biographer, George was evidently more fond of good books and the outdoors than he was of business—"As a business man, although unsuccessful, he was active, industrious, and honorable."

Henry, 22 and painfully shy, had learned printing in The Courant from his father. Alfred E. Burr, who had learned at Henry's side, remembered him as a "high-toned gentleman," who "shrank from notoriety," and who never married "we think on account of his inborn bashfulness." Wrote Burr:

> He was in The Courant office, overseeing everything, besides setting up weekly advertisements and arranging the headlines compactly, but with nice precision. He was remarkably neat, and his office was as clean as a milliner's shop. One line of 'pi' would not be allowed to remain five minutes. Even the old Ramage press was oiled and cleaned off daily, and its wooden halfsheet platen was planed smooth as polished glass about twice a year by Deacon Colton.

George, Sr., self-made, successful, outgoing, was at 58 the driving force of the new partnership. His sons, though men of the utmost probity, seem to have found the give and take of business life not especially attractive. But the Goodwins were a close-knit, loving family whose standards of conduct and opinions were well known to Courant readers—and approved by them.

In February, 1816, they proudly announced the purchase of a new Columbian press from George Clymer of Philadelphia. Gone were the days when the printer must make his slow impressions under a wooden platen laboriously lowered against the type by a turned screw. The Goodwins could not contain their joy:

> The different parts of the press are of iron, not excepting the platen,
> which ensures its strength and permanency . . . Being entirely composed
> of iron, it is far less liable to get out of repair and is obviously more
> durable than the common presses, and the impressions it gives are more
> uniform and distinct.

The Goodwins could now print two full pages at a single pull instead of a page at a time. The Columbian press was surmounted by an iron spread eagle attached to the heavy platen by a series of levers. As the platen moved, so did the counter-balancing eagle, considerably lightening the pressman's labors. Equally decorative, but less functional, was a symposium of alligators and other creatures garnishing the uprights and cross pieces of the machines. It was a press to be proud of, standing rather topheavily on five dainty feet.

George Goodwin & Sons had not been managing The Courant for long before disturbing events began to occur in Connecticut politics. The principles of the Federalist Party, indeed of George Washington himself, were being questioned. The new Democrats, or Republicans —the titles were interchangeable and amounted to the same thing— wanted to broaden the suffrage requirements, and had joined the Tolerationists, who wanted to get the Congregational Church out of politics. Furthermore, certain Episcopalians, defecting from the Federalist Party, had joined them.

This was political revolution, and the next order of business was to do what revolutionists generally do—reshape the foundations of government. In 1818 the General Assembly duly called for a Constitutional Convention.

The Goodwins, devoutly hoping that the old order would not be overthrown by a rabble of democratic politicians, waited broodingly for the outcome. They refused to predict what the delegates might do, but ruefully reported in September what the Convention *had* done:

> It has provided that every white male of 21 years of age, and upwards,
> who does military duty, or pays a state tax may be made a freeman, and
> be entitled to vote in all freemen's and town meetings during life.
>   It has abolished our laws obliging men to support any religious in-
> stitutions . . . and, last though not least, it has sat already twenty days
> at an expense to the state of about TEN THOUSAND DOLLARS, or
> FIVE HUNDRED DOLLARS A DAY.
>   We hope the result will show that this great sum is not worse than
> wasted.

The Courant told the Federalist faithful that the plan of making a new constitution was "perfectly unnecessary," as all friends of peace and tranquility could plainly see. On the two main issues, suffrage and separation of church and state, the delegates had clearly gone wrong. Extension of the franchise had placed political power in the hands "of such men as throng the cities for day labor, or with other less meritorious views"; and disestablishment of the church served to undermine the very supports that had "upheld and preserved the reputation of the people for wisdom, sobriety, and virtue." *The people* were, of course, the middle class. The middle class had been let down with a thump. The rabble had triumphed.

"How long the people will remain quiet under such a constitution remains to be seen," The Courant lugubriously observed.

When the Goodwins turned their attention from politics to business, the picture looked brighter. Between 1810 and 1819 United States production of paper jumped from 3,000 to 12,500 tons, and the Goodwins' East Hartford mills shared in this boom. The firm's correspondence in 1817 and 1818 shows that papermaking was regarded by the Goodwins as at least of equal importance with the newspaper business. Paper-making continued to increase in importance. By 1836 the Goodwins were ready to sell The Courant—but they kept the paper mills.

The trouble with the printing business was that anyone with $200 could set up a plant. Many did just that. Standard law books and inexpensive bibles and textbooks became so common that quality printers could not afford to make or even sell them. The market was expanding, but overcrowded.

Much the same could be said of the newspaper field. In Hartford, the *Mercury* (founded in 1784), the *Mirror* (1809), and the *Times* (1817) were all competing for readers in a city of between six and seven thousand population and a State that totaled about 270,000. It was a competitive business, destined to get more so. By 1841 Hartford had 11 competing newspapers.

Stimulating the multiplication of newspapers and the national demand for paper was the rapid improvement in communication. The 13,000 miles of U. S. post roads in 1795 had increased to 73,000 by 1820; post offices had increased tenfold, from 450 to 4,500.

It would be many decades before air travel, but in November, 1819, The Courant reported:

An illuminated balloon, constructed by Monsieur Prelubit, a French gentleman, was raised from the State House Square in this city, in presence of a large multitude of spectators. It ascended in handsome style, and soon disappeared, in a southerly direction. We have since been informed that it descended in Wethersfield, about six miles distant.

An accompanying advertisement promised that in a subsequent ascent a cage would be attached containing some living animal. This story and advertisement seem to be the earliest mention of aviation in Hartford.

November 15, 1823, the firm name became Goodwin & Company. The reasons for this new arrangement are not clear. His biographer states that George Goodwin and his eldest son, Richard, retired at "about 1825." This would have left George, Jr., and Henry, who were joined by their brothers, Charles, 32, and Edward, 23, in November, 1823.

The Goodwins shipped paper down the Connecticut River to Boston and New York and other points. When competition began to cut into the profits from the lower grades of paper, the firm went in for such specialties as bank bill paper and fine stationery. Bookselling declined and papermaking increased in importance to the firm, so Charles left his post as storekeeper and took to the road, canvassing paper distributors in major Eastern cities.

A foreman of one of the Goodwin mills, William Debit, invented a rag cleaning machine that saved the work of a dozen girls. The Goodwins acquired the patent rights, and sold the device to concerns along the Eastern seaboard. By 1830 the United States led all other countries in paper manufacture as well as in paper consumption.

The ships that carried the Goodwins' paper down the river and over salt water to market also carried silver and Britannia ware, bells, barrel staves and hoops, ironware, cordage, horses, mules, grain, butter, cheese and many other products of central Connecticut. Hartford was a seaport, the home of captains and merchants, and later of insurance companies formed to protect cargoes on the high seas. Almost any issue of The Courant during the first half of the last century lists the arrivals and clearings of brigs and sloops trading with the Barbadoes, Martinique, Guadalupe, Mexico, Savannah, Philadelphia, Boston, or other Atlantic ports. In the 1840's some 2,500 vessels a year berthed at Hartford, carrying, in addition to cargoes, 24,000 passengers arriving or departing.

These links with the outside world kept the Hartford community from becoming provincial. The Courant's proprietors and readers had nationwide, often world-wide, interests. Conscious of these interests, the Goodwins apologized when the state and local news grew in quantity. "We hope our readers in the neighboring states will excuse us," they wrote in 1818, "for devoting so much of our paper in the last few weeks to subjects of a domestic and local nature." Then, as almost from the start, most of The Courant's readers lived outside Hartford, and many outside the state.

Visionaries could foresee an almost limitless expansion of horizons. The Connecticut River—if the rapids could be by-passed—would conduct the world's trade from Long Island Sound to the borders of Canada. Robert Fulton had captured the imagination of a nation by taking his steamboat up river from New York to Albany. As steamboating increased on the Connecticut River, it was easy for the Goodwins to observe editorially that "Hartford, being at the head of ship navigation, is the Albany of New England, and like Albany she would become the depot of all the products of the extensively fertile country to the North of us." The Courant painted for its readers the alluring picture of a Connecticut river teeming with commerce "exploiting those exhaustless sources of wealth" lately opened by the republics of 'South America. This was heady stuff, enthusiastically read by subscribers who had been watching and dreaming since the steamboat *Fulton* had first ascended to Hartford in 1815.

When, in 1826, the steamboat *Barnett* tried the river above Hartford, The Courant followed its progress with as much interest as it later followed the first orbital flight from Cape Canaveral. The voyage of the *Barnett* symbolized the opening of a new era. There were skeptics, of course. Some said that the Enfield rapids could not be passed. Others pursed their lips and talked gravely of the Willimansitt Falls. But the doubters were more than overbalanced by the believers—and believers, as the Goodwins pointed out, with ready cash.

On Monday, November 27, 1826, the *Barnett* sailed upstream from Hartford. Courant readers learned that "as it passed up the river, it was greeted with loud acclamations from the inhabitants of the banks, who thronged to witness the novel sight; bells were rung; salutes were fired from all the principal towns." It is true that on Tuesday it took the tugging and hauling of two scows and about 30 men to get the steamboat past the Enfield rapids. But the believers argued that the vessel had not been designed to navigate rapids.

Once past the rapids, the *Barnett* moved triumphantly on to Springfield, Massachusetts, where "every man rushed to the landing . . . The Court of Common Pleas was then in session, and a lawyer at that moment arguing a cause; but so intense was the interest excited, that none were left in the courtroom but the judge, the jury, the speaker, and the adverse counsel. The boat was received at the landing with reiterated cheering."

On Wednesday the *Barnett* continued its triumphant trip at an increased speed, improvements having been made on the engine. At the Willimansitt Falls an enthusiastic crowd hauled the boat over the difficult places. At North Hampton, The Courant reported nearly 1,000 persons thronged the bridge, hoisting the flag in honor of the great occasion. Finding two freight boats bound for Brattleboro, Vermont, the *Barnett* took them in tow. And so the triumphant progress continued, past Brattleboro to Bellows Falls, where the gallant vessel was welcomed by 50 guns.

The next day, after a 124-gun salute, the *Barnett* headed down river again, having set all New England agog with the potentials of the machine age. Before long, steamboats plied regularly between Hartford and Springfield, Massachusetts.

Whatever the commercial value of the *Barnett's* pioneer trip, it helped to stretch Hartford's horizons, to help its merchants and traders and newspaper editors think in larger terms. Timely news of distant places now seemed more important than ever to the Courant and to its readers scattered throughout the State.

News came crowding in, so in 1825 The Courant resorted to supplements. These were giant single sheets, not bound with the paper, printed so that the reader could cut and fold them himself into eight pages of reading matter. The Goodwins had puzzled over space limitations. As they saw it The Courant's business was to present three principal kinds of reading matter: advertisements, without which the paper could not have made a profit; news or, as they put it, "a sketch of passing events;" and miscellaneous matter "intended for instruction and entertainment." If the miscellaneous matter was not to be squeezed out, the supplement was a necessity.

The Courant's Columbian press was hard put to keep up with the regular weekly issues and the supplements. By 1828 the paper was being printed on a machine that reduced the labor of the pressman. It incorporated improvements designed by John I. Wells of Hartford.

Late the next year, when the new President Andrew Jackson sent his message to Congress, The Courant not only printed the entire document verbatim—all seven and a half columns of it—but announced that the message had reached Hartford in the record time of 25 hours by express post riders traveling in relays:

> The express traveled from Brunswick to New York, a distance of 33 miles, in 1 hour and 42 minutes; from New-Haven to Hartford in one hour and 55 minutes; and from Hartford to Boston in 6 hours and 8 minutes. Such speed for so great a distance, is probably without precedent in our country.

The machine age was catching up fast, but it was not yet able to outstrip the express riders at their best.

The Goodwins announced that they would content themselves with reporting the facts about Andrew Jackson. It was not for them, they declared, to tell their readers that "the man who only nine years ago could figure as a bully and a ruffian" was not fitted to serve as President of the United States. The Courant would take the high ground. It would report the facts, even when the facts showed that Jackson had "violated the sanctity of the constitution, set at defiance the laws of his country and trampled under foot the rights of individuals."

The increasing doubts of Connecticut conservatives in the face of political change was matched by an increasing certainty that the country needed a general tightening up of its moral fiber. Religious days must be kept inviolate; intoxicating spirits must not be consumed; and benevolent institutions must be supported and encouraged.

In 1823 The Courant noted with approval that the Brick Meeting House would be open for divine services on Christmas, and that in Boston and many other places pious people "whose form of worship differs from the Episcopal Church" would be remembering the Savior's birth.

The Sabbath, too, should be kept holy. With regret The Courant noted that President Monroe had inspected a government warship on Sunday and President Adams had made a Sunday journey from Providence to Walpole. When the steam boat *Oliver Ellsworth* was scheduled to arrive at Hartford on Sunday mornings, The Courant's proprietors felt certain that many persons would "greatly lament this arrangement."

The Goodwins came to believe that a leading underminer of moral institutions was liquor. Although as late as 1824 they carried a front-page advertisement including a picture of the Hartford Brewery, by 1828, under the influence of the widespread temperance movement, they began advocating total abstinence.

Another target was the circus. The Goodwins found in the circus nothing "calculated to exalt the mind or purify the morals"; they lamented the exhibition of such "debasing buffoonery" and supported legislation to curtail these promoters of "immorality and vice." Lyceums, on the other hand, were greatly to be recommended. "A Lyceum," The Courant explained, "is a voluntary association of individuals for mutual improvement." The members met regularly to hear dissertations and read essays on the various branches of natural science and other valuable topics. "It is contemplated," the paper optimistically reported, ". . . to establish a Lyceum in every town." Hartford was clearly ready to explore new cultural horizons. In July, 1829, the paper printed a poem over the initials L.H.S., the first verses of the prolific Lydia Sigourney to appear in The Courant.

The Goodwins did not limit their sense of moral responsibility to Hartford. Their sympathy went out to the Greek people in their struggle for independence, and The Courant encouraged meetings for Greek relief, where the hat was passed and considerable sums were raised. When Georgia, with the concurrence of President Jackson, began to discriminate against the Cherokee Indians, the Goodwins denounced this bullying of an aboriginal people who had made "great advances in civilization." As a practical step to aid the Nation's colored population, the Goodwins supported collections for the Liberian project of the Colonization Society.

The general spirit of social responsibility led to the founding in Hartford of a number of lastingly beneficial institutions, all strongly supported by The Courant. Among them were the American Asylum for the Deaf and Dumb and the Retreat for the Insane, now the Institute for Living. George Goodwin, Sr., was a founder of the asylum for the deaf and a vice-president of the Retreat. The sons founded or supported the Hartford Female Seminary, The Hartford Orphan Asylum, the Hartford Sunday School Society, the Bible Society, and others. Not only were these institutions endorsed by The Courant, but its proprietors gave of their time and money. Their support of good works was well known, and contributed to public confidence in the newspaper.

From about 1830 on, Goodwin's newspaper business must have seemed less and less promising, while the prospects of papermaking looked better and better. American journalism had undergone an expansion unprecedented in the world's history. The number of newspapers published in the United States had risen from about 200 in 1800 to some 1,200 in the early 1830's—a six-fold increase. The United States became the greatest newspaper-reading nation in the world with the largest number of newspapers and the largest aggregate circulation. All this meant a greater demand for paper, and greater competition in the newspaper world.

Hartford's first daily newspaper appeared in 1833—the *Review*, which had been established as a weekly in 1828. It could print fresher news than its rivals—and it entered the political arena on the opposite side from The Courant. Journalism was becoming for the Good-wins a far from peaceful business.

The older Goodwin brothers could remember when Oliver Ells-worth, David Daggett, Chauncey Goodrich, Doctor Strong, Colonel Wadsworth and others had made The Courant office their headquar-ters when the Assembly was in session. The Courant had reported what these men discussed in the printing office. There had been no frantic rush to print daily dispatches. There had been no anxious waiting for packets delivered by steam boat. And there had been far less harassment from local opposition papers. Hartford had been blessedly comfortable.

To keep up with the onrush of events, the Goodwins in 1832 bought an Adams power press, the first in Hartford. This innova-tion, designed by Isaac and Seth Adams, could turn out 750 impres-sions an hour, and had a "fly" to deliver the sheets from the ma-chine. It also eliminated hand inking of the type face.

By 1836 the Goodwins were ready to get out of the newspaper business. The brothers might have sold The Courant had it not been for their father, who loved the business. They first offered the news-paper to Alfred E. Burr, working in their composing room. He was only 20 years old, but there was no question about his ability. He later was to move to the Hartford *Times* and to build that paper into one of the state's leading journals.

The Goodwins offered Burr The Courant on two conditions: that he change his politics and his religion. He must join the Whig party and the Congregational church. Burr, a man of principle, refused the terms. So the Goodwins sold the newspaper to John L. Boswell, aged 28, a native of Norwich. He had come to Hartford at about age 12 to begin his apprenticeship in The Courant office. In 1830 he had gone to Columbia, Pennsylvania, and there published the Columbia *Spy,* supporting Henry Clay against Andrew Jackson in the cam-paign of 1832. Here was a man the Goodwins knew well, experi-enced, an editor of correct political and religious principles. He be-came sole proprietor of The Courant in September, 1836.

The Goodwins' farewell on September 12 said: "In politics, we have defended those doctrines and measures which we believed to be identified with the stability and success of our free institutions, and the true interests of the country . . . we leave the paper . . . with a subscription list as large as at any period within the last fifteen years."

George Goodwin was more than 80. For thousands of readers he and his sons and the paper they conducted were symbols of all that was tried, and stable, and of good report. What if the old man sometimes did write wistfully of bygone days? Had he not seen the immortal Washington; supported and chronicled his country's fight for liberty; talked with the Founding Fathers? The Courant was a paper a man could count on, give to his wife and children for useful information and gentle entertainment. The choice of a successor to the Goodwins was a matter of interest to persons throughout the state.

Boswell proved a good choice.

1836-1854
From Weekly to Daily

C HANGE was in the air. The very month John L. Boswell took over, his newspaper ran an advertisement requesting bids for grading a railroad between Meriden and Hartford. Before long, this railroad would link Hartford more closely than ever with the outside world.

Then there was Boswell himself. Little in the editor's appearance suggested the vitality he was to infuse into the newspaper. He had big ears, a big nose, big hands, and narrow shoulders. His high, stiff, proper collars and firm, straight mouth suggest rigidity. And yet this enterprising young editor had managed The Courant for not quite a year when, in September, 1837, he began to publish it as a daily, continuing the weekly Connecticut Courant as before. It was a bold move. Hartford's only previous daily, the *Review,* had gone back to a weekly in 1835 after about two years. Boswell was not deterred by this nor by the major financial panic of 1837, when more than 600 American banks failed. In New York, banks suspended specie payment. Hartford banks followed suit. Boswell, characteristically, discovered in these distresses a reason for expanding his business. The news, he argued, was becoming so vitally important that people must be kept abreast every day. He cheerfully explained in The Courant of August 29, 1837:

> Having been requested by many persons in whose judgment much confidence may be placed, to publish a DAILY PAPER in this city; and believing that its population [about 11,000 at the time] and business [still shaky from the panic] are sufficient to support such a journal [the *Daily Review* having recently gone under], the proprietor of the Connecticut Courant, relying upon the liberality of the community, has concluded, with as little delay as possible, to commence such a publication . . .
>
> If we shall find, on the first of January, that the support received will compensate for our trouble and expense, the paper will be continued at the rate of $5.00 per year, or $30.00 to yearly advertisers, including paper.

Regular publication of The Daily Courant began September 12, 1837. There were perhaps 120 dailies in America. Their predominantly commercial nature is shown by the frequency with which the word *Advertiser* appeared in their names. Arthur M. Lee reports that from 1790 to 1820 *Advertiser* appeared in the titles of at least half the dailies. It appeared in 20 of the 24 titles in 1800.

One reason for the development of dailies was the increasing number of local weeklies published on different days. In Hartford, The Courant appeared on Tuesdays, the Hartford *Times* on Wednesdays, the *Northern Courier* on Thursdays, and the *Patriot and Democrat* and the *Review and Telegraph* on Saturdays. This meant that on four of the six week days the people of Hartford could read a fresh local paper—that is, if they bought four weeklies. It was an obvious step for one of the newspapers to try to sweep the field.

Boswell launched The Daily Courant with a circulation of 200. By January, after four months, he had not yet obtained the number of subscribers he thought necessary, but he decided to continue anyway, trusting to Hartford's growing population and the city's "favorable position for news,—(the mails arriving from some quarter almost every hour of the twenty-four)."

Just how favorable Hartford's position was in the mid-1830's is suggested by that indefatigable historian of Connecticut life of more than a century ago, John Warner Barber. Among the blessings of Hartford Barber included the bridge "1000 feet long" connecting the city to East Hartford. He counted eight small steamboats plying between Hartford and upriver communities, two of them carrying passengers between Hartford and Springfield, Massachusetts, and the remainder towing flat cargo boats of 15-to-30-ton burden as far as Wells River, Vermont, 220 miles above the city. Three steamboats formed "a daily line between here and New York." He counted 12 newspapers, including religious organs, two semi-monthlies, and one monthly. More than twice as many books, he added, were published in Hartford as in any other place of equal population in the United States—a book-publishing tradition that went back to Thomas Green's Almanack of 1764 and The Courant's amazing record in books.

Not only did news reach Hartford at all hours and from all directions, but as Boswell was fond of pointing out, it came fast. President John Tyler's message to a joint session of Congress, delivered June 1, 1841, arrived in Hartford at eight o'clock the next morning, coming "the whole distance (350 miles) in 20¼ hours—average over 17 miles the hour." The following table shows how news between Washington, D. C., and Hartford speeded up:

Year	Event	Date of Event	Date In Courant	Time Lag
1814	British sack Washington	Aug. 24	Sept. 6	13 days
1823	Monroe Doctrine	Dec. 2	Dec. 16	14 days
1829	Andrew Jackson's inaugural	Dec. 8	Dec. 15	7 days*
1837	Van Buren's first message to Congress	Sept. 5	Sept. 7	2 days**
1841	John Tyler's 1st message to Congress	June 1	June 3	2 days***

* The news reached Hartford in 25 hours, a record, but missed weekly publication date, and so had to be held until Dec. 15.

** Traveled 70 miles between Baltimore and Philadelphia by railroad.

*** The news reached Hartford in 20¼ hours, that is, at 8 a.m. on June 2, too late for morning publication that day.

Express riders galloping—or slogging—their way to The Courant kept the daily supplied with fresh news. In Connecticut's April, 1838, elections, The Courant received tabulations of votes from all but ten towns by 7 a.m. the next day. An hour and five minutes later, special riders set out from The Courant office for Boston and other points with news of the election results. The 700 extra copies printed that morning could not meet the demand. Said Boswell: "Our friends ridiculed the idea of hearing from Fairfield, New London, and Litchfield counties in time for our paper of Tuesday; but we were confident it could be done; and if two or three of the town expresses had not failed, we should have been able to have given returns from every town in the State." Scoffers could not disconcert Boswell, who was determined to maintain the paper's statewide appeal. If interest warranted, he would arrange even for special dispatches from out of state. In 1838 such was popular interest in New York state elections that Boswell engaged express riders from New York and Albany. He took pride in his aggressive reporting, especially of political events—and was always careful to let his subscribers know that such service cost money and effort.

Boswell lost an able newspaperman when Alfred E. Burr, foreman of the printing room, left to become a partner in the Hartford *Times* in 1839. This was the same Burr to whom the Goodwins had offered The Courant on condition that he become a Whig and a Congregationalist. So well did Burr manage the *Times* that by 1841 he was able to buy out his partner's interest and to establish the paper as a daily. Burr left The Courant with Boswell's good wishes for everything but his politics.

It was a year of newspaper changes in Hartford. On July 15, 1839, Boswell wrote:

> We understand that two daily papers are to be commenced in this city in the course of a few days. As one of them if not the other is to be an evening paper, we take this opportunity to state that it has been our intention for more than a year to make 'The Courant' an evening paper as soon as the rail road should be completed between Hartford and New Haven. We mention our plan so that we may not be accused of trespassing on occupied ground . . .

Boswell's threatened invasion of evening journalism probably frightened no one. The year saw the establishment in Hartford of the *News and Advertiser* and the tri-weekly Hartford *Evening Courier*. The field was undoubtedly getting crowded.

Boswell had threatened to invade the evening field as soon as the railroad was completed between Hartford and New Haven. In mid-December passengers began to move between the two cities despite heavy snow on the tracks. Reported Boswell: "The time occupied in coming from Meriden was only two hours. The passengers state that the sight caused by the throwing of the snow, (which lay in many places four and six feet in depth) twenty or thirty feet to the right and left, was grand in the extreme."

Trains leaving New Haven at 7 a.m. reached Hartford at about 1 p.m., a schedule that turned out to be more satisfactory to Hartford morning newspaper publication than to evening—1 p.m. was rather late for evening deadlines. Boswell said nothing more about making The Courant an evening newspaper; instead, he began to publish a tri-weekly for country readers. He announced on December 16:

> We also intend, on the first of January, to commence the publication of a paper, THREE TIMES A WEEK, *for the country,* which will contain all the reading matter of the Daily Courant. It is intended for our country friends who do not take a daily paper, but who desire to receive the news oftener than once a week. We have not concluded on what days to publish it, but shall probably fix on Tuesdays, Thursdays, and Saturdays.It will be sent by mail, or delivered to those who call for it at the office, at $3 per annum. No subscription received for a less term than six months. We shall have no carrier for the city.

At the same time Boswell's daily readers learned that their Courant for 1840 would be "considerably enlarged" and would be printed from "new and beautiful type" from the foundry of Messrs. George Bruce & Co., New York. When the enlarged Daily Courant appeared in 1840, it measured some 15x20 inches to the page (almost the size of a page today), leading its owner to remark, "We now believe it is the largest daily paper in the country for the price, 5 dollars a year." The three-issues-a-week Courant, "for our country friends," returned to once-a-week publication. The weekly was discontinued in 1914 after the Sunday Courant started.

The increasing volume of news that swelled The Courant's pages ranged, as ever, from the important to the trivial. Attempts to free slaves; Charles Dickens' visit to Hartford; murders; train wrecks; political tidbits. The Courant under Boswell made lively reading.

In July, 1839, a cargo of slaves in the Spanish ship *Amistad* staged a revolt, killed some of the crew, and seized control of the ship. The lives of two Cuban owners of the ship were spared, on condition that the ships be sailed back to Africa. The tricky owners tried to steer for Cuba, but missed their mark so far as to sail into Long Island Sound, where the vessel was seized and brought to New London. While diplomats and jurists wrangled, the slaves stayed in jail, some at New Haven and some at Hartford. The climate did not agree with them and many died. Eventually, in March, 1841, the United States Supreme Court ordered the immediate freeing of the Negroes, some of whom finally got back to Sierra Leone after a stopover at Farmington, where attempts were made to Christianize them. In addition to the news accounts, The Courant published lively comment from the friends of Abolition and the American Missionary Society.

When Dickens arrived in Hartford in 1842, The Courant described him for its readers, not from first-hand observation, but from an account in a Worcester paper. It appeared that the young author wore a brown frock coat and "trowsers" and a red waistcoat. At least that is what he had been wearing in Worcester.

When Dickens returned to England and came out with his highly critical *American Notes,* Boswell commented indignantly:

> Mr. Dickens is making himself more supremely ridiculous than we ever supposed possible. Bitterly chagrinned at the poor and meagre success which happened to the special object of his journey, the establishment of international copyright, he returned to foster the disappointment with what philosophy he might. . . His feelings find utterance in gross caricatures upon American society . . .

Also in 1842 The Courant carried the account of Hartford's first railroad accident:

> The brakemen of the early train of cars yesterday [December 14] were unable to check them as they approached the depot, on account of the rails being covered with ice, and the two forward cars broke through the partitions of the ticket office, passed through the office and out the

front part of the building, taking the stove with them. Fortunately no person was hurt.

In 1843 Boswell hired Chauncey Howard, whose name he bracketed with his own, as editor. It cannot be claimed that the paper's editorials at this period were outstandingly profound. The Courant charged in 1843 that the General Assembly had not only wasted money for writing paper and pen knives, but had used public money to buy two clothes brushes, at $1.50, and had had six pens mended at 37½ cents—"a gross and unpardonable outrage," said The Courant.

More significant was the paper's view of the generally depressed economic conditions of Hartford and the nation. It was Boswell's belief that Hartford was deficient in manufacturing. Steam power, he thought, might make it possible for manufacturers to locate in Hartford instead of in the back country, where streams supplied water power. A Hartford location would cut transportation costs and would bring "many men of business energy among us."

A man of business energy himself, Boswell promoted his paper by reducing the yearly subscription price for 1844 from $5 to $4, and the yearly advertising rate from $20 to $15 a square. "We have run expresses annually (with the exception of last spring)," he wrote, "on the night of our state election and also at the presidential election and given the result to our readers the morning following."

This kind of prompt reporting took money and energy, especially when the presses gave trouble. A few months before, in November, 1843, Boswell wrote:

> We owe our readers an apology . . . There are occasions, with which printers are familiar, where everything about a press goes wrong. Such a time we had yesterday. It was impossible to make our sheet look right and we had to send it to our subscribers as they received it or not at all. The foreign news was so unintelligible that we have reprinted it on our first page today.

Also unintelligible to many Connecticut readers, but for far different reasons, was the news coming in from the Mexican border. Here a group of American settlers in Texas was seeking admission to the Land of the Free as a slave state. Boswell tried his best to explain the annexation fever that had seized many Americans. The southern slaveholders, he wrote bitterly, were seeking to extend their territory and to maintain the power of slaveowners in Congress. The owners of Texas bonds wanted to make sure of their security. Warmongers, too, were abroad, hoping to start a fight between our government and that of Mexico. And over all hung the spectre of slavery spreading

out to the territories. The Courant was still a long way from propos-
ing the freeing of American slaves, but, like some other northern
papers, it had set out along the path that would ultimately lead to
the popular outcry for emancipation.

Increasingly the great issues stemming from slavery crowded the
columns of The Courant. Slavery, Boswell accurately foresaw, was
splitting the Union. The North, he said, "will not voluntarily become a party in the perpetuation of American slavery." He believed
it a mistake to identify the interests of slaveholders with those of the
entire South, as the slaveholders did not number more than 300,000.
When single women, widows and heirs under guardianship were
subtracted, "there are probably not over 125,000 slaveholding *voters*
in the entire Union!"

Success in one editorial campaign came to Boswell in December,
1844—the railroad was opened between Hartford and Springfield.
Boswell took the train to Springfield and back, reporting his pleasure
with a trip that took only an hour and five minutes up and an hour

HARTFORD AND N. HAVEN RAILROAD·

SPRING ARRANGEMENT.

UNTIL further notice, the Cars will leave Hartford and
New-Haven daily, (Sundays excepted) as follows:
Leave Hartford at 5½ o'clock, A. M.
  do.   do.   4 o'clock, P. M.
Leave New-Haven 8½ o'clock, A. M., and on the arrival of
            the Steamboat from New-York.

The morning line from HARTFORD arrives at New-Haven
in time for the Steamboat which leaves at 8 o'clock, and arrives in New-York at about 2 o'clock, P. M.

. MERCHANDIZE will be promptly forwarded between Hartford and New-Haven and the intermediate places, at reasonable rates.

N. B.—Powder will not be transported over the road under
any circumstances.

TICKET OFFICE at the Depot, foot of Mulberry st., where
passengers are requested to call and purchase their Tickets
before the departure of the train.   For further particulars
enquire of   VALENTINE REYNOLDS,
  j. 31   dtf   Agent, at the Hartford Depot.

WIDE HORIZONS, FASTER NEWS THROUGH STEAM POWER
Hartford train met the New York steamboat at New Haven

and ten minutes back. Rail traffic could now move from Boston, through Hartford, to New Haven, and thence by steamer to New York. Other rail-and-steamboat routes from Boston to New York lay through Norwich and Stonington; but while the distances along the three routes were approximately equal, the route through Hartford had the advantage that it was mostly by rail. Railroad trains could make about 25 miles an hour; steamboats, only about 13.

Still another advance came in June, 1846, when a telegraph line was completed between New York and Boston, running through Hartford. The Courant carried its first telegraphic material on June 23—not a news item, but an advertisement announcing that the "Magnetic Telegraph" stations had opened that day in Hartford. Copy for the advertisement, Boswell said, "was received from Boston yesterday, by the Telegraph itself." Three days later, The Courant carried its first wire news: brief notices of U. S. Senate debates on raising volunteers for the Mexican War, on the tariff, and other matters. Boswell said that this Washington news had been received "at fifteen minutes after 7 o'clock last evening." Connecticut readers began to expect news of national events within hours.

Telegraphic news cost money and established dailies enjoyed an obvious advantage. In 1845, while the telegraph line was being strung to Hartford, The Courant bought out the Hartford *Evening Journal,* a staunch Whig paper that in the Clay campaign of 1844 had carried the excited motto: "Whigs, arouse, awake, shake off the dewdrops which glitter on your garments, and march to battle and to victory." The Whigs lost. Four years later The Courant retired another competitor when it bought the weekly *Connecticut Whig.*

At first the telegraph hardly could have been called a dependable source of news. The lines broke. Storms snapped the poles or short-circuited the wires. Farmers in the back country chopped down the poles. And no one was allowed to monopolize the wires for more than ten minutes.

Boswell claimed an ever-increasing circulation. In 1846, in a dispute with the Democratic postmaster over The Courant's right to publish lists of advertised letters, he produced a sworn statement of circulation. This showed the circulation of The Courant to be 720 and that of the weekly Courant, 4,824, for a total of 5,544. As newspaper circulation statistics were seldom made public in those days, Boswell's repeated assertions that The Courant had a larger distribution than any other Connecticut newspaper must be taken as one man's opinion, though probably a correct one.

In 1847 The Courant's page size was again enlarged, to 17¼x22 inches, almost the same depth and about two inches wider than newspaper pages today. Boswell again engaged an associate editor, Lucius E. Smith, whose name appeared from April until June of the following year.

An arresting story in 1849 told of the arrival of the Messrs. Porter and Robjohn and their "serial steamer or flying ship," pictured in The Courant. The exhibitors hoped that their ship, something like a dirigible, would be able to cross the continent to California in five days. It was the right time to be talking about quick trips to California. Almost every issue of The Courant carried news of the Forty-Niners, some of whom reported finding as much as an ounce of gold a day, though Boswell doubted it.

To the special advantage of subscribers to evening newspapers, private homes in Hartford at about this time began to use gas for illumination. Newspapers could be read comfortably by good light even in the winter when darkness came early. In September, 1849, a city meeting approved a contract with the newly organized Hartford City Gas Light Company for 50 street lights, the company to light and extinguish the lamps and to furnish gas at $2.50 per cubic foot. Boswell gave no hint that the new means of illumination might be helpful to readers of evening papers. Gas light was helpful in the composing rooms of morning papers, where fine type had been set by the flickering light of lamps.

Business activity began to pick up. When the readers of The Courant opened their paper on January 1, 1850, they learned that "The subscribers have this day formed a copartnership of Boswell and Faxon, and will continue the publication of The Courant at the old stand." William Faxon, the new partner, had learned the printer's trade from Boswell in The Courant office. He was not quite 28 years old; Boswell was 42. Faxon's sentiments on the slavery question matched Boswell's.

The issue announcing Faxon's partnership also reported:

> The publishers of the daily 'Courant' and 'Times', in view of the greatly increased expenses . . . consequent upon the enlargement of their sheets and the procurement of news by telegraph, cannot in justice to themselves, continue to furnish their papers at the reduced prices at which they have heretofore been delivered. The terms will be $4.50 per annum—if paid strictly in advance.

The agreement suggests interesting thoughts about combinations in restraint of trade.

About the same time John P. Brace was engaged as an editorial writer. He remained with The Courant until 1861, making his office in a dusty library on a floor above the printing office, reached by a rickety stairway. In those days the term "editor" applied generally to everyone on the paper not connected with the mechanical departments. Brace was The Courant's "heavy" editor, which meant that he did most of his work at his desk rather than circulating about the city to gather news.

About this time, too, The Courant subscribed to the service of The New York Associated Press.

Also competing for space was the greatly increased local news of booming Hartford. The census of 1850 reported 13,555 inhabitants; for 1860 it was 29,152, more than double. In April, 1850, The Courant reported what it called "a good looking omnibus . . . now running the whole length of Main Street." It expressed gratification, too, for the plans for "a spacious and beautiful hotel" to be built by T. M. Allyn.

There were cultural stirrings, too. July 5, 1851, brought the immortal Jenny Lind to sing at the Fourth Church. The Courant had been expressing doubts that P. T. Barnum—a Connecticut native—really would bring Jenny to America or to Hartford, but arrive she did, much to the joy of the populace. The church windows were opened, and nearby fences and rooftops were crowded with those who could find no room in the church. A dispute started over the seating because too many tickets had been sold, and the program was interrupted by a riot that neither the mayor nor the chief of police could quell. The crowd began to break the church windows. Frightened, Jenny climbed out a rear window and dropped to the backyard, where she found two young women whom she paid $5 to show her the way to the railroad station. There she kept to her private car. So keenly did Boswell feel Hartford's disgrace that he wrote, "We have no heart for the comments which this sad and disgraceful affair crowd upon the mind."

The Jenny Lind debacle showed at least that there was an audience in Hartford for the performing arts, and that churches were not necessarily the best places for the performances. In 1852 the General Assembly repealed the law prohibiting theatrical exhibitions, permitting them if licensed by local authorities. In November, Hartford's Common Council was asked to license a theater in the city. The Courant, long opposed to theatrical exhibitions, printed a column-and-a-half remonstrance. "Experience has demonstrated that in a small city like Hartford, none but a most corrupt and pernicious stage can possibly support itself, so long as a majority of the people remain virtuous and Christian." It was asserted that the theater would increase drunkenness, gambling, and prostitution. The Council refused the license. But next April the Democrats elected their city ticket largely on the theater issue, and the Common Council approved an application for theatrical exhibitions in American Hall.

Boswell and Faxon also shook their heads over the increasing secularization of their city. There were plans afoot, for example, to run a Sunday mail train. When an opposition paper twitted them about breaking the Sabbath themselves—by setting type Sunday night for the Monday morning paper—they indignantly replied, "Such is not the case. The telegraphic dispatches in Monday's paper are placed in type on the morning of that day which makes the delivery of our paper somewhat later than usual that day."

Hartford can bless Boswell for one most important contribution to the charm and grace of the city. Late in July, 1853, The Courant made an editorial plea for public parks, and especially for "one Park on a large scale" on about 40 acres of the farm then owned by Messrs. Gillette and Hooker. In October, Dr. Horace Bushnell appeared before the Common Council urging the importance and feasibility of a public park or common for Hartford. The issue was brought before a city meeting in 1854, and the park was approved by a vote of 1,005 to 682. The claim is made that Bushnell Park is the first public park in the world created and paid for by a vote of the people.

The pressure of news and advertising caused Boswell and Faxon to enlarge their newspaper again in 1854 to 19x23½ inches, seven columns wide, giving The Courant the largest page in the State. This enlargement came none too soon; 1854 proved a newsy year. The superb trotter, Flora Temple, ran a mile at Kalamazoo in 2:19½ —smashing all records; and Pierre Soule, U. S. Minister to Spain, helped to draft the Ostend Manifesto declaring that if Spain would not sell Cuba to the United States, the United States would be justified in taking it by force. Autobiographical works were published by Henry David Thoreau and P. T. Barnum. Several clubs formed in New York to promote the relatively new game of baseball. John A. Roebling built a suspension bridge over the Niagara gorge. *Uncle Tom's Cabin,* the play based on the book by Harriet Beecher Stowe, a resident of Hartford and contributor to The Courant, opened in New York.

These events made good copy, but the issue of slavery overshadowed all other news. In February, 1854, a meeting was held in Ripon, Wisconsin, by a group of Free-Soilers, Whigs, and anti-slavery Democrats who adopted the name "Republican" for their political association. In April the Massachusetts Emigrant Aid Society was formed to encourage armed anti-slave emigrants to move to Kansas. May saw passage of the Kansas-Nebraska Bill, which greatly alarmed abolitionists, because it left the choice of free soil or slavery up to the inhabitants of the territories. In June the fugitive slave, Anthony Burns, was led through the streets of Boston, to be returned to captivity in the South. Bostonians draped their buildings in black and tolled the church bells. In the same month The Courant reported that an Anti-Nebraska convention of some 2,500 delegates at Worcester, Massachusetts, had passed strong anti-slavery resolutions "based on the idea that the slave power was determined to make itself dominant in the nation." The delegates called themselves Republicans.

In the midst of the alarums and excursions of 1854 Boswell became critically ill from an attack of erysipelas and died on July 30, after four days' illness at the untimely age of 46. "His mind was unclouded to the last—he was perfectly conscious of his situation, and was ready and willing to go, and died calmly and peacefully and without a struggle," said The Courant.

Boswell's death left William Faxon sole manager of The Courant, a circumstance he evidently did not relish. At the end of 1854 he sold The Courant to Thomas M. Day, of Hartford, a man whose rigid opinions were destined to get a good shaking up in the violent years that followed.

JOHN L. BOSWELL
Defied financial panic, began daily

WILLIAM FAXON
In emergency, kept the paper going

ABEL N. CLARK
Pressed for space, printed extras

THOMAS M. DAY
Supported Lincoln editorially

TORCHLIGHT PARADE OF "WIDE-AWAKES" ON HARTFORD MAIN STREET: 1860

Courant backed formation of these young Republican clubs throughout nation

1855-1864
Politics and Civil War

W HEN THOMAS M. DAY, 40, bought The Courant, he was opinionated, full of personal prejudices, and wobbly in his political thinking. When he retired from the management of the paper at 50, he had seen a nation at civil war, had heard Abraham Lincoln, and had matured in his political views.

Day took over the paper on January 1, 1855, with few obvious qualifications besides a facile pen and a willingness to work hard. A descendant of one of the original settlers of Hartford and son of a former Secretary of State and Judge of the Hartford County Court, he had always known comfortable living. After graduation from Yale in 1837, he had studied law in Hartford, being admitted to the bar in 1840. Deafness forced him to give up law, and he tried various enterprises before going abroad in 1850. Being well off, he did not engage in business again until he bought The Courant more than three years later. All previous publishers, except Goodwin's partner Hudson, had been practical printers, familiar with the mechanical as well as the business and editorial sides. Day, despite his lack of experience, thought he would like to run a journal, had the money to buy one, and he bought it.

His first editorial, January 1, 1855, ran a full column. As to party label, he could hardly care less. "We may be called Whigs [The Whig party already had one foot in the grave]; we may be called Republicans [The American Republican Party was an anti-immigrant group]; we may be called Americans [That is, Native Americans or Know Nothings, a not especially charming organization of xenophobes]." Under this anomalous banner, he proposed to "encourage every judicious effort to stay the encroachments of the slave power"; to uphold the prohibition of liquor; to help check the influence of immigrants at the polls; to support a high protective tariff; and to expect little good from President Pierce or his cabinet. Like many other citizens of Connecticut before the era of Lincoln, Day was politically adrift.

On the question of the kind of newspaper Hartford needed, Day held clearer and more forward-looking ideas. Hartford readers could learn much about the wide world from the Boston and New York papers, he wrote, "but there is a local field which no metropolitan sheet can hope to fill, and that local field we hope to occupy." He promised to employ reporters to collect "everything that everybody wants to know, particularly in our own city, county and state." This promise constituted a complete about face from The Courant's original practice. As late as 1825 the Goodwins had apologized to their far-flung readers for publishing so much state news. And even the largest metropolitan papers did not generally have reporters for local items before the 1840's. On reporting timely local news, Day was far ahead of his predecessors and of most of his contemporaries on comparable journals.

In his opening editorial Day promised his readers important typographical improvements—"an entire change of type"—and a new press using "steam or water power as a motor." John P. Brace would continue as a writer and A. N. Clark would keep the books and look after the business.

Readers soon were treated to large doses of Day's racial and religious prejudices. The editor praised the Native American party for going into political battle with the war-cry of "America for the Americans." He praised the party's twin aims: "a refusal to be governed by foreigners—a determination not to allow Romanism to decide our elections." He criticized other editors for not seeing that Irish and German immigrants could undermine the American labor market.

With even greater assurance he wrote:

> We believe the Caucasian variety of the human species superior to the negro variety; and we would breed the best stock . . . the caucasian variety is intrinsically a better breed, of better brain, better moral traits, better capacity every way, than the Negro, or the Mongolian, or the Malay, or the Red American.

The Native American motto "America for the Americans" had a different effect on some of the newspaper readers in The Courant's distribution area. They believed the issues of freedom and human bondage to be far more profound than those of native birth, and they began to look about for a political organization to give force to their view. Their search led directly to the founding of the present Republican Party in Connecticut and to the establishment of a newspaper, the Hartford *Evening Press,* that was destined to merge with The Courant and to infuse new vitality into the old paper.

Day was still blustering at non-Americans when, about 2 p.m. on a cold Monday, February 3, 1856, Joseph R. Hawley, a local attorney who years later was to become one of the owners of The Courant, and John F. Morris, cashier of the Charter Oak Bank, met at the corner of Main and Asylum Streets in downtown Hartford. The weather was stormy, the snow falling fast. Both men had the same problem on their minds—and it wasn't the weather. Both were deeply concerned about the possible spread of slavery into the territories of the West.

Morris, according to his own account published in The Courant many years later, abruptly asked: "Hawley, isn't it time that a Republican organization was formed here?"

"Yes, it is," Hawley replied, "full time, and we must be about it."

Later that afternoon Morris received a note from Hawley: "Morris —Can you come to my office tonight at 7 o'clock. A few 'republicans' will be there respecting organization. Please be punctual and hold your own counsel. Tell the bearer whether or not you can come."

Promptly at 7, Morris entered Hawley's law office at 297 Main Street. Presently Hawley arrived, soon to be followed by Calvin Day, James M. Bunce, David P. Robinson, Nathaniel Shipman, Judge John M. Niles, Gideon Welles, later Secretary of the Navy under Lincoln, and others. Day, Niles and Welles were Democrats who had become unhappy with their party over the question of slavery. Robinson, Howard, Bunce, and Morris were Whigs who felt that their party no longer stood for much. Hawley was a free-soiler, well known around the state for his stump speeches against slavery. None had ever had any connection with the Native American Party.

The little group talked about the crisis the nation faced—a crisis involving human bondage on one hand and liberty on the other. They decided that Judge Niles and Gideon Welles should draw up a circular calling for the organization of a Republican party in the state. There was no national Republican organization at the time.

Things moved fast. Eight days later an enthusiastic mass meeting was held in Hartford. An executive committee was appointed to send delegates to Pittsburgh on February 22, the first national Republican meeting ever held. A National Republican Committee was formed, with John M. Niles the representative from Connecticut. In June a National Republican Convention in Philadelphia put up John C.

Fremont as the party's first candidate for president of the United States.

These political stirrings had an important impact on The Courant. A manuscript belonging to the late Miss Katharine S. Day, of Hartford, shows that as early as January, 1856, definite plans were under way to publish a Republican newspaper, and that 76 signers had promised up to $100 each to meet the first year's losses. The Hartford *Evening Press* commenced publication February 27, 1856, just 24 days after the Republican meeting in Hawley's law office. Ten years later, *The Press* merged with The Courant.

Both *The Press* and The Courant supported Fremont, who carried Connecticut while Buchanan carried the nation. In view of the Republican success within the State—42,700 votes against 35,000 for the Democrats and a mere 2,600 for the Native Americans—it became clear that Republicanism was on the wax and Native Americanism on the wane. Day commenced a judicious retreat. He declared that the extension of slavery had become the single great issue facing the American people, and that beside this question "it sounds like child's prattle to be discussing the every-day topics of our previous politics"—such topics as those of "naturalization, of length of residence, of birth-place, of religious connections, of foreign allegiance."

On January 1, 1857, The Courant announced that Abel N. Clark had been taken into partnership. Clark had been with the paper nine years in charge of the financial department. He was destined to carry on the paper after Day's retirement and to help to bring about the merger of The Courant's staff with that of *The Press* in 1867.

Both Day and Clark seem to have had a surer feeling for local news than for national or foreign. Personal, domestic matters caught their fancy more than politics or economics. They told their readers that they wanted The Courant to be like a cheerful morning visitor:

> The character of journalism in America is every day changing. Thirty years ago, only the public doings of public bodies were chronicled in the driest way. Now-a-days, people . . . care more to know what is going on about their own homesteads. The local journal is becoming the chronicler of all the little local matters; the remembrancer, to call to mind the business of the day and jog the memory, in time for needful action. We think The Courant owes much of its success to the fact that it is eminently a family paper; is read at thousands of breakfast tables; contains something for both sexes; and is addressed to the young as well as the old.

A week after his famous Cooper Union address in New York City, Abraham Lincoln spoke in Hartford's City Hall, filled to capacity before the speaker appeared. When he took the rostrum the applause was long and loud. Lincoln began his remarks to a hushed audience. Frequently, as The Courant reported, his "quaint allusions and similes" brought laughter; frequently his arguments drew long applause.

Before Lincoln's appearance, political discussion in Hartford's papers had been marked by a notable crassness. A chief argument of the anti-slavery newspapers was that the very presence of black men debased society. Slavery ought therefore to be kept closely confined to the states where it already existed. Local abolitionists, of course, wanted to see slavery done away with, but they were commonly regarded as extremists who made more noise than sense. The pro-Southern papers, while disapproving of slavery, sought desperately to pacify the South, out of fear that northern manufacturers would lose their valuable Southern markets if the slave-holders became sufficiently angry. None of the parties adopted a noticeably lofty approach to the problem, and it was the practice of the more experienced politicos to side-step the slave issue whenever possible.

Lincoln changed all this in Hartford. The tone of editorial comment was never quite the same after his speech at City Hall. Lincoln boldly began: "Whether we will have it or not, the slave question is the prevailing question before the nation." He placed the value of the United States slave population, considered as property, at $2 billion, and he reminded his audience that a similar amount of property, if owned by northerners, would also have a great influence upon their opinions. He went on:

> Slavery is morally wrong . . . If, then, we of the Republican party who think slavery is a wrong, and would mould public opinion to the fact that it is wrong, should get the control of the general government, I do not say we should or would meddle with it where it exists; but we could inaugurate a policy which would treat it as a wrong, and prevent its extension.
>
> For instance, out in the street, or in the field, or on the prairie I find a rattlesnake. I take a stake and kill him. Everybody would applaud the act and say I did right. But suppose the snake was in a bed where children were sleeping. Would I do right to strike him there? I might hurt the children; or I might not kill, but only arouse and exasperate the snake, and he might bite the children. Thus, by meddling with him, I might do more harm than good. Slavery is like this. We dare not strike at it where it is. The manner in which our constitution is framed constrains us from making war upon it where it already exists. The question that we now have to deal with is, "Shall we be acting right to take this snake and carry it to a bed where there are children?" The Republican party insists upon keeping it out of the bed.

Lincoln also defended in his speech the shoemakers of Lynn, Massachusetts, in their right to strike for higher pay. The Democrats had made the strike a political issue. Said Lincoln, in what must have seemed pure heresy to many in his audience: "I am glad to know that there is a system of labor where the laborer can strike if he wants to! I would to God that such a system prevailed all over the world."

Lincoln's talk aroused Hartford as nothing had before. A young Republican organization, calling itself the Wide Awakes, held torchlight demonstrations and made speeches. The Wide Awake program caught on nationally. Soon The Courant was printing excerpts from the hundreds of letters from various parts of the country asking how to form Wide Awake clubs.

Day actually found himself defending the shoemakers and other strikers:

> The shoemakers of Lafayette have struck for more pay; the blacksmiths and machinists in large locomotive works in Philadelphia have struck for more time; and the boardinghouse keepers of Haverhill have struck for pay in advance; and the Hartford *Times*, great organ of the unterrified Democracy; is horrified!! It cries out— 'What can be done so long as there is an organized party in the North based upon *one idea* alone, and that idea hostile to the South?' If we have but one idea, thank God it is a good one. *Freedom* is our motto, and if the *Times* can suggest a better one we shall be thankful for it. If the idea of *Liberty* is offensive to the South, that is their fault—not ours. . . .

When Lincoln won the election in November, The Courant burst out in a flutter of crowing cocks, spread eagles, American flags, and pennants reading "GLORIOUS NEWS!" and "VICTORY! VICTORY! WE'VE GOT 'EM!"

It proved to be short-lived elation. In April, 1861, The Courant reported the attack on Fort Sumter:

THE LATEST NEWS.
BY TELEGRAPH.

THE LATEST DEVELOPEMENTS OF SOUTHERN CHIVALRY!!!

A Barbarous and Unprovoked Attack on Fort Sumter!!

CONTEST CONTINUED ALL DAY!!

TWO OF THE MADMEN WOUNDED.

THE FLEET IN THE OFFING.

A Violent Storm Raging.

Correspondence of Gen. Beauregard and the Confederate Secretary of War!

Charles Dudley Warner, an editor of the *Evening Press* and later of The Courant, has left an account of how Hartford responded to the war news:

In all the crowded churches with heavy hearts but with exultant patriotism they sang 'My Country 'Tis of Thee,' and at noon the whole town seemed to be gathered in State House square; it was packed with thousands, men, women, and children, and when the flag was raisd, the starry flag, which lots of people had scarcely ever seen before, and few knew how to make, the great hymn of 'My Country' went up, while tears streamed down the cheeks of the singers. . . .

All that day and the next, men and women were cutting out and making uniforms for the volunteers. On Monday morning came Lincoln's call for 75,000 men. The Hartford company—how the crowd cheered and cried at the station—departed for the camp at New Haven, with Barnham Captain and Hawley Lieutenant. And war was to be learned, and be the chief occupation for four years.

It seems like a dream now, those years of excitement and dread when one sat at the end of a telegraph wire that seemed to burn the brain. After the first Bull Run there was almost war at home. The City arsenal had to be protected by the City Guard. The *Press* Office was threatened, and prepared itself with a stock of loaded rifles for defense. More than once during the war the office was practically cleared of editors and compositors by volunteering. But it battled along. News increased mightily in quantity. Where there had been before the war a quarter of a column of telegrams, there were now many columns.

The demand for newspapers rose sharply and circulations rapidly mounted. So did costs—for paper, for labor, for gathering news. The news poured into Hartford in increasing volume, some of it late, some of it inaccurate, all of it bulky.

When Day retired as editor at the end of 1864, he noted that The Courant's circulation had trebled in the ten years of his management. At a conservative estimate, this meant the combined daily and weekly circulations amounted to 30,000 by the end of the war. Day claimed, perhaps with some exaggeration, that daily circulation jumped from 17,000 to 26,000 within a month after the firing on Sumter.

The enlarged circulation proved too much for the old Adams press, and Day bought a steam-powered Hoe. The cost of paper went up, from about $7\frac{1}{2}$ cents a pound at the start of the war to 22 cents in 1863, after which prices became rather unstable. News gathering was expensive. Day wrote: "It has not been sufficiently understood heretofore, that we have *all* the telegraphic information within reach of the Associated Press in New York. Of course, we pay for it, and pay handsomely."

Subscription rates for the daily were raised from $5.00 at the start of the war to $8.00 by war's end. Annual advertising rates in the daily were increased from $20.00 to $35.00 for a square.

The problems of newsgathering were enough to exasperate the most patient editor. The Courant was betrayed, at one time or another, into proclaiming the capture of Vicksburg and Richmond when neither place had been taken, of assuming that Jeff Davis had died when he was very much alive, and of giving currency to rumors that General Beauregard had been killed and—twice—that the Southern General Ben McCullock had died.

News of the battle of Bull Run appeared in The Courant the day after the event, but it was erroneously hailed as a Union victory. The next day the story of the same battle bore the heading, "Disaster and Retreat." News of the battle of Wilson's Creek appeared four days late. It was almost two months before any clear account of the fighting near Richmond appeared in The Courant. As for the battle of Gettysburg, early dispatches arrived on Friday, July 3. But Saturday, the 4th, being a holiday, The Courant took a long weekend, and had the pleasure of informing its readers on Monday that "The news of federal successes seems almost incredible."

Day, like other editors, had his troubles with censorship. Sometimes news arrived in letters from the front giving battle plans in great detail. At other times the telegraph wires were blocked for no discernible reason. What most annoyed Day was the government's reluctance to publish bad news. In August, 1862, he disgustedly headed his telegraph column:

More Mystery.

NEW YORK, Midnight.—Various rumors are afloat here relative to army movements, some of them stating disaster, but the War Department will not allow anything relative to the movements of our army to be telegraphed.

Editors found it hard to resist armchair generalship. Day thought Baltimore should be placed under military rule. On first learning of the appointment of General Sherman, Day dispatched the whole business with the remark, "He belongs to the tribe of do-nothing generals."

Day loyally supported the Northern war effort, tried to arouse patriotism, called for volunteers, publicized mass meetings. Democrats, in particular, came under his suspicion. The more he thought about the Democratic press, the more excited he got. At one point he intemperately declared that the Hartford *Times* was the strongest proslavery paper that could be found in the country. He seemed to have forgotten the *Times'* many protests against the institution and his own former belaboring of the Negro. He thought he could see subversive newspapers scattered throughout New England.

Half a year before the war ended, The Courant reached its one hundredth anniversary, October 29, 1864. From the pages of the newspaper and from reminiscences, it is possible to recreate some of the events that probably took place at The Courant that day.

The working day began at about 1:30 a.m. when, his lantern bobbing and flickering along Pratt Street, compositor Jacob Turner arrived at the office.

Unlocking a heavy wooden door, he let himself into a hallway even blacker than the night. He closed the door behind him, making sure that it was left unlatched, and mounted the wide, creaking stairway to The Courant's low-ceilinged mechanical department.

Lighting the lamp in the center of the room, he glanced at the marble imposing stone on which his chief, W. H. Goodrich, was accustomed to leave directions. Not much there—only a small sheet of copy paper and a few strips of telegraph tape.

Turner blew out his lantern, hung up his coat, gave a hearty shake to the grate of the coal stove, and threw in a shovelful of coal. He was ready for business.

The copy paper on the imposing-stone bore a message from Mr. Goodrich. Goodrich hoped Turner could squeeze in the few late telegraph dispatches from General Grant, which had come in just before the closing of the telegraph office at 9:15. Turner would find the inside pages partly made up, but should feel free to rearrange them. Mr. Day had crowded things a bit by writing a long editorial on the paper's one hundredth anniversary.

Turner picked up the narrow strips of telegraph paper. As usual, they had been only half decoded: "At evry pnt enemy found entrenched and his wks manned I shl keep our troops out where they are untl toward noon tomrow in hopes inviting attack Sig U. S. Grant Lt Gen"

There were almost six column-inches of this sort of thing, Turner estimated, and if Mr. Goodrich was running true to form, he had left only four inches of space.

Turner took the strips over to the type cases and began setting the words, swaying easily from side to side as experienced hand setters do, throwing the type into his composing stick and snapping it home with his thumb. It was the custom of reporters to write their own headlines. But as no reporter had seen these late dispatches, Turner made up headlines as he went along. The words formed quickly:

THE MILITARY SITUATION

Reconnoissance of Gen. Grant.

A DECIDED SUCCESS.

THE ENEMY ATTACK AND ARE REPULSED.

PRICE ROUTED.

The click of the type soon was interrupted by the slam of the door downstairs. It was Tom, an apprentice come to heat the boiler in the cellar to provide steam power for the press.

Goodrich had more and more turned over management of the

composing room to Turner, who at 28, proved himself far more dependable than most compositors. These fellows generally traveled in packs of three or four, appearing in town without notice, staying at work for a day or a month as the spirit moved them, and vanishing as abruptly.

Turner, a craftsman to his fingertips, was another breed. He joined The Courant staff in 1856. Death severed his connection with the paper in 1924—68 years later.

A sharp hiss of steam, audible through the shaft that housed the belt from the basement steam engine, announced good progress with the boiler. Turner set the last type in the page—it fitted better than he had anticipated—and locked up the form.

As for the past 100 years, the regular edition of The Courant still consisted of a single folded sheet—four pages. The outside, pages one and four, seldom carried anything but advertising, and were printed days in advance. The inside pages carried the reading matter: city news and editorials on page two and telegraphic news on page three.

Mr. Day's editorial was indeed a long one: "A century has rolled away since the Connecticut Courant commenced its visits to the hills and valleys of this staid old State," it began; and ended 26 inches later with the flourish, "The Courant: esto perpetua!"

Turner proceeded to fill up the remainder of the editorial page with the material Goodrich had left him. But there was an inch and a half that no stories seemed to fit. Turner decided, as he had often done, to fill the space with his own composition. His eye fell on the long wooden tables stacked with the sheets for the morning's edition, covered with advertisements on one side, and blank on the other, ready for the material he was just then making up. This morning's issue carried a single column of reading matter on page one, a special Saturday feature. Here was inspiration. He set his thought in type: "See First Page for a column of interesting reading matter, including an article from the St. Louis *News.* . ."

A few minutes later, the page was locked in its chase, and the forms for the Courant's centennial issue were on the press.

By now, the sounds from the cellar had taken on the urgency that boilers express when the pressure is up and the steam hisses through the gauge cocks. Turner went to the speaking tube, pressed his mouth against the opening as if he were about to play a trombone, and blew hard.

From the cellar came a whistle and "All set down here, Mr. Turner."

"Good," said Turner. "Get her started, then come on up here."

Tom stepped to the flywheel of the little upright engine (which, as The Courant told its readers, delivered five horsepower), grasped a spoke, and gave the wheel a turn. Slowly at first, but with rapidly increasing speed, the engine puffed at each stroke of the piston. Tom took the loose belt, connected far above to the press, and with a deft twist slipped it onto the engine's drive wheel, pulling his fingers out of harm's way in the nick of time. Upstairs the press leaped into noisy motion.

Tom went up to the composing room, and the two men soon were printing the blank side of the large sheets.

By dawn the stacks of printed papers stood high on the tables, and the room was filled with the bustle of half a dozen newsboys. A couple of men were counting out papers and addressing bundles for the mail.

The boys took their papers to tables, deftly folded them, sharpened the crease with a smooth stick and inserted facsimiles of The Courant's first issue, which had been prepared in honor of the Centennial. Then they took their papers and went out on the street.

By mid-morning, the entire Courant staff was assembled. Editor Day was reading his centennial editorial to see how it looked in print. With him in the cramped office overlooking Main Street were the telegraphic editor, Henry Woodward, and the entire city staff, Albert Hotchkiss. These three were The Courant's only regular staff writers. They took care of the three departments that supplied the standard reading matter: editorials, "City Intelligence," and "THE LATEST NEWS: by The American Telegraph Company's Lines."

A fourth occupant of the "little 7 by 9 room" as Turner once called it was Abel N. Clark, co-owner and business manager. Clark, indefatigable, also helped edit telegraphic matter, even hiking down to the telegraph office to pick up dispatches.

Day turned to Hotchkiss' column, "City Intelligence," miscellaneous items of local news, interspersed with paragraphs of editorial comment. Hotchkiss, city reporter and city editor combined, contributed opinion as well as fact. Day noted with satisfaction that the Democratic Hartford *Times* had been brought to book in several of the items. The *Times* had recently gone so far as to accuse an abolitionist living on Pleasant Street of felling a tree in front of his house just to obstruct a Democratic torchlight parade. Hotchkiss had investigated and found no evidence of tree felling. "Lie number '197'," his column read. "There wasn't a tree felled in Pleasant Street. 'Tell another.' "

Day smiled, but stopped as he noted a quizzical glance from Hotchkiss. There was nothing wrong with casting barbs at an opposition paper, but Hotchkiss needed no encouragement.

Hotchkiss left on his rounds, expected to net a good 24 to 36 column inches of city news before suppertime. Even the opposition press acknowledged that Hotchkiss was a superb newspaperman. He had been on the Courant for only a little longer than a year, but already the legend that no important story could elude him was developing. There was the night the Democrats had held a secret caucus in Talcott and Post's Hall, all reporters barred and all Democrats attending sworn to silence. Next morning, Courant subscribers were treated to a verbatim account of the proceedings. Hotchkiss had found a hole in the ceiling through which a chandelier was suspended. While the secret proceedings were in progress, Hotchkiss crouched at his listening post, rapidly taking notes.

Afternoon brought a lull. Day, having finished his editorial labors before noon, had departed, as was his custom. Woodward, who disliked the cramped quarters, had retired to his room in the Allyn House, where he preferred to do most of his work. Hotchkiss was out gathering items.

But afternoon brought no quiet to the "practical" department, or to its superintendent, Goodrich. When he was not finding space for new advertisements, he was making up the news pages, ordering paper, preparing the presses, combing the town for a compositor to supplant one who had suddenly departed, attending to any one of a hundred details.

Turner, meanwhile, was urging on his crew of compositors and apprentices. They rummaged through the box into which all news copy was dropped, until they found a story to their liking—preferably one written unhurriedly and in a neat hand. The faster the typesetting, the more the pay for the day's work. They were paid about 30 cents a thousand ems, and a good compositor could set seven to ten thousand ems a day, worth perhaps $2.50 a day on the average.

By 9 p.m. the telegraph office closed, and the compositors quit shortly thereafter. The lights went out, the key was turned and another working day ended at the offices of The Courant.

A hundred lively years lay behind, and another hundred even more lively lay ahead.

1864-1869
Rocky Road to Broad Highway

B ETWEEN its centennial celebration in 1864 and the beginning
of 1870 The Courant management changed almost yearly,
moved to a new building, tried an eight-page format for a
while only to return to four, and joined in the publication of an evening daily. It reported Lincoln's assassination, the alarums and excursions of the Fenians and the Ku Klux Klanners and the carpet-
baggers, the impeachment of President Johnson, and the New York
Stock Market's Black Friday in 1869.

The Nation was growing fast. Between 1860 and 1870 the population of the United States rose from 31½ million to 38½ million,
or about 22 per cent. Hartford grew even faster—from 29 thousand
to almost 38 thousand, an increase of about 31 per cent. Communication, too, was getting faster. In 1866 the first really successful Atlantic cable was completed; in 1869 a golden spike joined the East and
West Coasts by rail; the same year, the Suez canal was opened. The
nation's telegraph lines, strung hither and yon during the war, now
connected remotest villages. The steadily increasing volume of news
over these wires demanded more and more columns of space. The
Courant reported in May, 1865, that there was now continuous telegraph communication between Washington and Macon, Georgia,
which meant that news from the deep South, relayed through the
Nation's capital, could reach Hartford in a few hours. No newspaper man worth his salt could have resisted the temptation to add
to his paper's reading matter.

Advertisers, too, were demanding more space. These were boom
times in the North. Day after day big advertisements appeared, seeking investment money for an expanding country. Oil companies, insurance companies, railroads promised larger and larger dividends in
larger and larger type.

Finding space for all the news and advertisements became a daily
struggle. The presses in most newspaper offices were not big enough
to turn out papers larger than eight pages at most.

It was all very frustrating. The important news in 1864 under the
headline:

The Old Flag Still Waves!

GLORIOUS VICTORY!

ABRAHAM LINCOLN OUR NEXT PRESIDENT!

The Last Hope of the Confederacy Crushed!

Magnificent Majorities!

Republican Institutions Not a Failure!

had to share the limited space in The Courant's four pages with an
advertisement that read:

Thomas M. Day, when he wrote his editorial for The Courant's centennial issue, knew that he was to retire in two months. He had planned it ten years ago, back in the fall of 1854, when he had bought The Courant. Ten years as owner and editor, he had thought, would be enough. They had proved more than enough. He had not counted on the hardships of managing a wartime newspaper. When the war had been in progress a year, he had turned over to Abel N. Clark a large part of the management, and he was now ready to retire from active journalism, though he retained a financial interest in the newspaper for another 15 years.

Clark was a good man for the job. Forty-six years old when he took command, he had already been on the paper 17 years. During this time his chief concern had been to manage the business end. He also helped with the editing of telegraph matter and tried his hand at an occasional local news item. Acquaintances said that when he undertook a job it was as good as done.

An almost ascetic face rather belied Clark's businesslike nature. A dark beard ran from ear to ear under his chin, framing an elongated, pale, intellectual countenance. Little hint here of the man's practical side.

In addition to managing the business details, he devoted a great deal of time to practical Republican politics. His obituary notice said of him that he had probably done more work in a quiet and unobtrusive way for his party than any other individual in this state. That was saying something, in those flamboyantly political days.

In his introductory editorial Clark told readers he was assuming entire responsibility. The Courant's views on public affairs would be those which "in the judgment of the conductor" the public welfare demanded. But Clark wrote that the future path of The Courant would not change much.

It was a promise he could not keep. The volume of news increased so rapidly that it soon overflowed four columns on Page Two, the principal news page, leaving a bare two and a half columns for advertising. Telegraph news on Page Three often ran to nearly three columns. Restricted to four pages, Clark was offering more reading matter, but at the expense of the advertisements that kept him in business.

Here was a stubborn problem. Advertisements were still being sold by the square, which in those days measured 14 lines in one column. A square could produce a yearly income for The Courant of anything from $35 to $234, depending on whether the advertiser bought a square for a year at $35 or paid for single insertions at the rate of 75c an insertion. The puzzle the editor had to solve was how to increase his news columns without running himself out of business. Every 14 lines of advertising permanently lost to reading matter reduced The Courant's income.

Something had to give. On Saturday, March 18, 1865, The Courant appeared with an additional sheet, which it called an "extra," bringing the total number of pages to six. Clark told his subscribers:

> We present our readers this morning with an extra quantity of reading matter, much of it original. The pressure upon our columns of late has been so great that we have found it difficult to do justice to all. We shall from time to time relieve the pressure upon our columns by furnishing extras.

But Saturday supplements were not a real solution. The newspaper was crowded every day, not just on Saturdays; and the insertion of extra sheets and pasting them in along one edge took time and money.

On April 3 Clark came up with a more practical solution, announcing a change to eight instead of seven columns a page, with the additional comment that "The Daily Courant is now the largest paper in New England, with perhaps a single exception in Boston." The Saturday supplements also continued to give some relief to overcrowding.

Of course, the news and advertising problems of The Courant had their sunny side. Said Clark in August, 1865: "The Courant was never so successful as now, and never furnished a greater variety of reading matter . . . It is our aim to make The Courant second to none of its contemporaries."

But Clark was not destined to carry out his high hopes: he came down with a sickness he could not shake off. The following spring he sailed for Savannah. But health did not return; and, finding it increasingly difficult to keep up, he admitted William H. Goodrich, head of the composing room, into partnership on January 1, 1866. This was the third change in The Courant's management within thirteen months.

Goodrich was to remain on The Courant, with one brief interruption, for a quarter of a century. An item in the 150th Anniversary issue, which was published while Charles Hopkins Clark was editor, says that:

"Mr. Goodrich was of the old school of publishers, more careful to prevent a dollar going out than to get two dollars to come in, and, though the paper was a paying proposition throughout his management, it neglected the opportunity for growth of which those who came after him have made such good use." This was written 20 years after his death, and it may be a reasonably accurate characterization of Goodrich in his old age. It does not apply to the man in his younger years as partner.

Goodrich, who learned his trade as a compositor on the Hartford *Times,* was thoroughly familiar with newspaper work. It is a good thing he was, too, because Clark was never to be a well man again. Goodrich immediately tackled the problem of newspaper size. His solution was a radical one for Hartford. He made The Courant an eight-page paper.

This departure, on July 2, 1866, required some explanation. The eight-page form, Goodrich told his readers, "is chosen in preference to the four-page 'blanket' sheet because of the greater ease with which it is handled and read, and also on account of the better position it gives to all advertisers. . . . Hereafter telegraphic news will be found on the first page, and the eighth page will be occupied by local intelligence. Thus the most important and generally interesting news matter will be contained upon the outside of the paper."

These were sound reasons for an eight-page format, but Goodrich soon found the Hartford business community objecting. Advertisers were not pleased with news on Page One—right where they wanted their advertisements. Furthermore, the eight pages were uncut. They were a single huge sheet folded once to make four pages and then folded once more to make eight. Readers had to tear or cut the edges to get at the inside matter. Advertisers did not like that either. After 18 months The Courant returned to four pages—enormous blanket pages, to be sure—but only four of them. And the advertisers were back in full force on Page One.

Though he may have shown poor timing in changing to eight pages, Goodrich showed good news sense. He put the news where it could be found most conveniently— on the outside—and he gathered items from towns around Hartford and arranged them systematically on a single page. Further, he retained a correspondent in Boston and one in New York, who sent letters of big-city news.

It quickly became evident to Goodrich that he would have to share the burden of the business. The doubled number of pages in each day's issue called for tremendous efforts. Clark was dying of cancer. And Goodrich, competent in all phases of newspaper work, was chiefly interested in the business and mechanical side.

He and his ailing partner agreed to merge the venerable Courant with the youthful Hartford *Evening Press* and to publish a daily morning and daily evening newspaper. The weekly editions of the two papers would be combined into a single weekly called *The Connecticut Courant.*

The ownership announced this step December 6, 1866:

> General Joseph R. Hawley will be the Editor in Chief of both papers; Mr. Charles D. Warner will occupy the position of Literary Editor; and Mr. William H. Goodrich will be the business man and practical printer of the establishment.
>
> The firm name will be Hawley, Goodrich and Co.

The consolidation took effect in January, 1867.

Many years later, Charles Hopkins Clark (no relation to Abel N. Clark), who became editor and publisher of The Courant and who published a history of Connecticut newspapers, said of the transaction:

> When in 1867, the *Evening Press* was merged with The Courant, the name of the latter was retained, but the personal force and spirit of *The Press* took control of the journal. . . Anyone who looks up the old files and compares The Courant with *The Press* will see that *The Press* was the more attractive paper of the two, more alive and decided, and it ought to have made its way, but it didn't. Even then The Courant had such a firm hold on the public that there was no disturbing it.

The new proprietors had almost more business than they could handle. They were running three newspapers: the morning Courant, the *Evening Press,* and the weekly Connecticut Courant, which was made up of stories taken from the two dailies. At first, the staffs of The Courant and *Press* worked more or less separately, greatly complicating the business. Hartford, meanwhile, was demanding more news than ever.

The proprietors had planned from the beginning to move their merged papers into new quarters on Pratt Street. In the meantime, to make room for a new press, the *Evening Press* advertised for sale its Taylor power model.

The merger undoubtedly involved dislocations of the workers. About this time the compositors of The Courant went on strike. Amos B. Stillman, on The Courant from 1866 to 1870 in the capacity of "office boy as well as city editor," has left a sketchy account. The compositors quit work at 9 o'clock one night. Stillman went down to the telegraph office a few blocks away and wired Hawley, who was in New Haven at the time. Hawley immediately wired back, "Give the boys what they demand," and the strike ended then and there.

March 18, 1867, the slow process of moving to 14 Pratt Street began. For The Courant this meant going only a few doors from the corner of Pratt and Main Streets. The proprietors begged the indulgence of subscribers, explaining that there might be some delays in delivery. The new press was in place, "but as there is some delay in the removal of our engine and boiler, we are compelled to rely on 'hand power' instead of steam with which to print The Courant for a day or two."

To the proprietors, moving from the cramped *Press* quarters in the old wooden Fisher building and from the single-floor Courant office, the new rooms seemed commodious indeed. The newspaper occupied several floors on one side of the five-story building owned by Talcott and Post. A new steam elevator ran between the composing room on the fourth floor and the press room in the basement. The Courant was proud of this modern convenience—despite an accident one day that dropped the forms for the inside pages from the composing room to the bottom of the elevator shaft, entirely destroying four pages of type, and costing hundreds of dollars. For a few days the newspaper had to be reduced to four pages.

On the first floor were the business office and a free reading room where newspapers from New York, Boston, Albany, and other cities were kept on file. The new Hoe double cylinder press in the basement could handle an eight-page newspaper, cut in sheets, printed one side at a time. The paper first had to be wetted down. One man, the feeder, slid sheets into place by hand. Each sheet had to go through the press twice. The paper, like a pancake, was done first on one side and then turned over. Supplementary sheets had to be printed separately, each side in turn, and then folded into the newspaper. Not for a quarter of a century was any substantial improvement generally adopted in this cumbersome procedure.

The only ones not pleased were the advertisers. They still remembered wonderful front pages devoted to nothing but advertisements. They expressed their complaints and the proprietors did their best to accommodate. Advertising kept increasing, however, until by August, 1867, the newspaper had settled into this usual pattern; page one, advertisements only; page two, perhaps a column of literary and miscellaneous items, and the rest advertising; page three, advertisements only; page four, mostly editorials and news of the day, a few advertisements; page five, all advertisements, except for paid notices

of births, marriages, and deaths; page six, a column or so of financial news and the rest advertisements; page seven, advertisements
only; page eight, general city news, New England news, and advertising.

No matter how much money this advertising brought in, the arrangement did not satisfy the proprietors who were, after all, trying to run a journal of news. The newspaper had been changed to
eight pages in the first place to put page-one news where it belonged. With great reluctance the proprietors decided upon what
seemed to them in most respects a backwards step: they decided
to go back to four pages. This meant adopting a huge inconvenient
blanket sheet opening to a full spread of 30 inches by 46 inches,
twice as wide and twice as long as a conventional newspaper today.
In the larger cities, blanket sheets were the butt of jokes, and were
rapidly going out. "The weather is too cold to read it in the apple
orchard," *The American Journalist* facetiously remarked of the
blanket-sized Toledo *Blade,* "and the paper is too large to unfold
in any ordinary house in Ohio." Still, Hartford's advertisers were
not ready for big-city journalism. They wanted to bring in customers, and in their opinion, an advertisement in a blanket sheet was
the way to do it.

On New Year's Day, 1868, The Courant abandoned its eight-page
form, not to return to it for over 19 years. The first issue in the new
size carried this reluctant announcement:

> Our new and somewhat enlarged form is adopted purely for business
> reasons, in order to accommodate our advertisers in the best manner and
> at reasonable prices, and leave us sufficient space for the other purposes
> of the paper. To adopt a smaller sheet would compel us to charge higher
> prices for advertising, thus excluding many, or to reduce the space de-
> voted to reading matter, or both. Had we any desire to make this the
> largest paper in New England, a trifling addition to our present size
> would suffice, as only The *Boston Advertiser,* and that by a very few
> square inches, now surpasses The Courant.

On the face of it The Courant should have begun about now to
settle down to a long period of orderly growth. Much was in its
favor. One of the oldest papers in the nation, the second largest in
New England, it was under the direction of able, experienced, energetic proprietors. But there was still a stretch of rocky road ahead.

Early in 1868 Warner, who had carried the main burden of the
Evening Press during and since the war years, decided that a trip to
Europe would be good for his health and left for what turned out to
be a 14-month tour. Hawley, meanwhile, was getting more and

more involved in politics. He had served as Connecticut's Governor in 1866 and 1867. And this, 1868, was a presidential campaign year, and there were dozens of meetings and scores of speeches to be made for Ulysses S. Grant. Hawley was up to his political ears and loving every minute of it. When Grant's victory was assured, The Courant announced the fact in a story garnished with eight line-drawings running from top to bottom of the page: an American flag, six spread eagles, and a crowing cock. Hawley served as chairman of the Electoral College that made Grant's victory official.

Warner's absence in Europe and Hawley's political involvements left the management of two dailies and the weekly up to their associates. This didn't please Goodrich, who began to talk about leaving.

The proprietors decided that they were trying to do too much, and sold the *Evening Press* in 1868 to the *Morning Post,* which then changed to an evening paper. The Courant declared that "two experienced editors who have been hitherto devoted to the *Press* will now be employed upon The Courant exclusively." It said also that the New York and Boston correspondents who had been with the *Press* would now be retained by The Courant. No employees were released, despite the sale of the *Press.*

Although dropping the *Press* eased the load, Goodrich resigned at the end of 1868 "because," as a notice explained, "other inducements promise a somewhat easier life than any man can hope for on a daily, and especially on a morning paper." Stephen A. Hubbard, who had been on the news staff of the *Press* since 1861 and who had become a partner in 1867, took Goodrich's place as business manager, but not for long. Hubbard did not enjoy business details, and Goodrich, after a few months, began to think that newspaper work was what he liked best after all. He therefore approached Day, still an inactive partner of the firm, and bought him out. Thus Goodrich returned as business manager of The Courant, and Hubbard went back to more congenial editorial duties.

The rocky post-war road was behind The Courant; a broad, smooth highway lay ahead. Not for more than 20 years was there to be another change in its management through death or retirement. Hawley, Warner, Hubbard and Goodrich, a remarkable quartet, were to work together in remarkable harmony—and with remarkable results.

1870-1890
Gentlemen of the Press

ON THE MORNING of April 13, 1870, The Courant electrified the ladies and gentlemen of Hartford with the headlines:

Prize-Fight Broken Up!

**Prompt Action of Governor Jewell—
The Military Ordered Out!**

A LARGE CROWD OF ROUGHS ARRESTED —RESPECTABLE (?) YOUNG MEN IN THE GANG!

**The New Haven City Hall Filled w.th
the Victims—Strong Guard of
Soldiers and Police!**

ETC., ETC , ETC.

It was an unusual story.

Prize fights were no everyday occurrence in Connecticut—and for a good reason. The law said anyone engaging in a prize fight might be imprisoned up to five years, and that every person who aided a prize fight, whether present or not, might be jailed up to two years.

This stiff medicine had the whole-hearted endorsement of the four gentlemen who managed The Courant, and probably of most of their readers. As a rule, The Courant did not even mention prize fighting. Even when the great John L. Sullivan came to town and gave a demonstration, The Courant ran not a line on the whole unsavory business.

However much the gentlemen of The Courant might deplore prize fights, no newspaperman could have omitted the fight story on this particular April morning. The Courant informed its readers that the Sheriff of New Haven County had appealed to Governor Jewell, and that the Governor had given authorization for calling out all troops. Wrote a special correspondent:

A prize fight was announced to come off, at Charles Island, Milford, this morning at six o'clock, between James Kerrigan of New York and one Toughey of the same city. About forty of the worst kind of roughs arrived . . .

In the morning Sheriff Hotchkiss received a dispatch from Milford asking for protection from the roughs that were prowling about the village. . . The New Haven Grays, the Governor's Foot Guards, the Montgomery Guard, and the New Haven Light Guard were ordered out and left on a special . . . The sheriffs and militia . . . captured 68, who were marched to Milford Station and placed under guard. . . Your reporter noticed among the crowd several young men from Hartford, whose parents are among the first business men of our city.

Joseph R. Hawley and his associates wanted Courant readers to make no mistake as to how the newspaper regarded such shenanigans. The Courant was produced by gentlemen for gentlemen and their families. The young roughs had got what was coming to them. "Nearly all of them are in jail," an editorial observed. "Now let there be no twaddling or thimble rigging justice."

This view reflected the philosophy of the proprietors. Hawley, Warner, Hubbard, and Goodrich thought of themselves as journalists, of course; but, quite literally, they thought of themselves as gentlemen of the press. Journalists might, and often did, invade the privacy of individuals, play up the sensational, and even fabricate stories. Not so a gentleman. For the four proprietors, gentlemanliness was a compelling idea, a guiding editorial principle.

Their emphasis on gentlemanly standards stood in marked contrast to much that was going on in American newspapering at the time. The decades between 1870 and 1890 witnessed a remarkable increase in sensationalism. "Keyhole journalism" flourished—especially in the bigger cities. The interview was developed as a reportorial technique. If the persons interviewed turned out to be involved in bizarre crimes of one sort or another—well, that was the way the chips fell. Sex scandals, monstrosities, and disasters of all sorts began to crowd less spectacular news as the "new journalism" arrived in this country.

The proprietors of The Courant looked at the new journalism and found it part good, part bad. On the credit side was its emphasis on lively writing, properly directed crusades, forthright editorials, and increased use of pictures. On the debit side were foolish and sensational stunts, the frequent invasion of privacy, over-emphasis of the trivial, and a preoccupation with anything that would boost circulation.

To the gentlemen of The Courant, interviewing, as practiced by such metropolitan newspapers as the rambunctious New York *World* and New York *Herald,* was a stench in the nostrils. In 1870 they reported with sad head-shaking that the New York press had "fallen in respect to courteous and reliable journalism—and it has been disgraced by an access of personalities, and the vile invention of 'interviewing.' "

Four years later The Courant was just as doubtful. An editorial in 1874 asked

IS THERE ANY PRIVACY?

The conduct of the modern newspaper is beginning to fill many people with alarm, and that not without reason. It seems to be taken for granted that one who holds any sort of public, though not necessarily official, relation to his fellows can have no privacy . . .

The primary duty of the newspaper is to print the news, but not to make itself an inquisitor to find out private secrets for the gratification of a morbid or prurient curiosity . . .

When the New York *World* reported an exclusive interview with the distracted sister of a wife murderer, The Courant deplored the whole sordid business under the head "UNGENTLEMANLY 'JOURNALISM.' "

The Courant did more than point a finger. It practiced what it preached. For example, in April, 1871, it showed how it could apply gentlemanly principles in reporting an unusually sensational crime story in Litchfield.

TERRIBLE CRIMES IN LITCHFIELD COUNTY.

The Most Sickening on Record—Incest and Murder—A Brutal Father Debauches Six of His Daughters.

Another Horrible Case---Murder in the First Degree.

The Courant, coming to the core of the story, told its readers only that:

Perkins has had six daughters and two sons. The oldest daughter is now 28 years old, and has given birth to five children, the fruit of her father's unnatural crime. Two of these children are now living, one a boy of seven years, and the other an infant, born since the father's arrest. The other three have, it is charged, been murdered by the father immediately after birth, the girl testifying that she never saw them but that she heard them before they were removed from the room by their father. . . . Perkins is now 54 years old.

Here was sensation made to order. Murder, sex, six daughters to be interviewed, not to mention the seven-year old boy and gossipy neighbors. But The Courant, which had a reputation for thorough follow-ups on important stories, chose only to report the basic facts. Nor did it keep the story alive with day-by-day stories on the unfortunate victims of the tragedy.

Presently, though, it was taken to task by a Hartford clergyman for even mentioning the crimes. The Courant replied with an editorial headed

WHAT NEWS SHALL BE PRINTED?

There are newspapers whose only object seems to be to pander to public curiosity. Concerning these we have nothing to say.

But what business have newspapers with the publication of crime or its details? Why not leave them to the law and the courts? . . . A law not backed by public opinion is not worth the paper on which it is engrossed. Public opinion is, or ought to be, enlightened, founded upon knowledge; and that not simply of what is sweet and agreeable, but of a great deal that is foul and terrible.

There is no record that the clergyman had an answer to this argument.

That the four proprietors should consistently apply their gentlemanly policy and manage the innumerable details of a lively daily newspaper through two decades without faltering or falling out is remarkable. Especially so because, aside from their common concern for gentlemanly journalism, they were in almost all respects poles apart. They were able to work harmoniously for such a long period partly because they saw eye to eye on fundamentals and partly because their personal abilities, and even their personal limitations, supplemented each other.

Hawley, first among the four equals, gave an air to The Courant by his very presence. This dashing former editor of the *Press* was widely known as the first man from Connecticut to volunteer after Sumter was fired on. In 24 hours he helped form Rifle Company A, First Connecticut Volunteers, personally engaging the needed rifles, and was mustered in as Lieutenant of the company. After the Battle of Bull Run he helped to form the Seventh Regiment, Connecticut Volunteers, which was thereafter known as "Hawley's Regiment." He saw much action, including the siege of Charleston and the battle of Olustee, Florida, then was mustered out in January, 1866, having been breveted major general during the war.

Hawley succeeded, too, in the arts of peace—as Governor and later as U. S. Senator from Connecticut. He served as senator for six terms. In 1876 he was President of the great Centennial Exposition in Philadelphia, famous as the first successful world's fair in America, a wonderful show that did much to awaken America to its role in the new age of technology.

Hawley's name was placed in nomination for President of the United States in the Republican National Convention of 1884. Picking up support, he remained in the running through four ballots. After a heated contest, the nomination went to James G. Blaine.

One Courant legend has it that whenever Senator Hawley returned from Washington and was seen on the streets of Hartford, the word would quickly get about that "the General is in town." Next morning, the editorials would seem to sparkle wlth fresh vigor, and husbands would tell their wives over the coffee, "Hawley certainly can get to the core of a problem."

The fact is, Hawley seldom wrote editorials. It was Warner, for the most part, right along.

But Hawley had the dash and color and character that people liked and admired and trusted. When he did occasionally write editorials, his favorite theme was the proper conduct of the national government. "Uncle Sam must be a gentleman," he told his readers. And when the question of the national debt came up, he promised that The Courant would "contend without quarter for the payment of every dollar of the National debt, in the good faith that would best become a nation of Christian gentlemen."

He liked to prepare himself for the editorial task with an evening snack—an enormous Swiss cheese sandwich washed down with a seidel of beer—in the dark-beamed grill room of Heublein's Hotel. He would usually bring with him some congenial soul from the newspaper office.

Even Hawley's weaknesses turned out to be assets. According to Amos B. Stillman, member of The Courant's staff, Hawley found writing extremely arduous, and would sometimes put off starting his lead editorial until past midnight. The General blamed himself much for this laziness, as he called it, and yet his reluctance to wield the pen undoubtedly helped to keep him and The Courant out of political hot water. An indiscreet editorial from Hawley, his friends found, could embroil the newspaper in endless wrangling. Even as it was, if The Courant spoke in his praise, word got about that Hawley was glorifying himself. On the other hand, there were always solicitous friends who feared that this or that editorial policy was "hurting Hawley."

Hawley was probably harder to hurt than they imagined. He enjoyed a remarkably stable place both in politics and in journalism. A lithograph of 1882 published by Root and Tinker of New York, showing "Representative Journals and Journalists of America," places a portrait of Joseph R. Hawley first on the top row among such notables as Whitelaw Reid of the New York *Tribune,* Charles A. Dana of the *Sun,* James G. Bennett of the *Herald,* Joseph Medill of the Chicago *Tribune,* Henry Watterson of the Louisville *Courier-Journal,* and others.

It sometimes happens that the most colorful and conspicuous officer in an organization has the least to do with its operation, while one of the least conspicuous is the mainstay upon whom everything depends. The man upon whom everybody on The Courant depended was Stephen A. Hubbard, one of the most beloved managing editors who ever sat up with a newspaper.

Hubbard looked like an Old Testament prophet—wavy dark hair, deep eyes, sharply aquiline nose, and flowing beard that spread over his shirt like a bib. He had, too, some of the prophet's dedication and spiritual vitality. Warner, in an obituary editorial, expressed the consensus of his associates:

> Dear friend, noble heart. The world was sweeter and better that you lived in it. You helped our faith in humanity and in the everlasting goodness. We shall all be better the closer we walk in the spirit that guided you. How small and petty, indeed, it seems to have any other spirit, in this presence.

Hubbard contributed what none of his partners could, in anything like the same degree: infinite patience with detail and with the human weaknesses of his associates on the paper; a long familiarity with newspapering that commanded respect from cubs and veterans alike; an intimate acquaintance with the city and state.

Hubbard was a self-made man who had begun setting type on the *Hampshire and Franklin Express* of Amherst, Massachusetts. After working on other small New England papers, he went to the New York *Evening Post.* In 1853 he started the Winsted *Herald,* which became, under his ownership, one of Connecticut's leading papers. When he came to Hartford, first on the *Evening Press* and, after the merger, on The Courant, he brought a broad knowledge of journalism. He had been a typesetter, reporter, editorial writer, and publisher. He knew journalism in the cities and in the hinterland. When he spoke, he spoke as one who knew.

Hubbard, like Hawley, wrote little. The partner who set the pace for the writing staff was Charles Dudley Warner, whose books and other writings were well known to the American reading public. His complete works, published by The American Publishing Company, of Hartford, in 1904, occupied fifteen volumes. Warner's titles included such then favorites as *My Summer in a Garden, Being a Boy,* and the book he wrote with Mark Twain, *The Gilded Age.*

The Gilded Age, which gave a name to an era, apparently was written in response to a challenge thrown to the two friends by their wives. Twain's wife, Livy, and Warner's wife, Susan, were discussing current novels they liked one evening, the two authors pooh-poohing such modern trash. The wives challenged the men to do better, and *The Gilded Age,* published in 1873, was the result. Twain wrote that he and Warner each received $18,000 from the book's sales; and Twain was later to get a reputed $80,000 or more from the play rights.

At The Courant, praise from Warner was catnip to a reporter or junior editorial writer. Warner took great interest in the literary quality of The Courant and loved to discuss points of style with members of the staff. He himself was a frequent contributor to *Harper's,* the *Atlantic, Scribners,* the *Century,* and others. For six years he conducted the "Editor's Drawer" department of *Harper's.* He then succeeded William Dean Howells as conductor of the "Editor's Study" department for another six, until July, 1898. In the 1880's he had edited Houghton-Mifflin's distinguished biographical series, *American Men of Letters.* This work brought Warner in touch with well-known literary men—Oliver Wendell Holmes, for example, did the biography of Ralph Waldo Emerson. In the 1890's he served as Editor in Chief of the *Library of the World's Best Literature,* published by Peale and Hill.

Warner was filled to the brim with a delicious, spontaneous humor. Just as his friend Mark Twain, around his own billiard table, used to throw away on his friends more witty sayings than he ever published, so Warner in The Courant office sparkled involuntarily. A restless soul, he would wander about the office and at length come to rest at some busy writer's desk, draping his limp, tweedy form over a nearby chair like a rag doll. There was a shaggy look about him. His thick hair was always tousled, his eyebrows bushy, his moustache drooping at the corners. His beard usually looked as if it could stand the clippers.

He would gaze at the writer through deceptively sad eyes. There was something about his expression that suggested the half-depressed, half-quizzical face of a St. Bernard. Presently he would begin to talk, and the writer, however preoccupied with a deadline, would quickly fall under his visitor's charm.

He was an easy man to live and work with, largely because he took life good humoredly as it came. Courant tradition maintains that the familiar saw commonly attributed to Mark Twain, "Everybody talks about the weather but nobody does anything about it," really belongs to Warner, appearing in an editorial on August 27, 1897. Hawley said after Warner's death: "We have lived as brothers, without a single controversy or passage of ill feeling, for 57 years."

Hawley, Warner, and Hubbard had all come over from *The Press.* The fourth member of the partnership, William H. Goodrich, had been on The Courant a little over 16 years at the time of the merger. Starting as compositor, he had worked his way up to foreman of the composing room. From foreman he rose to business manager, and held that position until his retirement in 1891.

There was a marked no-nonsense look about Goodrich's somewhat chubby face that appeared above a stiff, businesslike collar. He looked like a calculating cherub. If Goodrich had any warmth in his makeup, his associates have been remarkably silent about it. He stood near, but not in, the circle of warm friendship that included his partners and other lesser lights on the paper. To him, The Courant was a business. It needed to be run in a businesslike way. And, Heaven knows, if the details of dollars and pennies had been left to Senator Hawley, or Warner, or the tender-hearted Hubbard, the till would probably have stood open and empty half the time.

Goodrich disconcerted his associates because, in his coolly objective way, he could take The Courant or leave it alone. Twice he resigned from it. After the first resignation, which lasted only through the year 1869, he bought back in. He was welcomed by his former associates: they needed his good business sense.

During the early years of the partnership, the newsroom staff comprised only two persons: a city editor and a night editor. The latter's job was to wrest some kind of coherence out of the telegraph

CHARLES D. WARNER
Publisher, editor, noted author

JOSEPH R. HAWLEY
*General, Governor, Senator,
publisher*

MARK TWAIN
*Nook Farm neighbor of Warner,
Hawley*

STEPHEN A. HUBBARD
To his partners: "dear . . . noble"

CHARLES H. CLARK
Improve product, stick to principle

WILLIAM H. GOODRICH
Two dailies, two weeklies: too much

dispatches as they arrived in fits and starts. Everyone on the writing end, if not a proprietor, was an editor. It was all chiefs and no Indians. The fact that one of the lesser chiefs liked fire water has given rise to a legend that explains how a gentleman of great consequence was added to the staff.

According to the legend, it all began on a night in 1871—the night of the great Chicago fire. Unfortunately, a key man on the small reportorial force had chosen this of all evenings to indulge too freely in alcohol, and The Courant found itself badly hampered in handling the biggest news story of the year. Fire news was crowding in over the wires and, as word spread, insurance-conscious Hartford waited for each successive dispatch.

Things had just about reached a state of chaos when a self-possessed young man entered the office, where the proprietors were in desperate conference, and inquired mildly if there was a job available for an inexperienced lad just graduated from Yale.

It took the proprietors a split second to come to a decision. Was there a job? Indeed there was! Chicago was burning down, and they wanted the young man to get to work on the story right away.

It was a hectic night, but the young man did a splendid job. Next morning The Courant ran a complete story, covering the fire from every important angle.

Thus (so the legend goes) did young Charles Hopkins Clark, on the very first night of his employment, show those qualities of diligence and steady good sense which were to carry him to the editorship of the Hartford Courant.

This legend, existing in several printed versions, turns out on examination to be badly garbled, but seems true to the spirit of what actually happened. The facts, as gathered from Clark's own reminiscences, from correspondence, and other sources, were something as follows:

Charles Hopkins Clark, a graduate of the Hartford Public High School and of the class of 1871 at Yale, applied early in October, 1871, for a job as reporter on the Hartford Courant. Hawley, who interviewed him, liked his looks and academic record, which showed distinction in writing and literature, and suggested to his partners that the young man might be well worth hiring. The partners agreed because Albert Hotchkiss, that star reporter, had just gone off on one of his periodic binges, leaving the paper high and dry for a couple of nights. They didn't want to fire Hotchkiss, who was the best reporter they had ever known. On the other hand, they wanted to insure themselves. It seemed that even an inexperienced reporter could tide them over, so Hawley wrote Clark the following letter two days before the Chicago fire:

"October 5, 1871

"Dear Mr. Clark:

We want you to begin next Monday, if you will—a.m. We think *very* well of you as a beginner, but of course it is only as a beginner, and we believe you will come to be a ready and useful newspaper man, but we do not feel willing to offer any beginner more than $20 a week. I should wish to have you feel entirely satisfied with whatever bargain we make, and shall be glad to have you with us.—This is after a conference of all four of us on this and various matters.

Hastily Yours, J. R. Hawley

Late Saturday night, October 7, the first of two huge fires broke out in Chicago, and all through Sunday the dispatches jammed the nation's telegraph wires. As fast as they came in, The Courant set them in type. Sometimes the messages contradicted one another. No matter. There was no time for the niceties of editing. As soon as each dispatch was set, it was placed in the galley below the earlier accounts. There was something breathless about the way the columns read:

First Dispatch!

Chicago, Oct. 8-2 a.m.—The most terrible conflagration that ever occurred in this city broke out about 11 o'clock tonight, and burning swiftly over six entire blocks, is still raging with almost unabated fury . . .

Second Dispatch:

2:30 a.m.;—The Fire is apparently raging as fiercely as ever . . .

Third Dispatch.

The Fire Under Control.

About one o'clock this morning the fire in the western division was under the complete control of the fire department . . .

The Latest—The Fire Still Raging.

Chicago, Oct. 9—12:30. The Fire in the west division is now raging with unabated fury . . . At this hour it still seems beyond control . . .

Before long The Courant office was crowded with Hartford insurance executives, who jammed the little quarters and made a hard reporting job harder than ever. D. E. Clapp, the night editor, was at his post handling the dispatches, and Hotchkiss, now back on his job as city editor, was covering the Hartford angles.

Managing Editor Hubbard decided to call in the cub reporter Sunday night, instead of waiting for Monday. Clark came in and was put to work tracing the burned areas on a large map of Chicago. This map immediately became the focus of attention in the office.

From it the insurance men could make estimates of their losses. It was futile to try to get telegrams into the stricken city. The best they could do was to match street addresses on their insurance policies with the areas Clark was blackening on the map.

By Monday morning this map had become such an important document that The Courant decided to run a cut of it. In those days cuts appeared only rarely in most American papers, and up-to-the-minute news pictures and maps were rarer yet, because it took so long to make the hand-cut engravings. Nevertheless The Courant decided to run Clark's map of Chicago.

The engraver looked and shook his head. There was a lot of detail on that map. He could never finish it in time for Tuesday morning's paper.

Well, could he just rough it out? The engraver was doubtful. Engraving is not a matter of roughing out. It requires painstaking care. And after all, a craftsman has his pride.

The upshot was that the engraver agreed to do what he could, and the people at The Courant waited nervously. By press time early Tuesday morning, a cut was ready, showing the center of Chicago. It was an ugly cut; a big black rectangle. Lake Michigan showed a solid black at the right, and the City in black crisscrossed by thin white street lines. Said The Courant: "The engraver, though he has necessarily done his work hurriedly, has given us a very good and accurate map of this portion of the city."

As soon as the presses stopped printing on Tuesday morning, the cut was rushed back to the engraver. On Wednesday, the same block appeared in The Courant, but this time greatly refined. The burned area was still black, but all the rest of the city now showed in light shading. Lake Michigan was no longer an inky sea, but showed in clean white contrast to the land mass. Wednesday morning's map told a much clearer story.

Clark, of course, got full recognition. Totally inexperienced, he had helped to produce the map which was a key item in The Courant's coverage. It was good service, which the proprietors never forgot. Nothing more was heard about his being just a "beginner."

The newcomer was well suited to his job. Intelligent and hardworking, he loved to write, he knew the city, he shared the enthusiasm of Hawley and the others for politics, and he was every inch a gentleman. It was not long before he felt himself quite at home among the other gentlemen of the press.

As time went by, the whole working force of The Courant under the influence of Hawley, Warner, Clark and the rest, felt itself drawn together in a common bond, hard to define but none the less real. A good many Courant men have written about the spirit in the office during the proprietorship of Hawley and his friends, but perhaps Clifton Sherman, who joined the staff in 1893, has come as close to the heart of the matter as any. There was about the place, he wrote, "an atmosphere of *noblesse oblige,* of a cultivated gentlemen's club, of a literary society of learned men."

In off hours, the gentlemen of The Courant moved in the social set that had as its focus Nook Farm, then a nationally known literary center. Nook Farm was near the corner of Farmington Avenue and Forest Street. Here lived Joseph Hawley and Charles Dudley Warner in a distinguished literary colony that included Mark Twain, Harriet Beecher Stowe, the historian J. Hammond Trumbull, and other notables. The Nook Farm leaders attracted many eminent men. President Grant was a visitor as were Bret Harte and Rudyard Kipling. Matthew Arnold came as a guest of Mark Twain.

Twain and Warner, visiting back and forth as neighbors, kept up a friendly rivalry over pay rates for their writing. Twain got the highest rates of his day, and Warner kept pressing editors to raise his own rates. Mark Twain established the rule of thumb that he be paid double Warner's fees. When Twain found that *Harper's* had paid his neighbor $100 a page for articles on California, he raised his own price to $200, remarking: "If I ain't worth (commercially, not literarily) double what Warner is, I want to be finding it out right away."

Back in 1878, while The Courant still occupied quarters on Pratt Street, the newspaper put in one of the first telephone lines in the city—to the homes of Hawley and Warner, and thence to Mark Twain's residence. This was before anything like today's telephone exchanges: the wire amounted to a private tie among the three families and The Courant. The man who helped to install the wire, John M. Knox, recalled the episode vividly in a memo now in the files of the Southern New England Telephone Company:

> On our way to Twain's I can remember going through skylights, clambering over roofs, and climbing trees—poles being used only when necessary. There was some commotion when we tried to install the telephone in his home . . . While work was in progress he strode about the room and uttered something like the following:
> "The voice carries too far as it is. If Bell had invented a muffler or a gag, he would have done a real service.

"What's the idea of attaching a long-distance feature to anyone's mouth? He's crazy.

"Put the thing near the window so that I can get rid of it easily."

Twain had tried to buy into The Courant in 1869, before coming to Hartford. Hawley and Warner had given his proposal careful consideration, had discussed it with Samuel Bowles of the Springfield (Mass.) *Republican,* and had finally turned it down. Twain evidently regarded the refusal to sell a share of the newspaper as a personal rebuff, and for a while after coming to Hartford he treated Warner rather coolly. But it was hard to know Warner and not to like him. The two were soon collaborating on their novel, and before long Warner was Cousin Charley to Twain's children.

Twain shared more than social and literary interests with the proprietors of The Courant; he was keenly interested in the mechanical and business sides of publishing, too. Frank Marshall (Cap) Jenks, whose career spanned more than 70 years in The Courant's composing room, told how Twain rounded up four substantial businessmen from Boston to witness a demonstration of the Paige type-setter, in which the author had an interest. The complicated machine, according to Jenks, had about 16,000 parts. When Twain and his Boston financiers assembled, the author directed Jenks and his fellow compositors to go to work. The machine whirred and clanked—and a piece flew out the window. "The four capitalists walked right out the door," Jenks remembered. Twain lost a reputed $300,000 on the machine.

After the success of *Innocents Abroad,* Twain bought an interest in The American Publishing Company of Hartford, a firm that published several of his titles as well as those of Charles Dudley Warner, Harriet Beecher Stowe, and other Nook Farm residents. The American Publishing Company was one of the most enterprising publishing houses in a city that boasted some 20 of them. At about this time Hartford publishing firms employed a huge army of agents —some 50,000—who traveled to every corner of the United States selling books. Sales of 150,000 to 200,000 copies of individual titles printed in Hartford were not uncommon. When Twain and Warner talked about publishing under the imprint of the American Publishing Company, they were talking about real money, as their returns from *The Gilded Age* testify. The American Publishing Company's imprint appeared on Warner's *My Winter on the Nile,* Twain's *Tom Sawyer,* and Harriet Beecher Stowe's *Men of Our Times.*

The general public regarded the residents of Nook Farm with

something akin to awe, and would turn out in crowds to see them when they appeared in public. Once, in May, 1875, the Asylum Hill Congregational Church invited Twain, Hawley, Clark, and others to participate in an old fashioned spelling bee. The crowd completely filled the church, the chapel, and the adjoining rooms. The occasion was covered for The Courant by Hotchkiss, whose account taken in his own method of shorthand has preserved Twain's decidedly unconventional views of spelling. Twain said:

> Ladies and Gentlemen—I have been honored with the office of introducing these approaching orthographical solemnities with a few remarks:—The temperance crusade swept the land some time ago—that is, that vast portion of the land where it was needed—but it skipped Hartford. Now comes this new spelling epidemic and this time we are stricken. I don't see any use in having a uniform and arbitrary way of spelling words. We might as well make all clothes alike and cook all dishes alike. Sameness is tiresome: variety is pleasing. I have a correspondent whose letters are always a refreshment to me, there is such a breezy unfettered originality about his orthography. He always spells Kow with a large K. Now that is just as good as to spell it with a small one. It is better. It gives the imagination a broader field, a wider scope. It suggests to the mind a grand, vague, impressive new kind of a cow . . .
>
> I have a relative in New York who is almost sublimely gifted. She can't spell *any* word right. There is a game called verbarium. A dozen people are each provided with a sheet of paper across the top of which is written a long word like kaleidascopical, or something like that, and the game is to see who can make up the most words out of that in three minutes, always beginning with the initial letter of that word. Upon one occasion the word chosen was cofferdam. When time was called everybody had built from five to twenty words except this young lady. She only had one word—calf. We all studied a moment and then said, "Why, there is no l in cofferdam." Then we examined her paper. To the eternal honor of that uninspired, unconscious, sublimely independent soul, be it said, she had spelt that word caff. If anybody here can spell calf any more sensibly than that, let him step to the front and take his milk. . . .

A literate gentlemanly journal, the proprietors of The Courant believed, could be just as enterprising as any sensation-mongering sheet. And could make money, too.

An account book covering the period from January, 1876, to January, 1887, has survived in The Courant's archives. It shows that on the first day of each year the partners balanced their assets against their liabilities, and divided the profits as friends and gentlemen should.

The first page of the book, for January 1, 1876, records under

"Assets" a total of $39,593.16 for such items as cash on hand, stock, and accounts due. "Liabilities" are shown as $14,911.42, including an estimated $11,000 for "accounts vs. the office." The same page shows liabilities subtracted from assets, for "Est. profits" of $24,-681.74 to be divided among the four proprietors.

Because the account book limits itself to first-of-the-year inventory, it omits a good deal. Under "Bills Payable," for example, appears an item of $5,980.80 for paper, but without any indication of how many months the bill covers. Estimated town and city taxes for the year 1876 amounted to $225. The telegraph bill for December, 1875, amounted to $385. This suggests that the partners were spending between $4,500 to $5,000 a year for telegraphic news, an amount that amply justified their frequent claims of high outlays for wire stories. For special dispatches from Washington during December, 1875, they paid General H. V. Boynton $30, indicating an annual cost for special Washington news of about $360. An item for George H. Munroe's Boston letters amounts to $130, without any indication for the number of months covered.

The sum and substance of the inventory for each year is that news costs were substantial, taxes were low, and profits were a joy and a delight.

Costs remained fairly constant during the '70's. The gas bill did go up from $83 in December, 1875, to $100 in December, 1879, but the telegraph bill remained about the same, as did town and city taxes and payments to correspondents. The inventory of January, 1877, shows an item of $105 paid to Miss Mary Mackay for correspondence from London over an unspecified period.

This account book gives the first clear indication of how much money the proprietors made personally out of the company. The January, 1880, inventory shows that Joseph R. Hawley had received $875 to cover three months' salary in 1879. For the full year his salary would therefore probably have amounted to four times this amount, or $3,500. In addition, the four proprietors had, during 1879, split $6,000 in profits which, evenly divided, would have amounted to $1,500 apiece. Hawley's total salary and profits, then, probably amounted to $5,000. At that time, the average family income in New England amounted to less than $800 a year. So the Gentlemen's income was on the gentlemanly side, too.

Although readers of The Courant were used to having their gentlemanly newspaper quote from other leading journals, it must have

come as a mild surprise when, on September 27, 1887, they were offered the following untranslated comment from the *Amsterdamsche
Courant*:

> Indianen uit Utah zijn, met oorlogszuchtige bedoelingen, de grenzen
> der Vereenigde Staten overgetrokken doch werden door de troepen terug-
> gedruven tot Colorado. Negen Indianen en tal van blanken zijn gedood.
> Een oorlog tusschen blanken en roodhuiden schijnt nu onvermijdelijk.

The Courant obviously expected its subscribers to take their medicine straight; if a reader happened to be ignorant of Dutch, too bad
for him. He might never learn that the Utah Indians had been driv-
en into Colorado by the U.S. forces, and that several of the redmen
had been killed.

This scholarly attitude was shared, more or less, by the entire editorial staff. It was particularly personified in Charles Hemenway
Adams, a bearded bibliophile who joined the staff in 1881, and remained to become the paper's most prolific editorial writer. Adams
came to The Courant with a highly respectable journalistic background. He had served with distinction on the New York *Sun* under
the great Charles A. Dana; on the Springfield *Republican,* under
Samuel Bowles; and on the New York *Evening Post,* under William
Cullen Bryant. He was a newspaperman's newspaperman.

He was also a scholar's scholar and carried his Euripides in his
pocket. Greek, Latin, French, and German he read almost as easily
as English. His desk at The Courant was surrounded with well-
tabbed volumes of the Congressional Record, and not the least of
his accomplishments was his ability to recite from memory the gist
of little-known Congressional debates of yesteryear.

The men in the city room, glancing through the door of Adams'
office during the evening hours—he usually worked until one or two
in the morning—beheld a portly figure bent over his desk, unhurriedly writing with a quill pen that he dipped into his inkwell after
every two or three words. Adams had no use for steel pens; much
less for the newfangled typewriters. "You can't do a good job in a
hurry," he would tell youthful reporters, stroking his bib-like beard
and squinting through small, round, Pickwickian glasses.

Some of the gentlemen in The Courant's newsroom in this era
went on to most distinguished careers. Watson R. Perry, an editorial
writer, served as U. S. Minister to Persia. Frederick C. Penfield, a
reporter from 1880 to 1885, entered the diplomatic service as a con-
sul, was Minister to Egypt and later to Austria-Hungary. John Addi-

son Porter, another reporter, was appointed secretary to President McKinley after the 1896 election.

If Adams approached his tasks with calm deliberation, so did his colleagues. Every week, more or less regularly, came a thick letter from Boston, over the signature of "Templeton." "Templeton" was the pen name of George H. Munroe, whose letters from the Hub during the course of almost three decades gave a vivid and intimate picture of happenings in politics, literature, society, and everything else worth mentioning in Boston. The only trouble with Templeton's letters was that they were written in a frightful scrawl. Charles Hopkins Clark would begin the deciphering, usually calling for help in the city room. There was something about Templeton's violet ink that made a bad scrawl seem even worse. As a last resort, Jacob Turner was summoned from the composing room. But, as The Courant proudly told its readers, Templeton's letters were so good that even the Boston papers copied them.

The quiet self-assurance with which the paper went about gathering and reporting the news was of a piece with the self-assurance of the times. By 1890, life in central Connecticut, as reflected in the editorial pages, came pretty close to heart's desire. Said an editorial: "A drive of no greater extent than to Cedar Hill, a stroll no longer than along our sightly Prospect Avenue, on a late afternoon or early evening nowadays, may do as much in the way of uplift and refreshment as will traveling many miles." We needed a Connecticut Valley Wordsworth, the editor thought.

In the same year, readers were reminded that "Hartford has always been a pleasant and attractive spot, but it has lately taken a new start, and is going to be even more attractive than it has been. There is more public spirit in the air. A thousand signs show it."

But there were small signs, both within The Courant organization and in the world outside, that boded change. In 1881 General Hawley went to Washington, to begin a 24-year career as U. S. Senator from Connecticut. He had already practically retired from active participation in the daily affairs of the newspaper, and from 1881 on he was almost a stranger in his own office. The Courant staff began to look upon Hawley, when he came in, more as a visiting Senator than as a fellow newspaperman.

Hawley's move was to place heavy responsibility on the shoulders of young Charles Hopkins Clark, the ablest all-round man on the paper. Charles Dudley Warner still held the position of editor in chief, but it was Clark who provided much of the real driving force.

The more Clark's voice was heard in the councils of The Courant, the more he insisted that the paper keep up with the times. He reminded his colleagues that big blanket sheets were relics of back-country journalism, that improved printing presses were being installed every year on metropolitan journals, that workable typesetting machines were just around the corner, that pictures were some day going to appear on every page of every newspaper. His elder colleagues listened patiently to these young ideas. But rapid changes were in the wind.

1870-1890
A New Home and New Horizons

FOR YEARS, the weekly Connecticut Courant had been a familiar friend in villages and towns throughout the State. The daily was now also beginning to reach far beyond Hartford. Commuters and their trains were bringing the habit of reading the daily morning paper to towns where a morning newspaper had been unknown.

The ringing of each new railroad spike under the blows of the sledgehammer was music to the ears of the proprietors who encouraged the builders like the chorus in a Greek play: "Build away, rich men, as fast as you think it will pay; we never heard of a railroad that in the long run hurt the people it accommodated," and much more to the same tune.

Meanwhile, Hartford's population was growing: from 37,700 in 1870 to 43,300 in 1880. So the newspaper readers in Hartford were increasing at the same time that the railroads were extending the effective demand for a daily paper far beyond the city limits.

Even before 1870 The Courant had growing pains. The paper had been at 14 Pratt Street less than a year when the proprietors gleefully complained that they were not able to keep up with the demand for The Courant. In January, 1868, they announced that circulation was rapidly approaching 10,000. By 1871 they were claiming one of the top circulations in New England.

The Courant's claims of rapid growth cannot be verified. Circulation figures, before the days of the Audit Bureau of Circulations, were a newspaper's most closely guarded secret. But there is no reason to doubt that the paper was growing: it was well established in the growing capital of a growing state.

One of the newspaper's promotional devices during this period was *The Courant Almanac* which appeared from about 1873 to 1899. In addition to the information usually available in these books, *The Courant Almanac* ran full-page portraits on almost every other

COURANT COMPLETED THIS NEW BUILDING IN 1880

page, displaying such beauties as Mary Stedwin holding a book of poetry, her eyes cast up to heaven, Theresa Vaughn with a banjo and Miss Archmere looking lonely on a stone park bench, her arm tenderly embracing a tennis racket.

By 1878 the proprietors were thinking about new, larger quarters. Early in January, 1879, they bought the property at 64-68 State Street, the historic printing site which many Hartford journals had called home. Plans were readied at once, construction of a new building started in September, 1879, and The Courant moved in on June 19, 1880—just thirteen years after their previous move into new quarters.

A handsome building it was—five stories high, dwarfing the Hartford National Bank and the National Exchange Bank that flanked it. The front windows on the top story looked down on the historic Old State House, and far beyond, down river, to the delightful hills of Glastonbury. In fact, much of Hartford and the surrounding countryside could be seen from The Courant building which gave its staff a grandstand view of some spectacular goings-on, including what was probably the most dazzling of all, the burning of the old wooden bridge across the Connecticut River.

The Courant building was in the latest architectural style, "modern Gothic," done in red brick and red mortar, garnished with bands cut in diaper patterns. The upper windows were spanned with wide brick arches. Inside were modern conveniences: an elevator, reputed to work "at any hour," a communication system made up of a complicated combination of telephones and speaking tubes, and an engine room in the basement to supply power for the presses and for the manufacturing concerns that rented space not used by The Courant.

When the building was first occupied the editorial rooms were on the fifth floor, "above the noise and dirt of the street, the most commodious and convenient quarters occupied by any newspaper in New England outside of Boston." Stairs and an elevator led to these quarters; stairs for the timid and the elevator for the courageous. The Courant assured its patrons that the elevator was equipped with an air cushion which guaranteed the safety of passengers "even if the car should drop from the fifth story to the basement." It was hydraulically operated, using pressure from the municipal water system. According to The Courant: "When first put in, the car was dropped from the fifth story, about 60 feet, without spilling a drop from a glass of water placed on the bottom of the car. . . . Eggs were also placed on the floor . . . in a box containing brickbats and thin glass tumblers; not an egg or a piece of glass was cracked."

The visitor, whisked safely to the top of the building, found a door opening into the quarters of Managing Editor Stephen Hubbard. Hubbard presided at a large desk, squarely in the middle of the room, surrounded with gadgets and aids, not the least of which was a large wastebasket. Two of the paper's three telephones hung on the east wall of this room at a height convenient for the tall Hubbard, which meant that lesser men had to stand on tiptoe and yell. One of these phones, on the Bell System, led to the private residences of the editors; the other on the Edison System led to the general telephone office and thence to the city and neighboring towns. The third telephone was downstairs in the business office.

Among the proprietors, opinion was divided on the merits of telephones. Hawley had seen a telephone demonstrated at Allyn Hall, and being an impulsive and imaginative person, had decided that here was the communication of the future. He was about to put some of his savings into the development of the telephone when his friends got wind of his plan. They talked him out of it and thus saved him from becoming a rich man with all the perils of riches here and hereafter.

In 1878 The Courant reported that "The telephone is making constant progress . . . There are about 50 in Hartford, and everyone using it is delighted with its novelty and usefulness." The newspaper said that 250 to 300 miles was about the limit that words could be heard.

Hubbard also presided over a set of speaking tubes which carried his voice to the business office, the press room, the composing room, and the lower hall. A lift from the business office below brought up copy and messages. Over his fireplace hung a large portrait of the poet William Cullen Bryant.

The Managing Editor's room held the pivotal position on the news floor. The two connecting rooms to the north were given to the reportorial staff, and the two to the south to the Editors-in-Chief. Hawley was the Editor-in-Chief when in town—which was not very often—and when he was away Warner took over.

One of the two rooms to the north sufficed for the city staff, consisting in 1880 of George D. Curtiss and the telephone editor, T. P. W. Hull. The other was occupied by the two "general editorial staff" members, Charles Hopkins Clark and John C. Kinney.

THE CITY ROOM, 1895
Instead of typewriters, pen and ink

The city and "general" rooms were as innocent of typewriters as they were of telephones. It is remarkable how slowly the American press took to these two indispensables of today's journalism. In 1896 the New York *Times* had only two telephones, one of them for the use of the advertising department, and no company-owned typewriters.

Well into the '90's, any young reporter who showed up with a typewriter was looked upon with mingled contempt and amusement. Of course, in the early days, when typewriters looked much like treadle sewing machines, they were cumbersome, but even after better machines came on the market, the old hands on city staffs regarded them as noisy contraptions.

The Courant's writing force on the fifth floor, with the staff in the business office on the second floor, supplied news and advertising each day to fill a huge blanket sheet on both sides. The editors estimated that the paper contained from 60,000 to 100,000 words a day, the equivalent of an average novel.

Copy for each issue, some of it as easy to decipher as the fine cop-

perplate hand of Joseph Hawley, some as bad as the scrawl of
Charles Dudley Warner, was sent to the rear of the top floor to be
set in type by Jacob Turner and his men. The Courant was proud of
its new composing room. The furnishings were not much different
from those of a century earlier, but the quarters provided a fine,
spacious work space with windows on three sides. The compositors
worked far into the night, the windows gleaming gas light, making
The Courant a lighthouse for the center of the city.

Copy from the editorial rooms was stacked in a basket, where
compositors could shuffle through it and take their choice of hand-
writings. Each compositor set the headlines and then filled the rest
of his stick with the body of the story. It was understood by reporters that, except for major news, stories should not run over a stick
long. The result was that few stories exceeded five inches or so. On
the compositors' side, the man who got the first "take" was responsible for setting up the entire story, even if it ran to several sticks
and was in all but illegible handwriting.

CHARLES DUDLEY WARNER'S ROOM
"Above the noise and dirt of the street"

Turner and his crew set by hand; practical typesetting machines were not to come for a while. In 1878 The Courant reported:

> Pratt and Whitney Company have just shipped the last of 13 pairs of type setting and distributing machines for Mr. W. H. Green, of New York, which they have been constructing and perfecting . . . So much money has been spent in . . . search of machines of this class that practical printers look with incredulous pity upon one who says he has found the secret, as upon one who says he has squared the circle, started perpetual motion, or found the philosopher's stone . . . But they do say that the machines will work, and the proof is, they are working.

The Green type-setter was not to be the solution. The honor of finding a practicable type-setter goes to Ottmar Mergenthaler, developer of the Linotype. The first Linotype set up in a newspaper office was in the New York *Tribune* in 1886.

Meanwhile, compositors throughout the world continued to set by hand, as Jacob Turner had done on The Courant for 25 years. By 1893 The Courant had typesetting machines. Turner's two principal assistants were Ebenezer Williams and John Mather. Among them, the three could count 55 years of service in one concern, a remarkable record considering the notorious restlessness of compositors in the days of handsetting.

When the pages were in type and ready for the press, they were sent down to the press room on the first floor by a steam elevator at the rear of the building. The Courant's press was the same Hoe double-cylinder purchased 13 years earlier when the paper had moved to No. 14 Pratt Street. It was to serve another 12 years. As long as the paper did not exceed four blanket sheets, the double-cylinder was good enough. A 20-horsepower Wheelock steam engine in the basement supplied power.

By modern standards, The Courant's quarters in the new building were remarkably uncomplicated. The newspaper managed without a circulation department, or advertising department, or classified department. In 1880 there was no need for typesetting machine operators or stereotype operators or photographers.

In the city room, staff writers did not even have separate desks— they sat around a large, flat-topped table. The era of sports, financial and women's departments and other subdivisions of the newsroom had not arrived.

The arrangement reflected the simple organization of the news sheet itself. Reading matter fell under broad headings: editorials, "New England News," "News of the State" and within this loose and comfortable plan, the city items—politics, theater, clubs, sports, and what not appeared in no predictable order under the broad embrace of "Hartford and Vicinity." National and international news was under "By Telegraph." Fugitive items of various sorts might appear under "Chaff of the Day," "Social and Political" or "News and Notions."

In 1880 not a writer on the full-time staff would have wanted to be known as Sports Editor. Stories of baseball, walking races and boating appeared from time to time scattered among other miscellaneous items, but it would have occurred to nobody to provide for a sports department in the new building any more than for a photographic department. The proprietors looked on sports news with less than enthusiasm. "We are as ready as anybody else to throw up our hats in honor of the knights of the bat and ball, but we don't want to be called upon to do it every day of our lives," said an editorial. They hoped that the rapidly developing baseball craze would decline just as rapidly.

Furthermore, organized sport led to professionalism. "The smart American has found out how to do it," Warner resignedly noted in 1874. "As usual, he hires somebody to do it for him . . ." Baseball had gone professional. It was better to watch, Warner acknowledged, and it was certainly less demoralizing than bullfighting, but it was not better for individual participation. Warner held that a truly American, truly amateur, truly absorbing national game was needed. Throughout the '70's and '80's the proprietors looked for the development of a bona fide national sport. An editorial in 1873, under the heading "WANTED: A NATIONAL GAME" said half in resignation: "We are waiting for a great American novel, for an American opera, and a drama worthy of the name. We must also wait for our national game."

Having written off baseball, the proprietors next threw their handkerchief to boat racing. Here was a colorful sport for gentlemanly, nonprofessional American collegians seeking the sheer joy of competition. But the regattas soon began to develop troubles. In the summer of 1873 the paper reported a dispute over the Springfield Regatta, in which Yale, Wesleyan, Trinity, Harvard, Amherst, Bowdoin, and other colleges had taken part. First, second and third places were at length awarded to Yale, Wesleyan and Harvard, but not before almost everyone was angry. The oars had fouled at the turns around the stake boats. Officials tried to solve this problem by eliminating turns: the races were made straight-away. But this led to another difficulty. Persons witnessing the start could not see the finish. The Courant proposed a separate stake for each racing craft, so that there would be no fouling of rival oars.

Rifle matches next received editorial favor. The Courant even went so far in 1877 as to run a one-column cut of a loving cup to be shot for annually at the Willowbrook Range. By 1879 walking contests held the stage. The Courant had its doubts about walking for prize money, but it reported the spectacular contests in New York. A story in March, 1879, said that "The great event of the season is the contest now in progress at Gilmore's Garden, New York, for the Astley Belt, which is worth $2,500 and carries with it the championship of the world."

By 1881 The Courant was almost in despair over finding a truly National Game. "Baseball . . . has developed its school of professionals who work for pay. Boating . . . developed, when racing began, the professional racing oarsmen . . . Pedestrianism bears the same kind of fruit. Horse racing, which touches its prime in the friendly brush between two road horses . . . (owned respectively by the parson and the doctor) has grown to be a trade by itself for which horses and drivers are bred and in which there is involved a wonderful total of iniquity and demoralization." Small wonder that no provision was made for a sports department in the new building.

Finance, in contrast, was entirely respectable, and The Courant in 1880 carried a regular financial section on page three under "Finance and Trade." It was natural that financial news outstripped other news in departmentalization: it was important to a lot of people and it required special presentation, as in stock market quotations. Nevertheless, no special quarters were provided in the new building for a financial department. This news was long supplied to the paper by T. T. Fisher, a respected figure in local financial circles and former owner of the site on which The Courant building stood.

Most American journals of the day had a distinctly masculine slant. As late as 1886, the famous magazine editor, Edward Bok, expressed the view that "Women are not newspaper readers, because there is no matter distinctively for women." Bok was exaggerating, but substantially correct. As far back as 1867 The Courant had tried a column that appeared occasionally under the somewhat patronizing heading:

FOR THE LADIES.

GOSSIP OF THE BOUDOIR AND THE DRAWING
ROOM.

The gentlemen who ran The Courant held no grudge against the fair sex. Far from it. Up until the 1890's, when it made a right-about-face in policy, The Courant strongly favored women's rights and woman suffrage. It reported, with obvious approval, the argument of Susan B. Anthony's lawyer that "No greater absurdity, to use no harsher term, could be presented to the human mind than that of rewarding men and punishing women" for voting at the polls. And when an occasional woman lifted up her voice against the abuse of rum, or embarked on a career in medicine, or the ministry, she could be sure of The Courant's good wishes.

The Courant frequently referred to itself as a "family paper," which meant, among other things, that it would print nothing offensive to ladies, and that it occasionally ran short stories obviously aimed at women readers. Some of the advertising, too—though in nothing like the proportion today—was designed for women shoppers. The publishers felt no need for a women's department in their new building.

The considerable portion of the building not occupied by The Courant was for rent. The dual purpose of the structure was an accurate reflection of the way in which the four proprietors sized up the economy of their home town. Hartford's prosperity, they saw, depended largely on two kinds of business activity: manufacturing, and banking and insurance. Of the two, they had greater confidence in manufacturing than banking and insurance. "The prosperity of Hartford is largely due to the industrial pursuits which it has fostered," they commented in 1871. They believed that banking and insurance, though lucrative, were also chancy, especially while the silver maniacs were at work trying to undermine the gold standard.

In an editorial in 1880, entitled "HOW TO MAKE HARTFORD GROW," The Courant listed many manufactured goods that carried the name of Hartford to the corners of the world: Colt revolvers, Collins axes (trademarked "Hartford"), Hartford carpets, Weed sewing machines, lawn mowers, the products of Billings & Spencer, the fine tools of Pratt & Whitney. There was stability here; much more so than in the risky business of insurance. Said the editorial:

> A community (a small one) can get rich in betting against fire and death . . . but these are riches of the kind that can leave town when they wish and that bring with them only a small measure of municipal growth. The real thing most to be desired is the presence of factories with their hundreds of employees, with all the necessary demand that follows for homes, food, fuel, clothing, etc.

The fact of importance in 1880 to the four proprietors, however, was that The Courant owned a handsome new home of its own. Six weeks after they had moved in, the proprietors were ready to invite the public to an open house. On August 11, 1880, they ran a page one engraving of the building, and a full page story on the history of The Courant. Heading the page was a box that read:

AT HOME.

THE COURANT,

64 TO 68 STATE STREET.

Charles Hopkins Clark, the young reporter whose enterprise had meant so much to The Courant on the night of the Chicago fire, felt as proud of the new building as anyone else. But, more keenly than any, he felt that a new building was not enough. What really counted, he urged, were modern ideas.

In 1883 The Courant's arch rival, the Hartford *Times,* stole a march by modernizing its format. The *Times* abandoned the old-fashioned blanket sheets forever and went to eight pages, neatly cut, folded, and pasted so well that the paste still sticks today. Knowing that newspaper readers would remember the Courant's earlier failure with the uncut 8-page form, the *Times* went out of its way to explain the advantage of its new format:

> . . . The reader has easy access to every column, and the advertisements as well as the news and miscellaneous matter come readily to the eye. This form of daily and weekly journal is becoming popular, especially since the invention of cutting open the pages. It is evidently becoming the standard form. The papers all over the country have adopted it.

All this was salt in Clark's wounds. What the *Times* said was all too true, yet he could not get his colleagues to bring The Courant up to date. They, on the other hand, pointed out that a change to 8-pages would mean cutting and pasting—a slow and expensive operation. Not until 1887, four years after the *Times,* did The Courant change—for the second time—to an 8 page layout. And in 1903 it was still pasting its pages together. It took a long time for publishers to believe that readers would accept newspapers with loose pages.

Meanwhile mechanization of the American newspaper industry was going ahead rapidly. Almost every year brought something new in presses, or typesetting machines, or in reproduction of pictures. In 1882 the Hoe Company installed a press in the New York *Herald* that could deliver 24,000 12-page papers an hour. Seven years later it had a press that could double this output. But The Courant continued to struggle with its aging press, requiring the paper to be cut into sheets and wetted down.

It was equally important, Clark clearly saw, for The Courant to keep abreast of developments in newspaper illustration. One of the paper's earliest was a map published on August 16, 1869, to show the alternative routes being proposed for the Connecticut Western Railroad. It had been a woodcut, a far cry from the spot news pictures of today; but it did illustrate a current, live story. By 1873 newspaper illustration had reached the point where a Canadian firm of engravers felt bold enough to found the New York *Daily Graphic,* an eight-pager carrying about four pages of timely news pictures —electroplated line drawings. The Courant took note of this development by warning of the difficulties in making pictures fast enough and good enough: "In an illustrated daily of the kind the *Graphic* is and expects to be, the pictures must be as fresh news as the letter press, and must as accurately report the news."

Picture services sprang up, offering to mail newspapers the illustrations they needed on a fee basis. It did not take these agencies long to discover that some of their subscribers were fairly gullible. Newspaper pages began to blossom with stock line-drawings of faces identified as those of emperors, businessmen, or leading artists. The Courant, suspicious, ran a survey in 1886, on which it wryly reported as follows:

> Some people like humbug and are glad to buy it and pay for it, and treat it as they do any other commodity. 'Illustrated Journalism,' as well as other phases of the same trade, shows this interesting fact suggestively . . . At this office, where a number of illustrated dailies come in by exchange . . . two lines of inquiry were pursued with about equal success. One was to follow the same face and see how many different names it was called as it traveled over the country, and the other was to take the same name and see how many different faces were attributed to it . . . The same female would figure as a murderess's victim, as a noble woman who had slain a villain, as the belle of the mountains or of the sea shore, as Mrs. Cleveland, and as a foreign princess.

But newspaper pictures were clearly on the way. In 1889 the paper carried its first halftone, not in its regular pages, to be sure, but in a glossy-paper supplement celebrating the inauguration of President Benjamin Harrison. The photograph showed the Nation's Capitol; Harrison appeared in a line cut. Halftones on regular newsprint were still in the experimental stage at the end of the 1880's. In 1890 The Courant ran a story under the heading, "Amateur Photography Now An Important Pastime." All the illustrations for this story were line drawings.

If the partners had their doubts about the new journalism, they also had their reservations about other aspects of the American scene. In July, 1883, thousands of telegraph operators across the country went out on strike. This they did, according to The Courant, "in obedience to an order flashed over the wires from the central committee of a secret trade society of which they are members." Although all newspapers were hard hit, the Editor was inclined to sympathize with the telegraphers on the ground that the owners of the "telegraph monopoly" had been unreasonable and unjust. The Courant reminded readers that many telegraph operators worked 14 to 16 hours a day, without extra compensation for Sunday work, and that the average pay was $54.43 a month.

After a month the strike failed and many men went back to work. The Courant said that the public should hold the owners responsible for smug indifference to the demands of the workers. Smugness, indeed, was the bane of the country and there was plenty to be smug about in Connecticut. Still, in the panorama from the editorial office the editors could see disturbing things.

Railroads, for instance, linked Connecticut with the rest of America. The state was becoming more and more dependent upon railroads and railroads could easily fall into the hands of unscrupulous managers. The Courant hoped that Connecticut's railroads would never come under the control of a Jay Gould or a Jim Fisk. Furthermore, railroads were dangerous. Almost every day the newspaper reported frightful railroad accidents, many of them in Hartford. Public safety demanded that something be done.

The Courant's campaign took two directions: one against the abuse of power by railroad managers, and the other against accidents.

Freight rates on the Boston, Hartford, and New York run were anything but reasonable. As rival lines competed, they set rates between Boston and New York for far less than it cost to move the same freight from Hartford to New York. Said the Courant:

> Let grocers charge $10 for a barrel of flour, $20 for half a barrel, and $40 for a quarter of a barrel . . .

Let workmen be paid $1.50 a day or $3. for half a day . . .

When the public once get used to this sort of financial arithmetic, they will cease to grumble because the freight rate to Boston is scarcely more than half what it is from New York to Hartford, though the distance is more than double.

The Courant urged the passage of a "Short Haul Bill" which would provide that the same load should not be charged more for being carried a lesser distance. When, on April 3, 1884, a Short Haul Bill was defeated in the State Senate 13 to 8, the Editor angrily called the defeat "a significant sign of the supremacy of lobby over logic."

The second prong of The Courant's campaign was directed against the mounting toll of train accidents. On September 5, 1882, Charles Miller was "killed by the cars" at the Windsor Street crossing; on the 16th Thomas Doyle was killed at the tunnel; on November 23, Andrew Bradie was killed on the track near the Flower Street crossing; and so it went.

Most Hartfordians thought the Asylum Hill crossing the most dangerous in the city. During the 1880's the rails crossed Asylum Street at street level. This meant that they also crossed the tracks of the horse car line that went out Asylum Street and up Asylum Hill. A curve in the railroad tracks obscured the intersection until the train was nearly there; and traffic coming down Asylum Hill on a slippery night might easily end up on the railway just as the train was pulling in.

The station, which stood then, as now, just north of Asylum Street, had enormous, elegant, and entirely useless towers at its four corners. It was adorned with loggias, balustrades, and tall, round-arched windows. An ornate cornice ran around the top. The building was indistinguishable from an elegant Italian villa—except that the railroad ran through the middle of it. Trains from New York entered the city in wide, sweeping curves, and then, near a tiny round house, took one final swing to the north around Lydia Sigourney's place, clattered across the horse tracks on Asylum Street and roared into a tunnel in the center of the station, filling that elegant edifice with smoke and din. No bar gates, no fences, no obstructions of any sort kept pedestrians or street traffic off the tracks. Trains leaving for New York came puffing out of the tunnel into the midst of street traffic. In 1886 The Courant reported a plan that turned out to be the solution to these hazards:

Vice-President E. M. Reed of the Consolidated Road, while abroad, was at Hanover in Germany and was much struck with the way in which

there a difficulty very like ours at Asylum Street had been overcome. The
track had been elevated and a two-story station put up for passengers.
The waiting rooms are on the ground floor; the cars come in upstairs.

Soon this two-story plan was adopted, and the station was completed in 1889, to the accompaniment of persistent urging by Clark.

The Courant had to campaign much longer before another public
danger was removed. By any standards, the Park River was a menace
to health. Winding prettily between tree-lined banks through the
center of the City, it carried sewage from outlying towns and picked
up all kinds of filth from Hartford's own sewers. In the early days,
this stream had been affectionately named the Little River, and a
charming arched bridge had been built across it on Main Street to
accommodate travelers to Wethersfield. Later, when Bushnell Park
was laid out along its picturesque banks, it was called the Park River.
But as Hartford had grown, the once-clear stream became an open
sewer. People started calling it Hog River.

The Courant favored construction of an "intercepting sewer" par-
allel to the Park River, which would collect waste and drain it off
into the Connecticut. It took until the late '90's to win this battle.

The Blizzard of '88 began innocently on the night of Sunday,
March 11. Early in the evening, with the temperature around 40 de-
grees, the snow began to fall. By midnight, when about two inches
covered the ground, there came a lull.

But soon after 2 a.m. the storm took hold again with violence,
the snow coming in blinding sheets. South of City Hall, across from
The Courant, a mammoth drift reached ten feet. Snow covered the
store fronts. Howling winds kept up until near nightfall on Tuesday. In all, the Great Blizzard lasted about 48 hours.

The Hartford Courant was the only newspaper published in the
city without interruption during the great blizzard. Managing Editor
Hubbard was a prisoner in his home all Monday, and reached the
office Tuesday noon. J. A. Turner, foreman of the Composing Room,
could not get in until Wednesday. For a quarter of a century he had
been as prompt and punctual as the sunrise. The veteran head of the
press room, Horace C. Havens, climbed half a mile over snow drifts
to reach the office near midnight on Monday. Reporters were put up
in nearby hotels, and ate in restaurants.

The Circulation Department had its headaches. Most of Hartford
had been shut up, at home. And everyone wanted to know what had
happened. The regular carriers were promised double pay if they

COURANT WAS ONLY PAPER BLIZZARD DIDN'T HALT
Drifts blocked front door; steps (left) led to business office

would cover their routes. Several showed up soon after daylight
Tuesday. Horses could not be had; all deliveries had to be made on
foot. In Prospect Street, and some others, The Courant was on the
doorsteps before 8 a.m.—long before the snow shovels had accomplished anything. By noon, Main Street between Park Street and the
Tunnel had its papers, as well as Asylum, Park, and Prospect, and a
good many others. Any subscriber who called at the office in person
not only got his copy but was asked if he would be willing—as all
were—to leave copies at the houses of his neighbors. Hundreds of
Courants were sent to readers in that neighborly way.

For newsboys, the day meant a fortune. There was a steady stream
of them at the office, and all bought their papers at the regular news-
boy price of two cents apiece, the regular retail price of the paper
being three cents. But on that memorable day some of the boys
were able to sell their Courants for fifty cents a single copy. This
scalping The Courant cheerfully regarded as free enterprise at work:

> To show how money rolls up under successful business management,
> take one little fellow who came into the office with no capital at all. He
> was given three copies on condition he would deliver a few to sub-
> scribers. Shortly he came back and bought six, and before long he was
> back to buy ten more. These made nineteen Courants that had cost him 32
> cents. He sold them, as he said himself, for from five cents to half a dol-
> lar apiece, and as he left the office the last time he said he had more money
> than he ever saw before.

Looking back at the Great Blizzard a year after the event, The Courant expressed what was probably the feeling of most Hartford inhabitants:

> Everybody remembers the scarcity of milk, the abundance of snow, the paralysis of trade, the shovel brigade, the flight of the men who had season contracts for cleaning the sidewalk, the mutual aid, the universal good feeling, the exhilaration that one somehow caught from the bigness of the whole affair. It was a great time. May we never have another like it.

In February, 1889, less than a year after the blizzard, downtown Hartford experienced a disaster that was to have far-reaching consequences both for the city and for The Courant.

The Courant's front page carried the headlines:

A SAD DAY.

Hartford in Mourning.

The Park Central Hotel In Ruins.

Efforts at Rescuing the Victims--An Unprecedented Catastrophe--The Probable Result of Criminal Carelessness--The Boiler Blows Out the Front and the Whole Building Topples Down.

PROBABLY 30 PERSONS KILLED.

AT LEAST A DOZEN INJURED.

The Courant's report of the Park Central disaster, interesting in itself, has a good deal of additional interest as an example of American
newspaper writing outside the big cities near the end of the last century. The account has warmth and a feeling of the reporter's in-
volvement in the tragedy. No attempt is made at a who-when-where-
why-what opening; the fact that the Park Central Hotel stood on
High Street is not even mentioned. There are dark allusions to an
"incompetent engineer" of "dissipated habits." The Park Central
fire was a tragedy that struck very near to many Hartford families,
and the account of it was obviously written by Hartfordians for
Hartfordians. This was no impersonal story for the wire services:

> A sudden shock, as the vibration of a light earthquake, the sound of
> a sharp explosion, and then instantly, the Park Central Hotel, with its
> precious human freight, sank into a mass of rubbish and ruins, of which
> not one brick remained upon another in its proper place. . . In this pris-
> on of horrors, bound down by the confused mass of wreckage, crushed,
> mangled, or imprisoned in stifling smoke or gas, were some forty or
> fifty human beings, including not a few widely known and greatly loved.
> . . . The great force of the explosion of yesterday seems hardly credi-
> ble for a sixteen horse-power boiler. But if an incompetent engineer left
> it at midnight with a heavy fire and too little water, it might have got in
> such condition by 5 o'clock that the sudden turning on of water would
> cause an explosion . . .

The night of the explosion, Stephen Hubbard, who always "sat
up with the paper," had gone home at about 3 a.m. When news of
the disaster spread through the City shortly after 5 a.m., he at once
rushed to the scene to give help. At six p.m. he remarked to a friend
that he had not thought to eat since midnight. For about 18 hours
he had gone without food; in 29 or 30 hours he had had only two
hours' sleep. He never recovered from the effects of that day, with
its strain on his sympathies and on his physical energies. He died at
his home on January 11, 1890, in the arms of his friend, Major "Jack"
Kinney of The Courant.

Hubbard's death, attributed by all his friends to his selfless rescue
work in the disaster, brought the first break in the 20-year partnership of Hawley, Warner, Hubbard, and Goodrich. These men had
added Charles Hopkins Clark to their number in 1888, when he had
bought a fifth interest in the firm, but there had been no deaths
among the owners during the two decades.

The death of Hubbard brought very clearly to his survivors the
difficulty of conducting a partnership amid the uncertainties of life,
not to mention adjusting relations with an estate. Accordingly, they

got a charter and organized The Hartford Courant Company in December, 1890. Hawley, Warner, Goodrich, and Clark each held a quarter of the $200,000 capital stock. The first officers of the corporation were: President, Charles Dudley Warner; Secretary, Charles Hopkins Clark; and Treasurer, William H. Goodrich.

Under the charter The Hartford Courant Company had very broad powers to carry on the business of "printing, publishing, book binding, lithographing, stereotyping, engraving, stationery, and other work incident thereto . . . and to manufacture and deal in materials, machinery, and tools pertaining to said business . . . and also for mercantile purposes." Wide as this latitude was, it was nothing new for The Courant. Founder Thomas Green himself had run a variety store in connection with the newspaper a century and a quarter earlier.

1890-1900
Modernization

F AR-REACHING CHANGES followed Managing Editor Hubbard's death in 1890. Charles Hopkins Clark temporarily took over Hubbard's duties—just long enough to hire young Clifton L. Sherman, who was in a few years to become the paper's dynamic managing editor. Clark first turned over the managing editorship to William A. Ayres, thus freeing his own energies to put some progressive ideas into practice.

Full of ambition for The Courant and, at 42, 19 years younger than any of his co-owners, Clark chafed under conditions which compelled the paper to edit much of its news into the wastebasket. The Courant, in 1890, was still hand set and still printed on a flat-bed press, although many leading papers, by that time, had installed typecasting and stereotyping machines, and rotary presses. He had been promised that a new press would be bought at once when he put his money into the paper in 1888, but the purchase had been delayed.

In 1892 R. Hoe & Co. shipped a newly designed press to The Courant. This machine could turn out 24,000 eight-page papers an hour, or 12,000 sixteen-page papers, all of them, as The Courant breathlessly announced, "cut, pasted, and folded and made into one complete newspaper and neatly piled up at the foot of the press." Goodrich retired in December, 1891, and his stock was divided among his former associates. His brother, General Arthur L. Goodrich, and Frank S. Carey, who had come to The Courant as a bookkeeper in 1876, were also allotted some shares. Hardly waiting to roll up his sleeves, Clark proceeded to put some of his dreams into effect, with spectacular results for the newspaper that was his chief interest in life.

The new press, in particular, filled him with jubilation:

> The latest invention is called The Courant Press in recognition of The Hartford Courant, for which the first of these remarkable machines

was made, the only one as yet completed. It is the result of years of study and experiment and embodies the very latest and most advanced ideas . . . The Courant Press is a beautiful piece of mechanism . . .

The Courant even came out with color in advertising, a point that surprises newsmen today, who know some of the problems press-rooms can have with color. On December 22, 1892, in time for Christmas, The Courant produced a full page in red for William Rogers Manufacturing Company's silverware. Explained The Courant:

> The whole paper today is printed just as usual— all run off at once with one impression, the press varying the color of the ink while attending as ever to the business of printing. So far as we know, this is the only double press that has yet done any such piece of work, and experienced printers have been altogether incredulous as to such a thing being possible. Their doubts are probably at an end now.

Clark was spurred to further efforts. To make sure that The Courant kept pace, he hired young men. Perhaps the most far reaching move in this rejuvenation was the transfer, in 1893, of the 50-year-old William A. Ayres from the managing editorship to the editorial page and his replacement by the 27-year-old Clifton L. Sherman, who

THE "COURANT PRESS" OF 1892
24,000 8-Page Papers an Hour

proved of wonderful energy and enterprise. By March of 1893 under its new young managing editor, The Courant was proudly announcing many special features: "Our regular original copyrighted storiette . . . our always welcome Boston Letter . . . the Children's Page . . . the illustrated fashion article . . . gossip about society"

The next month, April, found The Courant adding still another feature: puzzles on the children's page. Prizes were books, skates, chessmen and baseballs. It was in 1893 that The Courant installed its first typesetting machines, which enabled reading matter to be set with what the newspaper called "a speed that is astonishing and . . . processes that are wonderfully clever." Meanwhile, writers of headlines were having their innings with such outlandish alliterative efforts as "FARGO FOOD FOR FLAMES" and "THE ALLEGED TURPITUDE OF TURPIN."

By December, 1893, The Courant was promising its readers a unique issue embodying "some features never before attempted by any newspaper." One of these was a narrow page, only two columns wide, carrying a William Rogers advertisement, in blue, on one side and an advertisement for Brown Thomson's department store, in red, on the other. According to The Courant, these advertisements showed "the wonderful capabilities of our press."

Anyone with a bright new idea could get a sympathetic hearing. Clark had been held back for years, and now he was proceeding full steam ahead with the throttle tied down. A woman's column edited by Edith E. Kibbe appeared in April, 1894. Still going strong, this column appears today under the heading "Feminine Topics." It is the oldest continuously published daily newspaper column in the nation. It features now, as it did at the start, fashion notes, chit chat, household hints, and brief paid advertisements of items for sale in local stores. Edith Kibbe, signing herself "Deborah," ran the column for 45 years. It appears today over the signature, "Jacqueline." Although Edith Kibbe has long since passed to her reward, the type for the column she started 70 years ago is still regularly identified today in the composing room proof sheets with the initials KB. Such is the force of tradition.

It pleased Clark that women liked to read The Courant. One day, it is said, Clark saw a Mrs. Robinson on Main Street, and mentioned the fact to his wife. "Why, you couldn't have seen her," Mrs. Clark objected. "She's still on vacation at Lake George." Later that day, Clark instructed one of the reporters to write a brief notice stating that Mrs. Robinson had returned from the lake—as she had. Next

morning his wife apologized: "Charles, I must have been wrong yesterday. I see here in the paper that Clara Robinson came back to
Hartford day before yesterday."

During the 1890's pictures began to appear in The Courant with
increasing frequency—etchings on zinc and chalk plates. In those
days, pictures, when they appeared at all, were usually line drawings
that might have been made years earlier. The Courant's new emphasis
on newsy pictures is illustrated by a chalk plate drawing of a fire
that occurred on the night of November 4, 1894, at the house furnishings store of Neal, Goff, & Inglis. The very next morning The
Courant carried a chalk-plate picture of the burning building, showing a Miss Clark and a Miss Turner climbing over the roof, "whence
they were rescued."

The chalk plate was a simple, widely-used process. To make these
pictures, a metal plate was covered with chalk, resulting in something that looked like a squashed marshmallow. The picture was
then scratched on the white surface with a sharp stylus. An acid
bath etched the picture on the metal.

The year 1895 saw The Courant's first editorial use of color. On
May 31 the editorial page appeared in the usual black, except for
a 2-column-wide box in brilliant red headed: "ADVERTISEMENTS
IN COLOR":

> An esteemed Boston contemporary made its appearance one day last
> week with two or three of its advertisements printed in color, while the
> balance of the paper was printed in black. The enterprise of which this
> is evidence is worthy of special commendation. But when it states, as it
> did with a great deal of flourish, that it is 'the only Boston or New Eng-
> land newspaper having the facilities for printing in color on the same
> press and at the same time at which black type pages are printed,' we feel
> obliged to take exceptions. It is nearly two years now since The Courant
> first demonstrated its ability to do just that thing and it has done it sev-
> eral times since.
>
> We have not an 'immense three-deck press' as our Boston friends say
> they have, nor do we claim ours to be the 'wonder of the age.' We have,
> however, come to look upon The Courant press as a very satisfactory
> piece of machinery. It is a 'Hoe' web-perfecting machine, and while we
> can claim for it only one 'deck' we are more and more convinced that
> under the skillful management of its master, Frank C. Stockholm, it can
> show more 'trumps' than any other press with which we are familiar.

The outrageous claim from Boston seemed to stimulate Clark to
even greater enterprises. On July 13 the paper came out in a 36-page
edition which according to its own claim was "the largest paper
and the largest edition of any paper ever printed in this state . . . The

length of the rolls of paper required for today's edition was, as near as we can figure it, about 450 miles."

Yet more dashing innovations lay ahead. In June, 1896, The Courant used its first two-column news headline—to announce the candidacy of McKinley and Hobart. For time out of mind, headlines for stories of whatever magnitude had been limited to single-column width. December of the same year saw the paper's first half-tone cut in the news columns—a portrait of the Rev. Clarence H. Barber, who had completed a 10-year pastorate of the Second Congregational Church of Manchester, Connecticut. January, 1897, brought The Courant's first editorial cartoon, showing the struggle between railroad interests. The "Steam Railroad Gulliver" in the picture is shown tied down by "the 'Electrics.'"

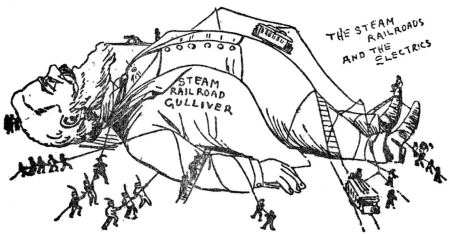

COURANT'S FIRST EDITORIAL CARTOON RAN IN 1897
Gulliver tied down by trolley wires

The Spanish American War of 1898 posed problems for all American newspapers. There was the sudden advent of news everybody wanted to read. There was the controversy over United States participation, some observers insisting that the whole thing had been stirred up by the sensational papers in New York. Atrocity stories had to be carefully screened out.

Managing Editor Sherman handled the war news with outstanding success. He was that rare item, a go-getter with a fine sense of balance. In addition to a deep respect for "hard" news, he had a real understanding of the value of background stories. He had both enterprise and judgment, a combination that paid off handsomely on a number of occasions, notably on the morning of February 16, 1898. At 1:50 a.m. word was received at The Courant that the battleship *Maine* had been blown up in Havana Harbor. At once Sherman sent a man in a horse cab to get The Courant's artist out of bed and to bring him back to the office at full gallop. Members of the staff were set to writing the history of the voyage to Havana and other pertinent stories. The result was that, with a story only a third of a column in length from the news wires, The Courant's extra had ten columns giving the news and its background on a subject that everyone wanted to read about. Clark also ran pictures of the Maine's Captain Sigsbee and Havana Harbor. It was far more complete coverage of the story than the Courant's exchanges carried that morning.

With the war, headlines began to grow. The paper's first 4-column headline appeared on July 2, 1898, and its first page-wide banner on July 4:

GLORIOUS VICTORY AT SANTIAGO

The Entire Spanish Fleet Destroyed by Admiral Sampson.

GENERAL SHAFTER CALLS ON SANTIAGO TO SURRENDER.

Clark strenuously advocated many civic projects. Among these were better public transportation for Hartford and a chain of public parks around the city. He also led a number of moral crusades. One of these was that favorite of Theodore Roosevelt, the campaign against huge trusts and "malefactors of great wealth." Another was a campaign against woman suffrage. Dead-set against giving women the vote, he kept up this fight until the bitter end.

On municipal transportation, Clark urged improved street railroads and better paving. In the spring of 1888 the street railroads of Hartford were all horse powered. About 800 horses served the city and suburbs. Rails ran along all the principal streets and converged in a great tangle at State House Square in front of The Courant office. The rails stood above ground level, like train tracks, making street cleaning difficult and hampering traffic. Citizens complained; the Society for the Prevention of Cruelty to Animals got into the dispute, stopping cars to inspect the horses' feet for sores. The railway people said these inspections took place with remarkable frequency in front of the Courant building, and suggested that the agents were attempting to get editorial attention.

In September, 1888, the first electric ran over Hartford rails. It was the beginning of the end for horse railroads. The Courant then began to oppose overhead trolleys, objecting that fallen high-voltage wires would be a danger:

> This is the first objection. Others are found in the damage to trees, the obstructions in the air, the bad effect on the good looks of the city, and the placing of still more wires where none should be at all.

It was a losing battle. In 1893 Clark ruefully admitted in an editorial that Hartford people obviously did not object to trolley wires. Soon almost all lines were electrified. In 1895 The Courant ran a story and picture of the street railway's one remaining horse-drawn car in operation in East Hartford. The next year The Courant ran pictures of the ugly tangles of overhead electric wires at various places in the city, and hopefully announced a movement to place them all underground. But trolley wires were destined to remain a part of Hartford's skyscape for many years. The Courant did get grooved rails flush with the pavement, so traffic could move freely. The Courant also recommended that the city take over the repair and cleaning of the pavement between the rails. Both recommendations were adopted.

On August 6, 1895, The Courant ran its first picture of an automobile, which it called a "French voiture automobile or automatic carriage." It was, the paper said, "propelled by petroleum vapor." In November of the same year the paper carried a picture of "the Duryea Motorcycle," a four-wheeled motorized carriage. This vehicle, going about 20 miles an hour, had won in the auto races at Chicago. By May 14, 1897, The Courant announced:

HORSELESS ERA COMES.

Columbia Motor Carriages
Shown to the Public.

RUN BY ELECTRICITY THROUGH
MUD AND UP GRADES.

It was the world's first public demonstration of a production-model electric auto. The Pope Manufacturing Company of Hartford had demonstrated it the previous day. The Courant was certain that an industry had come to town "which will surely develop into great proportions and add to the fame the city already has for first class mechanical productions." Two years later The Courant was to announce that New York's Fifth Avenue was to have "automobile coaches" run by electricity and manufactured in Hartford.

Clark campaigned early and late to have the rickety covered bridge linking Hartford with the east side of the Connecticut River replaced by a stone structure adequate to the needs of a growing community. By 1894 the old wooden bridge had reached such a sad condition that it inspired the Editor to the following sardonic reflections:

> The electric cars carry thousands of people daily over the so-called East Hartford bridge. What a joyous experience this is! The passenger hears the old timbers creak and groan, but he feels the comfortable human confidence that, if anything happens, it will be to the next person, not to him. Being thus reassured, and being somewhat shut off from a survey of outside scenery, alike by pine boards and by countless cobwebs stretched over what were windows early in the century, the traveler studies the inner decorations of this structure. . . Signs are all through it, signs of trade wherever space is sold, signs of age, neglect, and dirt where the space is still for sale. It is a shabby, cheap-John, discreditable approach to our beautiful city.

About 7 p.m., May 17, 1895, a fire alarm rang from Box 29 at the corner of Front and Morgan Streets. A moment later a shout was heard from the roof of The Courant building: "The old bridge is all afire!" Twelve minutes later Hartford's 76-year-old link with the east was broken, as a span collapsed. The fire probably could have been reported without a writer's leaving the newspaper building, the whole conflagration being in clear view from The Courant's roof. Nevertheless, seven men worked on the story. T. S. Weaver, later superintendent of schools in Hartford and namesake of a major high school today, wrote the lead paragraphs:

> The old bridge that since 1818 has connected Hartford with all of Connecticut east of the River went up in a sheet of flame last evening. . . . It was less than ten minutes from the discovery of the blaze before the flames had reached the west end, and the bridge had become, in the darkness of the night, for the first time in its history, a thing of beauty. . .
> There was the long skeleton of the bridge, its great wooden arches on either side and in the center, running east and west, glowing like bril-

liantly blazing rainbows, while the transverse supports of the roof structure, running north and south, stood out, each one of the hundreds of
them, like living hot golden ribs of fire—like the architectural beginning
of some fairy structure.

A four-column chalk plate drawing of the fire accompanied the
story. Charles Hopkins Clark regarded the picture as one of the best
examples of such work. The demand for The Courant that morning
was so great that the pressmen were recalled and the press run until
noon.

"GOLDEN RIBS OF FIRE" IN 1895—END OF THE WOODEN BRIDGE
Fine example of chalk plate reproduction

At the time of the fire the State Legislature was trying to make up
its mind what should be done about the old bridge. While arguing
continued on Capitol Hill, a temporary bridge was strung across on
the old piers, the trolley tracks were re-laid, and traffic resumed
over a structure hardly less rickety than before. On December 23 the
temporary bridge collapsed, about 200 feet of the structure being
swept away by an ice jam. Across the big gap where the timbers had
been swept away the street car rails hung over the water like a pair
of 200-foot cables.

The Courant, in a remarkable show of initiative and speed, ran the following morning a chalk plate sketch of what remained of the structure. An artist, sent to the scene in the small hours, sketched the wreckage by what meager light was available. The Courant hit the streets with the picture that morning. For a quick artist drawing a not too complicated picture, chalk plate was almost as fast as photography is today. The Courant immediately renewed its campaign:

> As we have said more than once before, the construction of a new bridge gives a great opportunity for improving and also for beautifying Hartford. . . The bridge, with a suitable draw, should . . . consist of stone arches, as permanent as the hills themselves—beautiful, safe, sure.

In May, 1896, a second temporary bridge was completed. Not until 1908 did a stone bridge take its place.

Clark was a strong believer in beautifying his beloved Hartford and Connecticut. One reason for The Courant's campaign for a stone bridge was that Clark thought stone arches across the river would be far more beautiful than steel girders. Hartford was a beautiful city, and he wanted to keep it that way. Today, one of Hartford's jewels is Bushnell Park, a fountained oasis in the downtown area with the State Capitol as a backdrop. When, in the '90's, the Rev. Dr. Francis Goodwin began an active campaign for more parks, somewhat as the Rev. Dr. Horace Bushnell had done in the '50's, he found The Courant again ready to support him every step of the way. The more Clark thought about it, the easier he found it to imagine Hartford one of the most beautiful cities in the country, bordered by a picturesque river and by a girdle of spacious parks:

> If the city of Hartford secures, while still it may be had, land south, west, and north of what is now the populous part, and lays out a chain of parks around the city, all future generations will be grateful. Such action would put Hartford ahead of any other city that we can recall . . .

The time was ripe. Hartford needed the parks and it had men of wealth and property who could give them. Some idea of the response to the campaign is indicated in an editorial Clark wrote on November 23, 1894:

> It seems almost to be raining parks these days, and the shower comes after a most protracted drouth. Nothing could be more welcome or more for Hartford's benefit.
>
> Col. Pope's gift in the south-western part of the city was announced last Friday morning. Everybody was delighted with it.
>
> Saturday morning came the announcement that Mr. Pond's gift [of Elizabeth Park] to Hartford could be accurately measured and that it amounted to his elegant home, ninety acres of beautiful land on the

west side of the city, and $200,000 with which to buy more land.

Now, a week later, comes the notice of Mr. Keney's still larger gift, and this is on the north side of the city. All of a sudden the hope and dream of those who have been most deeply interested in this much needed sort of improvement for Hartford seem to be comprehensively realized.

During the '90's it became clearer and clearer that Charles Hopkins Clark's ideas were chiefly shaping the paper's policy. Editor-in-Chief Warner was now an old man. Charles Hemenway Adams, though a prolific writer, was hardly the one to shape policy for a large and growing organization.

On the other hand, Clark was a journalist in the tradition of Bennett, Godkin, Greeley, Reid, Scripps, and a host of others. The paper bore the stamp of his personal interests, his likes and dislikes. There is a persistent legend that when Clark wrote a particularly opinionated editorial, indignant readers by the hundreds would cancel their subscriptions—only to renew them in a few days. Nothing in the records of the circulation department justifies this oft-told tale, although, like other legends, it probably has a kernel of truth. What The Courant printed really mattered to readers.

One highly controversial opinion that Clark held was that women should have no place in politics. In this he not only swam against the tide, but reversed longstanding Courant policy. Readers bitterly complained. Clark replied that he was trying to keep women clean and pure. He never abandoned the struggle until the Nineteenth Amendment forced him to surrender in 1920.

Since the mid-1800's, The Courant had looked favorably on the advances made in women's rights and privileges. It carried dozens of editorials supporting woman suffrage, despite uneasiness over Susan B. Anthony's somewhat disturbing tendency to make a spectacle of herself and to associate with Democrats. When women made news by practicing medicine or preaching, The Courant, prior to the '90's, had given its editorial blessing. It had reported, with respectful interest, "two experiments . . . now fairly inaugurated in the new education of women, one at Vassar and one at Cornell." When Mrs. Julia Ward Howe, at a Women's Suffrage Convention in Chicago in 1874, urged an equal place for women in business, The Courant approved, adding jocularly, "We believe in giving everyone a fair chance and hope no one will interfere with the speedy development of lady railroad managers who shall eclipse Vanderbilt." As late as 1891 the paper had bitterly rebuked the retail merchants of New York for the poor working conditions of their women employees.

In 1893, partly as a result of suffragette agitation, the General
Assembly of Connecticut passed an act giving women the right to
vote for school officers. Clark had his doubts about this act. He loved
the masculine rough-and-tumble of politics, the cigar smoke and in-
ner-sanctum excitement of political conventions. Deep inside, he
probably resented the intrusion of women. Besides, women belonged
in the home as symbols of all that is fine and pure. By 1895 he had
convinced himself that the women themselves did not want the vote.
He had watched their record at the polls since they had been granted
the right to vote for school officers, and had noticed with keen interest that fewer and fewer women had exercised their franchise.
He wrote an editorial in July, 1895, pointing out that the women's
vote on school matters had steadily declined. Citing figures for all
but three or four towns in the state, he showed that the women's
vote had dropped from nearly 4,000 to about 2,000. These paltry
figures he compared with the male turnout of about 164,000 at the
last general election.

Clark's editorials against woman suffrage, written over a span of
a quarter of a century, show every facet of conservative opposition
to an inevitable reform. They show a benevolent and kindly man,
certainly a loving husband and father, holding out to the very last
against what he regarded as a reform against nature. Sometimes his
attack was bitter, sometimes amused. But the intent was always the
same.

Through the mid-90's as America wallowed in financial doldrums,
The Courant, like other newspapers, reported one bank or business
failure after another. In the general uneasiness over "conditions,"
businessmen attacked newspapermen for undermining public confidence, and newspapermen came back with vitriolic attacks on
fraudulent business operations. When financier E. C. Benedict criticized newspapers for their "unbridled license" in reporting business
failures, Clark came back with a steaming editorial on the need for
ethics in business:

> Lots of changes must come, but they will be in the line of open hon-
> esty and not of the sort to facilitate operations in stocks or make it easier
> for the shepherds of Wall Street to shear the lambkins of the back coun-
> try. The 'unbridled license of the press' is helping on this day. That's
> one of its good works.

This was Clark's basic formula for the nation's economic woes:
morality in financial dealings and a vigilant press to keep the public
alert. If this thinking over-simplified matters, it nevertheless served

as the basis for much of the early 20th Century legislation upon which American finance rests today. It was founded on integrity, and integrity was a quality Clark had in ample measure.

Integrity in business, Clark believed, included decent treatment of workingmen. In 1894 he told his readers about two careful English experiments with the relatively new 8-hour day—experiments that showed no drop in production and that greatly improved the morale of the workers. Here, the exercise of practical understanding had worked to everyone's benefit. Clark had no basic quarrel with unions. He once wrote, "The labor union is the development of the self-interest of the employed against the selfishness of the employer." The rule to follow in management-labor disputes, he urged, was the Golden Rule.

On October 20, 1900, The Courant's Editor in Chief, Charles Dudley Warner, died suddenly while taking an afternoon walk. His companion of many years, Mark Twain, wrote the paper: "He was one of the old, old friends. This is a bereavement which falls heavily not only upon the family and friends but upon all the country. I wish to be at the funeral."

For a good many years Warner had had little hand in running The Courant, though he came into the office fairly regularly, and occasionally wrote an editorial or a book review. So warmly was he loved by his associates on the newspaper that years after his death they could still hardly believe he was gone. On the tenth anniversary of his death the editorial page carried a black-bordered obituary, exactly as if he had died the day before:

> Ten years ago today, men and women were saying to each other in Hartford . . . and in a thousand towns beside—'Charles Dudley Warner is dead . . .' He is still with us today . . . in the life of this ancient town which he loved and helped to make beautiful, in the books that will be read and prized for their fine sanity and delightful humor long after we have followed him . . .
>
> Once, we remember, he spoke delightedly of the 'afterglow' in the Alps; and a very beautiful sight it must always be to the nature lover. Incomparably softer, more lasting and more beautiful is the afterglow of such a life as Mr. Warner's.

Joseph R. Hawley succeeded Warner as President of the company, a position he held until his death in 1905. Charles Hopkins Clark became Editor in Chief. The years ahead were to be full of vitality for The Courant under Clark's leadership.

1900-1913
Editor Clark

C HARLES HOPKINS CLARK held all his opinions with a fierce conviction, evident in almost every line he wrote and still more evident to visitors in his office, who found themselves sitting across the desk from a towering, slightly stoop-shouldered man with a sharp goatee, a bristling moustache, and a piercing gaze. "No more independent editor ever sat in guidance over a newspaper in this or any other country," a reminiscent Courant editorial once said. It was an observation that many readers had already made for themselves, as was the newspaper's further comment that Clark "was in love with life."

Clark did not talk down to his readers. He threw out ideas, opinions, and prejudices and the subscribers could make the best of them. At one time or another during his editorship, The Courant supported and denounced civil service reform; favored and opposed a direct primary for Connecticut; argued that 1900 was not the first year of the 20th Century; announced that there were too many colleges for women; insisted that all wills should be made public; defended the right of women to smoke in public and the right of movie houses to show films and of hotels to serve liquor on Sunday; argued that any corporation should be required at any time to show any applicant its list of stockholders and the transactions in its stock ledger; pooh-poohed the moralists who feared the degenerating effects of modern social dancing; disparaged daylight saving proposals; and argued that too many newspapers were being published.

It is a measure of the respect in which Clark was held by his fellow newspaper publishers that he was appointed First Vice President of the Associated Press in 1906, and that he served on the Executive Committee on the AP's Board of Directors from 1910 until he died in 1926. On the board he knew well and worked with such outstanding newspapermen as Adolph S. Ochs of the New York

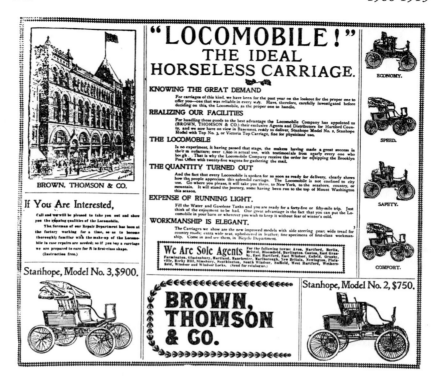

IN 1900 YOU COULD BUY YOUR LOCOMOBILE FOR $750 AT
DEPARTMENT STORE
Courant boosted automobiling, condemned "silly-rich" speedsters

Times, Frank B. Noyes of the Washington *Evening Star,* William L.
McLean of the Philadelphia *Evening Bulletin,* Clark Howell of the
Atlanta *Constitution,* and Victor F. Lawson of the Chicago *Daily
News.*

Though he did not seek public office Clark lived politics all his
life. He went to his first Republican National Convention in 1888
and never missed one thereafter. He believed that this country needed
two parties, one of them the Republican. But if Republicans got out
of line, they heard about it from The Courant, as when Theodore
Roosevelt incurred Clark's ire by breaking ranks to form the Bull
Moose party.

Bull Moose or no, Roosevelt remained for Clark "our greatest
man." In fact, there was a little of the Teddy Roosevelt in Clark.
Both men lived strenuously. Both liked to put ideas into force. Both
were inclined to believe that even the most complicated social and

economic problems were at bottom moral problems. When Roosevelt denounced "malefactors of great wealth" and launched on a spree of trust busting, he had no stauncher supporter than Charles Hopkins Clark, who tried to promote a little trust busting right in Hartford.

Although Clark held the position of Editor in Chief from 1900 and President of The Hartford Courant Company from 1906 to his death in 1926, the period of his greatest influence extended from the turn of the century until the first World War. After that, younger men began to make their ideas count. But, until his dying day, there was no question as to who was "The Chief."

Clark had been in the Editorial chair only a few months when the New York *Sun* lured his Managing Editor away. Clifton Sherman's departure during the summer of 1900 was a blow. It was especially hard on Clark, who had hired Sherman and who had had such tremendous confidence in him that he had made him one of the youngest managing editors in the country. As it turned out, Sherman's experience on the *Sun* proved to be a boon to The Courant. Clark managed to get him back again in 1904, after three and a half years. What Sherman had learned on the *Sun* about modern newspaper methods soon became evident in The Courant.

In the meantime Clark had little opportunity to feel sorry for himself. He appointed Charles W. Burpee Managing Editor, and the two soon had their hands full with a new four-page-wide press and folder that arrived from the Hoe Company during the summer of 1901.

During 1901 and 1902 the world of politics, too, kept Clark on the jump. President McKinley was shot September 6, 1901, and died a week later. In state politics the big issue was the revision of the constitution. Clark served as Hartford's representative to the Constitutional Convention. In June of 1902 the proposed new constitution went before the voters, to be rejected on the issue of representation of the towns in the General Assembly.

Then, in August, 1902, all Hartford was suddenly galvanized by the announcement that Theodore Roosevelt was coming to town. When the President arrived on August 22, he found Hartford in one of its most festive moods. Bunting fluttered from buildings all along the parade route. At The Courant, great swags of red, white, and blue hung from window to window; the building looked half suffocated in stars and stripes. As the parade moved through the city, the Governor's Foot Guard and other music makers kept up a lively

1898 POLITICAL RETURNS   McKINLEY ASSASSINATION
Stereopticon flashes results   *Front-door bulletins, 1901*

tune; a fleet of bicycle riders wheeled slowly in good order; Asylum Street, Main, Pearl, Washington, and Vernon streets were thronged, as was Pope Park, where the President spoke. It was a great day, and Roosevelt played his part to the hilt, waving his tall silk hat, flashing his famous smile, and bowing in all directions while the ribbons from his pince-nez fluttered over his shoulder.

Charles Hopkins Clark was determined to do justice to the occasion. The story received full news and editorial coverage, accompanied by a map of the parade route and other sidelights. But Clark felt that something special was needed. He consulted a local photo engraver. Roosevelt was scheduled to arrive at Union Station on the 4:18. There would be plenty of daylight. If the engraver could prepare a cut by press time at 3 a.m., the paper would be able to run what was then a rarity—a spot news photograph the day after the event. The engraver agreed, and The Courant engaged three or four local photographers. All arrangements were carefully made; it seemed nothing could go wrong.

But the planners had not counted on the unpredictability of the President himself. The train had barely pulled to a stop when a man jumped off. It was Teddy. Waving his hat to the crowd, he dashed over to the reception committee, shook hands all around, briskly walked along the platform and down the steps to where the parade was about to start. The photographers, swiveling heavy cameras on cumbersome wooden tripods, never had a chance.

Managing Editor Burpee, unaware of this hitch, had been snapping a few pictures himself. Amateur photography was in its infancy and a remarkably sturdy infant it was. Portable cameras had been on the market a few years, selling at prices almost anyone could afford. One popular model came equipped with a roll on which the user could take one hundred pictures. The user then sent the whole thing—camera, film, and all—back to the manufacturer, who developed the pictures. According to The Courant, there were countless amateur photographers in the crowd watching Roosevelt; "seemingly at every ten feet there was a camera."

When Burpee, returning to the office at 7 p.m., learned of the failure of the photographers, his first reaction was dismay. Then he began to think about what he might have in his own camera. He thought he knew enough about photography to develop his own films. Into the darkroom he went and worked out three good pictures.

It was now dark, and there was considerable doubt that the engraver could make plates in time by artificial light—or would if he could. Burpee took him the pictures, and the engraver went to work under sputtering carbon lamps. At midnight he said, "Half an hour more." At 2 a.m., "Ten minutes more." At 3 a.m., "Soon." Burpee held the page-one form, all put ,together except for an accurately measured place reserved for the engravings. At the last possible moment the plates were delivered, and The Courant came out the next morning with rare, on-the-spot news photographs of a most illustrious—and elusive—subject. They were the first spot news photographs to appear in The Courant.

In 1904 Burpee left the newspaper to go into insurance and Clark promptly asked Clifton Sherman to come back. In Sherman's absence The Courant had put in a new press, and Clark was eager to launch a renewed program of expansion and development. The challenge appealed to Sherman, who accepted Clark's offer and remained as The Courant's managing editor for 15 years.

Clark and Sherman put their heads together. There were experiments with headlines, new departments and features, special supplements. One new feature, "The Lighter Side of Life," appeared in

April, 1904, The Courant's earliest page devoted to jokes and cartoons. In May came a special "Automobile Supplement" showing the correct dress styles for women riders and the latest models of cars.

Clark himself loved to ride in an automobile and was of the opinion that "Nobody can spend a season with an automobile and not know more of where and how people live." On the other hand, he didn't want the automobile to be a plaything of the rich, and roundly criticized W. K. Vanderbilt for racing from Newport to Boston in his "Paris auto" at 61 miles an hour. The Courant ran annual automobile supplements, all the while attacking automobiles as threats to public safety. Readers became confused. Did The Courant favor the new means of transportation or not? In March, 1905, Clark wrote:

> We have shown a genuine zeal for automobiles by speaking out plainly against the silly-rich who abuse their privileges and make the automobile hateful . . . We are looking hopefully for the time when the automobile in Connecticut will be run properly and when the brainless young heirs of New York speculators will be put away among the bedbugs of back-country lockups if they defy the laws of Connecticut.

Although this shaft was aimed at brainless New Yorkers, Hartford's own record had been none too good. On June 11, 1904, The Courant had carried the headline:

WARRANTS FOR EIGHT AUTOISTS.

—

For Speeding on Farmington Avenue.

—

TO APPEAR IN COURT THIS MORNING.

—

POLICE GO ABOUT IT IN ARBITRARY WAY.

This was page one news. The Courant carefully explained:

> Early in the week, Bicycle Policeman Brown was sent out to measure off a course, and he chose Farmington Avenue as his scene of operations. Policeman Brown, when seen by a reporter last night, refused to say anything about his mode of operations, but it is understood that he put a tape measure on the avenue and decided that it was a quarter of a mile between Sisson Avenue and Woodland Street.
>
> Armed with a watch he proceeded on Wednesday to Sisson Avenue. He lay in wait and timed the automobiles that passed him. He could tell pretty well the moment that an automobile passed Sisson Avenue, but it has not yet been disclosed how he decided the exact time when it reached the end of a quarter of a mile. If he depended on his eyesight, he is likely to have been seconds off the way, yet it is not yet plain that anyone assisted him.

The automobiles, it turned out, had been proceeding at fifteen miles an hour. In later life, Clark loved to have his chauffeur drive fast.

In the spring of 1906 Hartford's three ice companies banded together, dividing up their customers among them, each declining to service the customers of the others, and all agreeing to fix the price of ice from 50 to 150 per cent higher than during the previous year. It was absolute monopoly.

Clark and Sherman flew to arms. The threat of the icemen hit home to every family, particularly those with infants needing milk. And the icemen themselves, completely unrepentant, made perfect targets for outraged editorials.

The Courant got its campaign into high gear on May 22, 1906:
ICE MEN SAY 'WHAT ARE YOU GOING TO DO ABOUT IT'

> Write your experiences with the iceman and send it to "The Courant." Tell how much your piece of ice has shrunk, tell what the iceman has said when you threatened to change to some other company . . .

Without a doubt, the ice trust had created an emergency in the city. Meat markets, grocery stores, restaurants, and saloons threatened to raise their prices. One liquor dealer showed a Courant reporter two bills for ice, one dated April 30 and the other a week later. The first charged him $4 a ton and the second $10 a ton. Clark, never one to pull his punches, accused the ice companies of saying, in effect:

> We now propose to make you pay double prices because we have got you where you've got to do that or see your babies and old folks and feeble generally die on your hands, for we've cornered the supply. Would you let your baby die for a half-dollar? Of course you would

not: then hand over the fifty cents! That's the size of it. It is as cruel as the ice is cold.

The liquor men acted first and for a few glorious days saloon keepers were the heroes of Hartford. They invited all Hartford merchants to join them in the formation of a rival supplier, to be called the Merchant's Ice Company. The Courant jubilantly announced, "ICE TRUST BUSTED; NEW COMPANY A FACT." Clark urged the new company to set up an artificial ice plant so the merchants would be independent not only of the trust, but of the whims of winter weather. Artificial ice, Clark argued, was also much purer than natural. But despite his counsel, no ice plant was erected. The new company simply bought its ice from a Massachusetts firm.

The Courant's campaign against the ice trust had an amusing sequel. Clark kept insisting on the wisdom of building an artificial ice plant, and when businessmen failed to build one, he urged the city to do so. But many Courant readers could see nothing but creeping socialism in this, or any, proposal for expanding municipal services. For the first and only time in his life Clark, who was nothing if not a bulwark of the Republican Party, found himself attacked as a socialist. The editor indignantly denied the charge:

> There is no more socialism in storing, supplying, and selling frozen water than in storing, supplying, and selling melted ice. It is the same thing; the difference is literally one of degree. Hartford can free itself from the monopoly just as soon as it will establish an ice factory of its own.

But the argument fell on deaf ears. Ten years later in 1919 Clark was still calling for an ice plant.

In these early years of the twentieth century The Courant had a circulation of about 11,000. A day-book showing daily press runs for the years 1905 through 1912 has been preserved in The Courant's archives. The record shows that the efforts of Clark, Sherman, and the rest of the staff helped increase circulation from about 11,000 in 1905 to 15,700 in 1913, when The Courant first entered the Sunday field.

The Courant, after Sherman returned from New York, began publishing more special editions. One of these celebrated the dedication of the new and beautiful stone bridge over the Connecticut River— the Bulkeley Bridge. The dedication was set for October 6, 1908. As early as April, 1907, The Courant began to plump for a big celebration. Clark wanted parades, and fireworks, and speeches, and dancing—a regular fiesta. As the great day approached, the newspaper kept building up interest with stories of the laying of the last stone, the taking down of the old temporary bridge, the meeting of the Celebration Committee, the erection of the grandstands, the hanging of the bunting. The bridge was declared the largest stone arch bridge in the world, nearly 1,200 feet long, the arches springing high above the water. Hartford felt great pride—its new bridge was a thing of beauty.

On opening day The Courant came out with the largest paper ever printed in Hartford up to that time. To a 16-page news section were added a 14-page Bridge Section, and a 10-page Industrial Section. If the Courant went all out over the new bridge, it had every reason to do so. Clark had been campaigning for a stone bridge for more than 13 years.

On August 14, 1913, The Courant, then in its 148th year, announced an innovation that was to bring vast change and infuse new vigor into the oldest newspaper in the nation. The headline that morning read, "A SUNDAY COURANT COMING."

By the time The Courant entered the Sunday field it was, by its own admission, "almost the only considerable American newspaper that we know of that has not already a Sunday edition." Hartford already had three Sunday newspapers: the *Journal*, founded in 1874; the *Globe*, dating from 1876, and the Sunday edition of the *Post*. None of these was healthy in 1913; the *Globe*, strongest of the lot, claimed a circulation of only 15,000. The Sunday *Post* was to be bought up the next year by the *Globe*. The anemic condition of these papers gave Clark pause, even though his colleagues on The Courant, and especially Henry H. Conland, the Secretary of the company, assured him that The Courant would succeed.

Clark felt no moral qualms about publishing on Sunday; he seems, in fact, to have felt something of contempt for the noisy local sabbatarians. But it did bother him that Sunday papers in Hartford didn't seem to stay healthy. In retrospect, it appears that the real trouble with Hartford's Sunday papers before 1913 had been the left-handed way in which they were operated. The *Globe* is fairly representative. It depended heavily on the week-end efforts of reporters from other local papers who were willing to sacrifice their Saturday nights in exchange for what they could get by writing a few news stories.

Clark proceeded with all the caution of a man handling a crate of high explosives. Every objection was carefully considered, the public pulse was felt and felt again, readers and advertisers were anxiously questioned, and the most careful advance publicity paved the way.

The August announcement held out the olive branch to the sabbatarians: "There is no moral obstacle, for everyone familiar with newspaper affairs knows that the Sunday paper does not call for Sunday work as the Monday issue does." Clark had assurances, too, for those who associated Sunday journalism with the trashy supplements of some metropolitan papers. "It will be in all respects a news-paper, and a first class one, giving the contemporaneous history of the world as gathered by that unrivaled agency, the Associated Press, and reflecting the life of Connecticut, social, industrial, and political, through its own army of experienced correspondents."

Clark allowed these assurances to sink in for about a month, then on September 13 told subscribers that "From a business standpoint the prospects of the Sunday Courant are already settled. It is going to be a success and a great success. Without exception the merchants of Hartford are pleased with the new advertising medium . . ."

A team of clerks, half way through the subscription list for the daily Courant, had not found half a dozen who had failed to engage the Sunday Courant. Clark promised that the paper would take on the character of an all-Connecticut newspaper, and that it would reach most of the State before the New York papers. He further promised:

> There will be no colored supplement and no freak or outrageous 'art' work. We aim to make a home paper, and as woman makes the home, the Sunday Courant will be careful to see that her interests are not neglected . . . Last—it should have been put first—is the intellectual side of woman's interests, the news about the manifold movements in which woman's activities find outlet.

On D-day—or S-day—minus five the paper put up a thousand posters showing a town crier advertising the forthcoming publication. When the fateful day arrived, The Courant appeared, a little thicker than usual, but in its familiar dress. There was the usual dateline, different only in that this one read *Sunday,* October 5, 1913. A box contained the announcement that the paper was in three parts. The first two parts, 28 pages in all, carried news, editorials, and financial reports. Not much novelty here. Part Three, 18 pages, was the Sunday supplement. This section, indexed in the box, contained:

> Thomas Hooker Cartoon and Interview
> Book Reviews
> Art and Music

Auto Trip to Nova Scotia
Playgrounds of Hartford
Records of Globe Circling
Letters of State Correspondents
Women's Interests
Social and Personal
State Politics
Farm, Garden, Poultry
Theater News of Hartford and New York
Automobile News and Views

A full-page drawing on the first page of the supplement was obviously aimed to quiet the fears of all but the most intransigent sabbatarians. The picture shows Thomas Hooker—Hartford's revered founding father himself, as solid a symbol of church and state as you could ask for—purchasing a paper from a young lad whose countenance shows to any discerning eye that he is utterly incapable of wickedness no matter how many papers he may sell from his bag labeled "Sunday Papers." With his right hand Thomas Hooker reaches for the Sunday Courant; in his left he holds a large bible. In the background the venerable Old State House looks down on the transaction. The caption reads, "Thomas Hooker: 'At Last, a Sunday "Courant." I must Purchase and Peruse It.. "

The Courant staff waited nervously for the public response. They did not wait long. The first issue of 25,000 sold off nicely at five cents a copy. And it was not long before readers began to write in their satisfaction. The staff breathed more easily. The heavens did not fall. But circulation did. It slid from the 25,000 of the first issue to about 16,000 in a few months. Hartford simply did not have the Sunday newspaper reading habit.

Then on February 21, 1914, an incident occurred that gave the Sunday Courant new vigor. A young lad, Christopher Harmon, working in the express office at Union Station, glanced up that Saturday to see flames and smoke in the room beyond. It turned out to be the biggest fire in Hartford in 50 years. Ten thousand people, The Courant estimated, stood in the snow to watch. The roof of the station was covered with snow, and icicles hung from the cornices. Jutting out at regular intervals from the snow-covered tiles were dormer windows, each spurting smoke and flame. The engines struggled through the snow-packed streets, several firemen were injured, the water from the hoses froze on the blazing building.

The next morning the Sunday Courant carried three full pages on the fire, illustrated by striking photographs. One shows the building

almost at the height of the blaze, the dormers belching smoke, firemen struggling. The Courant ran this remarkable picture five columns
wide on Page One. Here was something everyone wanted to read,
and there was The Sunday Courant with the news. People bought
the paper. And they kept on buying it. On its fifth birthday, the Sunday Courant sold 26,000 copies.

In the pre-Sunday-paper days, the custom of the staff was to assemble every Friday night in the old dining room in Long's Hotel
after the paper had been put to bed. Here they enjoyed their only
opportunity for two or three hours of relaxation together. It was almost a ritual. Each Friday night (or Saturday morning) they would
listen for City Editor Horton's half-cynical comment: "Gosh, this
bohemian life is great!"

For most of the staff, Saturday had meant a night off, although
some of the men spent their Saturday nights across the Old State
House green from The Courant, working in the office of the *Sunday Globe*. But The Courant's Sunday edition brought all that to an
end, at least for members of The Courant staff, whose nights off
were distributed throughout the week. The *Globe* rapidly declined
after 1913, finally being bought by The Courant in 1919. This left
The Courant the only Sunday newspaper in Hartford, as it is today.

1913-1919
War-time Changes

PUT A COPY of The Courant for 1913 alongside one for 1919 and the contrast is startling. The front page of 1913 has an air of calm. Every other column, one through seven, begins with a modest single-column headline. The news may be important, even world shaking—America on the brink of war with Mexico, Europe in turmoil—but the headlines seldom extend beyond one column. At the top of alternate columns, no headlines: just the continuation of the stories from the preceding columns.

In contrast, the front page of 1919 looks restless. Heavy black headlines stretch across three or four columns, calling attention to sometimes trivial news. The page is obviously designed to catch the eye of the hurrying pedestrian.

There is more news, too, than in 1913. An eighth column has been added and the paper generally has more pages. Some of these are increased advertising, but news, too, has increased. There are many more pictures, and—something new—cartoons: "Everyday Movies" on the editorial page and "Petey," perennially baffled by the century he finds himself living in, among the classified ads.

After the struggle in 1913 to launch a Sunday paper, The Courant staff devoted its next major effort to a 150th Anniversary number, which appeared on Sunday, October 25, 1914. It was a fine issue, a classic of its kind, worthy of the most enduring newspaper in America.

The Anniversary Courant, 114 pages in nine sections, took more than a year to prepare. Determined to put out the best issue of which the paper was capable, Clark and Sherman delegated the capable staff writer Frederick E. Norton to read the files—he had a year to do it—and write a year-by-year chronology of The Courant. Norton's efforts resulted in a highly readable 20-page account, to which Clark added several pages of his personal recollections of politics in Connecticut.

One section carried sketches of the earlier Courant proprietors. Twenty "old Courant hands" wrote their reminiscences, giving glimpses of persons and incidents that would otherwise have been lost forever. Still other sections told the histories of industry, banking, and insurance in Connecticut. Seventy-five thousand copies were printed, making this the largest edition published by any newspaper in Connecticut up to that time.

While the anniversary number was in the works, The Courant was getting some major stories. In April Vera Cruz in Mexico fell to the U. S. Marines. On June 29 The Courant carried the story of the assassination of Archduke Ferdinand, at Sarajevo, and from that time on the war news from Europe called for ever bigger and blacker headlines. Viewing the two conflicts, Clark found it easier to become exercised over the nearer. He thought our entire policy in Mexico mad. As far as the European struggle was concerned, that seemed to Clark to be largely Europe's business. In August, 1914, The Courant carried the headline:

GERMAN AIRSHIP DROPS BOMBS INTO PARIS, INJURING TWO WOMEN, DOING LITTLE DAMAGE

Modern warfare had entered the Air Age. Yet in The Courant's headline that morning there was detectable, to longstanding subscribers, an overtone of I-told-you-so. Since long before man's first practical flight, The Courant had tried to draw a clear line between the imagination of dreamers who saw the heavens filled with winged commerce and flying armies, and the practical reality of the early Air Age.

The judicious calm which The Courant, along with many other journals, adopted toward the European war abruptly ended with the sinking of the *Lusitania,* May 7, 1915. A bitter tone appeared in the war news. Captions over editorials read "BACK TO BARBARISM" and "THE LUSITANIA OUTRAGE." Presently war cartoons began to appear, showing evil-eyed Huns slobbering and baring their fangs while women and children bled to death in a tangle of barbed wire.

Few actual photographs pictured the war. To a large extent, timely cartoons, rather than often-delayed photographs, built up the public's mental picture of the goings on across the Big Pond. Clark never liked the war cartoons. Even photographs, he knew, were sometimes faked. He took a malicious delight in cataloguing the pictures of different persons identified as Pancho Villa in the newspapers that came across his desk. And if it was easy to fake photographs, it was still easier to convey false impressions in drawings and cartoons. Still, it may have been the Courant's war cartoons that helped to break Clark's resistance to what he considered the lowest of all art forms—the comic strip.

Clark detested comics. Salesman after salesman tried to sell him on comic strips in The Courant. Clark would listen just so long, then give his standard reply:

"You watch the obituary columns of The Courant. After you see my name there, you may be able to sell comics to this newspaper."

Beside some of the anti-German pictures of the Kaiser's beasts eating Allied babies, even the most offensive comics must have looked gentle indeed. Anyhow, Brigg's wistful "When a Feller Needs a Friend" began appearing daily in The Courant in March, 1915. In July scenes from American life drawn by the great James Montgomery Flagg began to be printed fairly regularly. They were huge pictures, a page wide. From these it was only a short—but for Clark a painful—step to the newspaper's first bona fide comic strip, "Millie and Her Millions," which began in March, 1916, in the classified section. Though various members of the staff had been urging the step for years, there were mixed feelings among Courant personnel. They were half sorry that the boss had given in.

Clark's feelings are not a matter of record. His name did not appear in the obituary columns that morning. But it is said that when the Sunday Courant began to carry a colored comic section, he insisted that it be removed before the newspaper was delivered to his door.

The romantic heyday of the newspaper City Room, which was to reach high noon in the late '20's and early '30's, was just dawning. The city room of the old State Street building felt the stirrings of this journalistic excitement, and her fourth-floor city room harbored a colorful assembly of talents and personalities.

City Editor William A. (Billy) Graham, dour and sharp-tongued, presided. This dapper martinet wore rimless pince-nez, and parted his curly hair down the middle. Known as "Doctor" by most of the staff (it was presumed he had a medical education), he was a forerunner of the hard-bitten city editor type later celebrated in novel, movie and personal reminiscence. Reporters quailed under his criticism and jumped to his orders. He had one absorbing interest outside the newspaper—the theater, although this was not generally known by his staff. Once his own city room was flabbergasted to see in a New York paper a photograph showing a smiling Graham backstage with a bevy of chorus girls.

Sitting back to back with Graham was Harry Horton, his assistant and later his successor. Pallid, sunken cheeked, and somber as an undertaker, Horton read copy at his roll-top desk and served as schoolmaster for the young cubs. Always mindful of the tightness of news space, he taught his charges to boil copy and to strive for accuracy. It was one of his cubs who later coined the admonition, "Accuracy, terseness, accuracy," still regarded as the City Room's copywriting maxim.

One night Horton asked a young reporter, "What have you got there?"

"Plumbers' convention at the Bond Hotel," was the reply.

"How much space will it take?"

"Well, about a column so far and another half-column will wind it up."

Horton's comment has become a Courant classic: "The story of the Creation took less than 200 words."

Like some of his staff and legions of newspapermen, Horton had literary aspirations. Mournful-faced, he would pick up a #2 pencil and dash off a quip that would later appear in *Judge* or *Puck* or *Town Topics*.

One of the most mild-mannered men ever to grace a newsroom was Elijah Shurter, telegraph editor for 52 years. Slight-statured and silver-haired, with a small silver mustache, and wearing rimless eyeglasses and the conventional green eyeshade, Shurter calmly edited copy on the astounding cavalcade of history. Stories from the Spanish-American War to the atomic blasting of Hiroshima received his impassive scrutiny. He would interrupt his scanning of the telegraph sheets to return a greeting pleasantly, but the boys in the City Room seldom got their first knowledge of world-shaking news from the imperturbable telegraph editor.

Max Farber, another veteran Hartford newspaper man, tells this cub story on himself:

One Christmas Eve he was assigned to cover police court. Later in the evening, Managing Editor Sherman noticed that the story was missing.

"There was no story, Mr. Sherman," Farber explained. "It was Christmas Eve, so the judge let all the prisoners go."

It was the classic "no news" situation. A Dickens-like story of Christmas Eve in the Hartford Police Court appeared in The Courant the next day, but it was written by veteran reporter Frederick Norton.

Financial Editor Daniel D. Bidwell once surprised everyone by challenging Nellie Bly's round-the-world exploit. Personally well off but frugal, he cut up old Liberty Loan posters to use for copy paper. When he died in 1937, he left an estate of nearly $300,000. But he loved to travel, and in August, 1911, while in Canada he impulsively took off round-the-world. The world's east-to-west record of 54 days was held by Cecil Gray of England. With a suitcase containing two changes of clothes and a volume of Kipling, Bidwell sped through Japan, Manchuria, Russia, Poland, Holland, England, and a good many other countries by boat and train, to set a record of 46 days, 23 hours, and 45 minutes. The whole trip cost him only $686, which may also have been a record. It pleased Bidwell that he had also beaten the west-to-east time of 72 days set by the New York *World's* illustrious Miss Bly in 1889.

Walter Brown became The Courant's first full-time music and drama critic in 1929, writing his column, "The Observation Post," almost until his death in 1932. He became a well known and respected figure in Hartford's growing musical life, familiar to audiences in the old Parson's Theater, the Union Hall, and Footguard Hall as he occupied his usual aisle seat, handsome, dignified, and silver haired. In his absence, Ralph R. Wolfe, a reporter who owned his own full dress, looked like a social lion and wrote gracefully, filled in.

A story that rocked Connecticut in 1916 was developed by Aubrey Maddock and others. It involved a series of mysterious deaths in an old people's home in Windsor. Maddock got a record of all death certificates of the home's inmates. These led to an inspection of the poison registers of Hartford and Windsor druggists, revealing a most striking coincidence in the sale of arsenic "for rats and mice" and the recorded deaths at the Archer Home.

Charles Hopkins Clark showed the evidence to Governor Marcus

H. Holcomb, who called in state police. Nearly a year later the murder story broke, on the morning of May 9, 1916. The headlines that
morning read:

POLICE BELIEVE ARCHER HOME FOR AGED A MURDER FACTORY
MRS. ARCHER - GILLIGAN ACCUSED OF MURDER OF INMATE
AUTOPSY SHOWS TWO WHO DIED WERE KILLED BY POISON

A dozen collateral stories filled in the background.

Clifton Sherman enjoyed finding young talent and then giving it
every chance to prove itself. He himself had made an early success
in newspaper work—Managing Editor of the nation's oldest newspaper at 27. One young fellow in the city room got his big opportunity when Connecticut troops were ordered to the Mexican border
in June, 1916. With the First Connecticut Infantry went Tyler Howe
"Tip" Bliss, a peach-cheeked Harvard graduate of 1911.

Connecticut troops wound up in Nogales, Arizona. The human interest stories Bliss sent home were masterpieces of their kind—vivid
vignettes of Connecticut Yankees in Pancho Villa's courtyard. Bliss
became an editor as well by arranging with the Nogales *Herald* to
print news from Connecticut. A slug showing The Courant nameplate
was sent to Nogales, and a brief summary of Hartford news was
telegraphed to Bliss. Next day Hartford news appeared in the *Herald* under the familiar "The Hartford Courant" title, below which
were the words, "Nogales Edition."

After Bliss got back from Arizona, he went out one night on a
routine assignment to cover speeches. At the first hall the speaker's
opening words were "Are there any Catholics in the room?"

No one responded.

"Are there any reporters?"

One of the ushers pointed to Bliss. Bliss left, phoned The Courant,
and immediately four other reporters went to the hall. One managed
to get in and reported a speech full of religious bigotry—a speech
that ended with the audience kneeling in rows radiating from the
platform, the right hand of each person on the right shoulder of the
man ahead, and all those in the front holding their hands on the
Bible. In this position all took the oath of the notorious anti-Catholic
"No Name Society."

The Courant's story shocked readers. But, before long, reporters
learned that another secret meeting was planned at Putnam Pha-

lanx Hall. Unable to wheedle or bribe the janitor, Aubrey Maddock slipped a microphone through an open transom, led the wires through the branches of a tree, and thence to the window of a nearby office he had rented. Soon, members of the No Name Society began to assemble in the hall. Next morning The Courant exposed full details of the meeting, the last to be held in the city.

A few months after World War I, Clifton Sherman resigned from the managing editorship of The Courant, having served the paper for a quarter of a century. His resignation caused people to wonder. The official view, as reported in his obituary in The Courant, was that "he resigned with the intention of retiring to his home in East Dover, Vermont." It has also been said that he resigned after trying, without success, to buy a share in The Courant.

Increasingly, over the years, Sherman found himself at odds with The Courant's entrenched Republicanism. By the end of the First World War he had come to the belief that there was something in the idealism preached by Woodrow Wilson, and that there was something decidedly lacking in the kind of Old Guardism represented in state politics by J. Henry Roraback, the Republican leader, and on the newspaper by the septuagenarian Charles Hopkins Clark.

Sherman came to his decision calmly and without rancor. He and the staff of The Courant parted friends and remained friends, even after Sherman accepted the managing editorship of the Hartford Times in 1919, within months of his resignation from The Courant. He lured some of his old Courant colleagues to his staff, including Max Farber, who later became Managing Editor of the Times. When Sherman retired in 1929, having risen to the editorship of the Times, The Courant gave him a banner head and spread the story of his career across eight columns. In 1939 Sherman wrote a long and affectionate memoir of his days on The Courant. Another Sherman—not related—Maurice S., then editor in chief of The Courant, wrote the preface: "Though his own modesty naturally prevents his saying so here, so capably did he discharge the duties of [his] office that at least one of his colleagues acclaimed him 'the best newspaper executive in the East.' "

When Clifton Sherman had returned to The Courant from New York in 1904, the paper's daily circulation had amounted to about 11,000, and there had been no Sunday Courant. When he resigned, daily circulation had reached 24,500 and Sunday circulation 28,800. Advertising in the year Sherman left totaled over 11 million lines for the daily and Sunday papers. The Courant was financially sound, and its circulation had more than doubled while the population of the State had increased by not quite one half.

Sherman's mantle as Managing Editor fell on a 25-year-old bundle of energy named Emile Gauvreau, a lame reporter with a large head, piercing eyes, and a nose that could scent news almost before it happened. His stories for the New Haven *Journal-Courier* had attracted Sherman's attention. In his autobiography, modestly entitled *My First Million Readers,* Gauvreau says Sherman went to New Haven and told him, "Boy, if you ever leave here, come up and see me. You can work for me anytime." Gauvreau did go to see Sherman and was put on The Courant payroll in August, 1916. The new man on the staff, according to his own account, was permitted to hunt out his own news stories.

A month after joining The Courant, Gauvreau, visiting friends in New Haven, met an old woman who lived in the cottage next door. The woman spoke casually of her many friends in Chicago and Washington society. Posing as a college student, Gauvreau discovered a sensational story. The woman turned out to be Mrs. Cecelia Hermione Wallace, a one-time Chicago philanthropist missing for eight years and rumored to be wandering about in tatters with a bagful of unset jewels. Clifton Sherman checked with a Chicago newspaper to confirm the facts, then sent a photographer, Harold Newsome, to the home of Gauvreau's friends. Posing as an itinerant cameraman, Newsome arranged the friends on the front lawn for a picture. The lady next door was coaxed into the scene. Newsome's picture of the missing diamond queen was blown up and run beside Gauvreau's story.

Gauvreau attracted off-beat news as a magnet draws iron filings. It was this gift that brought him to the managing editorship of The Courant—but sparks were to fly when young Gauvreau's drive for the bizarre clashed head-on with the traditions of America's oldest newspaper.

1920-1928

The Old Lady and the Flapper

PEOPLE HAD BEGUN to call her the Old Lady of State Street. For 40 years The Courant's front windows had opened on State House Square, and for more than a century before—long before Bulfinch had designed the State House—other Courant office windows had looked out on the Hartford scene. But the world was changing fast, and people wondered if the Old Lady could change with it. Critics, some of them on the paper's staff, believed the Courant catered too much to Old Guard Hartford, ignoring thousands of persons of foreign extraction and other relative newcomers. The new managing editor, Gauvreau, charged that the paper kow-towed to old-line aristocrats and persons of wealth. It was not a new criticism. As long ago as 1911 a prominent Connecticut newspaper had told its readers that "The Hartford Courant would favor a bill that required us to pay 5c for the right to breathe if certain corporations favored it." And in 1926, *Outlook* magazine, in a testy article, taxed Editor Clark with "intellectual indigestion in his occasional periods of non-somnolency."

A good many institutions, as well as individuals, found it hard to adjust to the Roaring Twenties. It was particularly hard for a conservative newspaper. And to make The Courant's adjustment more painful, the paper found itself with a young Turk of a managing editor whose policies were at variance with traditions built up over more than a century and a half.

Emile Gauvreau was 25 when he became managing editor. Clifton Sherman, who had been made managing editor at 27, believed in giving large responsibility to young persons. Gauvreau worked hard, often spending 13 to 14 hours a day, and turned up a number of good stories, served as legislative reporter, Sunday editor, and assistant managing editor—all within three short years. He was deferred from active service in the First World War because of a deformity that caused him to limp despite a shoe built up about three inches.

Easily the most experienced of the younger men, he was a logical choice.

In retrospect, however, there is something ludicrous in young Emile Gauvreau's trying to lead the Old Lady through the Age of the Flapper. He was, everyone agreed, a young man of tireless energy and resourcefulness. He was also immature enough to take each of his current opinions for eternal truth and to regard all who disagreed as fogies. This attitude did not endear him to his colleagues, though he could fire up a newsroom with his enthusiasm. He followed a story like a bloodhound and often turned up yarns where no one else had thought to look. An inveterate crusader, he wanted to make news happen. He expressed contempt for "printing the news after it had happened." For Gauvreau, the off-beat was prime news. As far as he was concerned, the great bulk of routine news—town and suburban, society and club, general wire news, obituaries, and, in fact, almost all news except the sensational—was dull as dishwater.

As managing editor he had trouble from the word "Go," and the trouble continued until he left the paper—also at the word "Go." Beginning with the view that Hartford and The Courant were stuffy and smug, that there was too much Republicanism abroad in the world, and that Publisher Clark's Republicanism was dictated by political boss J. Henry Roraback, he set out to reform the community, the paper, the Editor in Chief, and the Republican Party all at once. It was a tall order.

For most readers, the Gauvreau touch became evident first on the front page. As many as 18 or 20 stories, each under a 2-column headline, were scattered over the page. Many were of as little significance as the 2-inch squib that appeared under the large two-column headline: "HUSBAND ACKNOWLEDGES CHILD BORN TO WOMAN WHO IS NAMED IN SUIT." Occasionally the front page would be devoted to a single news event, as when the Dempsey-Carpentier boxing match occupied all the page except two-thirds of a column.

The Courant, long opposed to yellow journalism, began to look slightly jaundiced itself. As later events proved, Gauvreau had no rival when it came to editing a sensational paper. Going on from The Courant to edit the New York *Evening Graphic,* he boosted the circulation of that journal to half a million with a news policy that earned it the nickname Porno-Graphic. At one time, by Gauvreau's own computation, the *Graphic* was simultaneously fighting libel suits totaling $12 million.

The Courant never came anywhere near the abyss into which Gauvreau plunged the *Graphic,* but for months on end Hartford readers were served the kind of fare one might expect under such headlines as:

ARREST MAN WHO HELD WIFE ON TRACKS UNTIL STRUCK BY TROLLEY CAR

MISSING NIGHTDRESS TAYLOR MURDER CLUE; DRUG PEDDLER SOUGHT

In time, Gauvreau developed a strong partiality for the banner headline; staff reporters began to feel uneasy unless they were working on stories worth a page-wide head. The merest whiff of mystery would galvanize the managing editor. Disguises and impersonations, he thought, were standard reportorial procedure. He himself had posed as a college student when he had turned up the "Diamond Queen" story of Mrs. Cecelia Hermione Wallace. On another occasion he secretly sent a staff reporter, John R. Reitemeyer—later President and Publisher of the Courant—to get an inside story on a soldiers' home in the southern part of the state. For a month, Reitemeyer posed as an orderly. On another occasion when several persons in Hartford died from drinking wood alcohol after prohibition went into effect, Gauvreau sent out his entire news staff after the paper went to press, with directions to pick up every existing photograph of the victims. Gauvreau went too. Courant staff members collected an extraordinary array of photographs, effectively preventing all other newspapers from running pictures of the victims.

The Courant during the 1920's had a strong "period" flavor. It was during the twenties that the paper began, each Monday morning, to head one of its advertising pages with the banner line, "Firms Listed in This Section are Conducted on the 'American' or 'Open Shop' Plan." There followed a long list of firms in Hartford and elsewhere, the ads gathered by a free-lance advertising promoter. The Courant ran this type of advertising for about 10 years.

In April, 1922, 40 compositors—three-quarters of the composing room staff—quit, alleging, according to a page one story, that they "were unable to work any longer with men alongside of whom they had been working for years unless these fellow workmen voluntarily, or under compulsion by their employers, joined the typographical union." Soon the paper reported: "The men have quit and their places are being filled." Clark commented editorially:

> We shall maintain an open shop, where every man will have a fair and equal show, and where the managers will be those in charge of the work and no orders will be received from any organization or any inter-mediary. We have conducted our own business for 150 years and it has become a habit. Nobody else need apply.

The Courant started a temporary school for compositors, and by November about 20 graduates had qualified for permanent positions.

Gauvreau had not been managing editor long before he introduced new departments. Many of these proved sound and were encouraged by The Courant's Treasurer, H. H. Conland, who was eager to modernize the paper. In October, 1920, Gauvreau announced that, with the issue of Sunday, December 5, The Courant would carry an Art-gravure section of eight pages. He called it "a pioneer of its kind in this State, carrying news pictures of particular interest to Connecticut readers."

The section, when it appeared, lived up to its billing. Unlike some other journals, The Courant used illustrations that were locally interesting, not the usual syndicated material. The first Artgravure section carried pictures of Governor-elect E. J. Lake on the Hartford golf links, and of his family. There were also society pictures, as well as advertisements. The section caught on with the reading public and was continued until early in 1942 and wartime newsprint rationing.

Less than a year after the start of Artgravure, The Courant began publishing a Sunday magazine. Ever since the first Sunday Courant in 1913, the paper had carried a Sunday feature section, its pages the same size as those of the rest of the paper. The new Magazine appeared first on November 6, 1921, in tabloid size, 20 pages.

It wasn't sensational. No less distinguished a personage than Charles Evans Hughes was the subject of the lead story. There followed a book page, a cartoon page, a short story by James B. Hendryx, and other usual magazine material. But the magazine proved short-lived. By September 23, 1923, the full-size Sunday feature section was restored, although the section still carried the title of "Sunday Magazine" for a few weeks.

Another Courant departure was the paper's radio station, authorized in May, 1922, by Secretary of Commerce Herbert Hoover with the call letters WDAK. The Courant soon happily announced that its broadcasts could be heard clearly in Bristol and Plainville, and even in Greenfield, Massachusetts.

WDAK was the first newspaper-owned radio station in New England and the only licensed station in Connecticut. Pittsburgh's KDKA had gone on the air in 1920, the same year the Detroit *News* started the first newspaper-owned station. When The Courant's WDAK started, it was one of only 30 licensed stations in the country. Radio grew rapidly. By 1924 there were 500 licensed stations. And the public, on the receiving end, bought sets by the millions. In 1920 there had been, at an estimate, no more than a few hundred thousand receivers in the country. Ten years later there were 14 million; by 1940, 44 million.

The Courant's radio station gave Calvin Coolidge his first experience in a broadcasting booth. Coolidge came to Hartford on October 24, 1922, to give a speech. Clark and Conland persuaded him to come to the Courant building to say a few words over the airwaves from the paper's broadcasting room. The Vice President was skeptical about the contraption he found in the studio, but Clark, Gauvreau, and the station's operator, D. H. Morrill, showed him how it worked.

The "microphone" consisted of an upright desk telephone with a megaphone attached to its mouthpiece. To use the instrument, one put his face, up to the ears, into the big end of the megaphone and said his say. Coolidge decided to risk it and launched into his talk. Before he was done, a photographer entered, poured flash powder onto a pan, and took a picture amid blinding light and billowing fumes. This was too much for the Vice President who cut his speech short and staggered out of the room, gasping, "I hope they never put those damned things in the Senate!" As a crowning blow, it turned out that the station had been off the air during the entire speech.

As early as January, 1922, the paper began to carry regular wireless news on Sunday, in a section bearing the incongruous legend:

> # WIRELESS
> # NEWS
> # SOCIETY

This section also carried advertisements like the following:

The Following Cities have powerful wireless broadcasting stations which are heard nightly by hundreds of enthusiastic amateurs in Hartford and vicinity:—
Chicago, Ill.
Pittsburgh, Pa.
Newark, N. J.
New Haven, Conn.
Hartford, Conn.
Farmington, Conn.
Springfield, Mass.
Boston, Mass.

Equip Your Home With a

WIRELESS TELEPHONE

**Captures actual news, music and voices out of the air. Prac-
tically indestructible. Anyone can set it up.
Full information at our store**

The Courant also started paying more attention to photography. In
the 1920's, as now, much of the newspaper's photographic work was
done for advertisers. The Courant maintained a dingy studio on
Market Street, presided over by Bruce Lindsay, who had to take his
films to a dark hole under the stairs at the newspaper office to develop them. Not until 1936, with the hiring of the present head of
the photographic department, Philip J. Acquaviva, did The Courant
have a regular photographer for night assignments. In 1937, for the
first time, the photographic department was brought together in The
Courant building, where it was given half the third floor.

After Warren G. Harding took office in 1921, Charles Hopkins
Clark, then 73 years old, began to turn over more and more of his
responsibilities to others, particularly to Treasurer Henry H. Con-

land, whom he had long been referring to as "my partner." The Editor allowed himself to spend shorter hours at the office. He even cut down on his output of editorials, though his political interests remained keen as ever. From Clark's view, America in the 1920's had its seamy side—as indicated by the entrance of women into the hurly-burly of politics, and the appearance of cheap colored comic sections in newspapers—but to compensate for these the state and nation were solidly Republican, and seemed likely to adhere to sound Republican principles for quite a while. In politics, if nowhere else, reason had prevailed.

In 1923 The Courant improved facilities by increasing its capital to $450,000 through an issue of $100,000 of common stock. The composing room, press room, and mailing room were expanded. A new press and more type-setting machines were bought.

Promotion was the order of the day. The Courant flashed the results of the 1922 state elections from the tower of the Travelers Life Insurance Company, using a 2,500,000-candlepower searchlight to wag the message in a code explained in the newspaper. A section for boys and girls was started in the Sunday Magazine. Another stunt was to greet the New Year 1923 with an airplane flying overhead at midnight, the body and wings illuminated by strings of electric lights. A project that must had vast appeal for Gauvreau was a Missing Persons Bureau, established, he explained, because so many persons were disappearing and remaining "lost to sight."

Gauvreau and his superiors worked together closely, and for the most part amicably. But the managing editor's treatment of news kept raising the hackles of his colleagues. His handling of a major news story in 1923 finally prompted Clark to ask for his resignation.

The story developed when a special writer for the St. Louis *Star* arrived in Hartford that October, hot on the trail of a "diploma mill" suspected of selling false certificates to quack doctors. The writer, Harry T. Brundidge, had approached two papers in the state with his story. Both had turned him down. But Gauvreau sensed a sensational story and published Brundidge's account the next morning. A day later a 4-column head on page one announced:

GOVERNOR HAS EVIDENCE IN DIPLOMA MILL PROBE INVOLVING 142 DOCTORS

Soon State's Attorney Hugh M. Alcorn began an investigation and a special grand jury was called.

An 8-column head in The Courant for November 3 shouted:

CONN. MEDICAL LICENSE SOLD FOR $100
ALCORN PROBING EAST WINDSOR DOCTOR
REVELATIONS RIPENING FOR GRAND JURY

Gauvreau played the story to the hilt. If quacks were at large in the state, it behooved the paper to name names. On November 7, The Courant reported one Sutcliffe under suspicion:

Three Cans of Ether
Snuffed Out Life As
Sutcliffe Hacked Away

Banner followed banner; picture followed picture. The issue for November 13 showed a facsimile of the "type of fake high school diploma bought by quack doctors as first step to getting Connecticut licenses." On the 27th, under a 4-column head appeared a photograph of the chair in which A. C. Hoody had been strapped while Sutcliffe had given him three cans of ether. Hoody was taken to the morgue; the three cans appeared in the photograph.

Clark clamped down, pointing out that an investigation was under way. There was no need for "trial by newspaper."

Gauvreau promptly took the position that Clark, under pressure from Republican Boss J. Henry Roraback, was attempting to stifle the people's right to know. Bitterly the young managing editor reduced the headlines to a modest single-column each morning, and played down the sensational aspects of the story. In January, 1924, Gauvreau turned over a file of The Courant's stories on the "diploma mill" to the Grand Jury and received a routine letter of thanks. This he ran in facsimile on January 12, obviously with the idea that the letter could be taken as an endorsement of his handling of the story over the past months. And he gave it the lead position on page 1 the next morning: "MISSOURI DIPLOMA MILL TO BE SEEN BY GRAND JURYMEN." Not especially sensational treatment—but it was the inevitable last straw for Clark, who asked for and received Gauvreau's resignation.

During Gauvreau's brief regime, The Courant's daily circulation rose from 25 to 36 thousand, while Sunday circulation went up from 34 to 50 thousand, following the general rising trend of newspaper circulations in the nation. Advertising linage during the same period dropped abruptly, from 11.9 million to 10.4 million lines, then rose to 11.4 million, again following the U. S. pattern.

Looking back at his experience on The Courant, Gauvreau saw himself as a progressive editor victimized by entrenched old-guardism. He felt regret and bitterness at his failure to make a flapper of the staid Old Lady of State Street. He believed he could have built The Courant's circulation to towering heights. His later experience on Bernarr Macfadden's *Graphic* proved to him that he could build up a paper to a large circulation starting from scratch, using a formula of crime, sex, and photographs. It does not seem to have struck him as significant that the *Graphic* collapsed in 1932, only eight years after its founding.

The Gauvreau interlude shows the power of tradition on The Courant. Its long-standing opposition to sensational treatment of news proved too much for Gauvreau. He gave the paper a shaking up, which may have been good for it. But in the end, the Old Lady proved stronger and wiser than the young Turk. Gauvreau drew his last paycheck from The Courant on April 5, 1924. George B. Armstead was appointed Managing Editor, and next year, 1925, John R. Reitemeyer became City Editor. Both men had joined the Courant in 1920.

On January 21, 1926, Charles Hopkins Clark arrived at the office for the last time. Determined not to give up, he came to his desk that morning supported by a nurse and a male attendant. He sat there before his typewriter, but seeing it was no use, he allowed himself to be guided back to his car, and so passed out of the life of the paper he had served for 55 years. The distinguished President and Publisher of The Courant died at the age of 78 on September 5, 1926.

Treasurer Henry H. Conland succeeded Clark as President and Publisher of the Company, and Maurice S. Sherman (no relation to Clifton L. Sherman, former Managing Editor) was appointed Editor. Maurice Sherman came from the Editorship of The Springfield (Massachusetts) *Union*. Just as Clark, fresh out of Yale, had gone directly into newspaper work, so Sherman, fresh out of Dartmouth in 1894, had gone to work on the *Union*.

The new Editor wholeheartedly subscribed to putting the accent in *newspaper* firmly and clearly on the first syllable. In this he was

following the tradition set by his predecessors on The Courant, including Clark. But in some respects Sherman conceived the paper's
function far differently. Clark had been a man of decided tastes, a
strong party man who believed that the most good could be accomplished by working loyally for the organization. Sherman held that
a man is likely to come nearer to the truth if he listens with an open
mind to what is said by all factions.This is not to say that he was
without personal conviction, but simply that he held his opinions
humbly and with a due recognition of human fallibility, including
his own. He had not been in his chair at The Courant a month before the following editorial invitation appeared:

> The Courant will be glad to receive letters from its readers on any
> subject of public interest. It desires that its readers shall feel free to
> comment on men and measures, provided only that they do so without
> malice and in good temper . . .
> If the editor has a right to be heard, so have the readers, who ought
> not to be put in a defenseless position . . .

This view of the rights of newspaper readers shows how much the
intellectual temper of the editorial page had changed over the years.
Back in 1879 Charles Dudley Warner had denied any such right:

> Some time ago a 'greenbacker' was very much aggrieved because we
> would not admit a reply to a hard money editorial. He thought he had
> a 'right' as a subscriber to have his side heard. He had no such right.
> We utterly repudiate anybody's right to have his 'side' heard. If a man
> has been personally wronged by anything in the newspaper he has a
> moral claim to be set right or to try to set himself right. But if we wrote
> an editorial expressing the healthfulness of taking a walk on Sunday, we
> are not bound to admit a reply arguing its wickedness. If we denounce
> the opening of a dram shop on Sunday or the immorality of a variety
> show, we are not bound to admit a defense of either.

After Sherman's open invitation, the letters poured in and many
were printed in "The People's Forum," which appeared for the first
time on October 6, 1926. Previously, letters had appeared only from
time to time scattered through the news columns.

Because Clark had been known as a zealous party man, the opinion prevailed in some quarters that The Courant, at least on its editorial page, was little more than a Republican party organ. Sherman
determined that the editorial pages under his supervision should not
be, or even seem to be, stubbornly partisan. Three months after joining The Courant he wrote:

> To gather all the news worth gathering within its field and to present
> it without bias is The Courant's purpose . . .

In our editorial interpretation of the news and in our support of such measures and policies as in our judgment are predicated on sound principles it is only natural that some readers should find cause for disagreement. There can be no such thing as unanimity of opinion in matters pertaining to the political and social order, and it is not desirable that there should be unanimity . . .

This was a new tone for the editorial pages. It indicated a flexibility of mind that was to stand the paper in good stead as the '20's roared toward the abyss of October, 1929, and the vast economic and social changes that were to follow.

Two social developments of the 1920's, both the subjects of amendments to the U.S. Constitution, generated many news stories —oddly frivolous and serious at the same time. One was the amazing saga of prohibition after January 29, 1919, when the 18th Amendment went into effect. The other was the greatly accelerated infiltration of women into almost every aspect of American life after the 19th Amendment on August 26, 1920. The Courant, along with other newspapers, duly reported the gay doings of socialites made happy on contraband liquor and the cops-and-robbers pursuit of rum runners. It also reported the striking new developments in the world of women, applauded by some and denounced by others, as skirts rose to the knee, bare midriffs widened, and leading ladies in moving picture advertisements appeared in little more than "scanties"; as housewives began to smoke and make up in public and drink openly at cocktail parties.

The prohibition amendment soon came under attack as unconstitutional. While the Supreme Court upheld it, the public had its own ideas. The Courant sharply criticized the amendment and the desiccating idea behind it. Clark believed the amendment ill-framed and perhaps a threat to the essential concept of individual liberty in the Constitution.

By mid-decade the public could read almost daily about the dry-raids of the government agents. The Courant announced in March, 1924, that a "Dry Navy" was to operate out of New London. Soon the engagements between wets and drys in Long Island Sound began to read like Naval dispatches in wartime:

COAST GUARD CAPTURES $1,000,000 IN LIQUOR IN SIX MONTHS' DRY WAR

There was another disturbing side to the prohibition problem that the Courant did not overlook. Clark called the 18th Amendment a "monstrous invasion of state rights." On the tenth anniversary of prohibition in 1930 Maurice Sherman wrote that the law had "utterly failed" and had introduced evils that "far outweigh the particular evil it was designed to remedy."

Nor was the Old Lady of State Street silent about modern girls. The paper had opposed woman suffrage to the end, arguing editorially that it would make women less womanly; but on the controversial question of women smoking, the paper in 1921 said tobacco was no less a woman's than a man's prerogative. This was an advanced view. In the same year a New London judge had summarily told a mother to give up cigarettes or surrender the custody of her daughter.

As the decade went on, The Courant oriented itself more and more to its women readers, though not without backslidings. In May, 1922, appeared the paper's first section devoted to June brides. But in 1927 Editor Maurice Sherman was opposing jury duty for women as enthusiastically as Editor Clark had ever opposed woman's right to vote:

> We cannot believe that a great majority of Connecticut women wish to leave their household, business, and social duties in order to vindicate their 'right' and establish their absolute equality with men by sitting up all night and debating on the guilt or innocence of the prisoner at the bar of justice . . .

On March 3, 1929, a full page in the Artgravure section was devoted to a picture of a woman reading The Courant, with the heading "She Starts Every Day Right," and adding that The Courant was "replete with news and features of special interest to women." It was a justifiable claim. A typical Courant issue carried several columns of "Feminine Topics," large department store advertisements, columns of society news, grocery advertising, and a women's page featuring Dorothy Dix, Dr. Brady, and beauty and fashion notes. An editorial, "The Offending Knee," in 1929, chided the mayor of Lynn, Massachusetts, for ordering the arrest of all girls over 12 whose legs were exposed above the knee. The Courant, by tradition, opposed "that silly and super-puritanical zeal that delights in meddling with ordinary liberties."

But soon stories on ladies' limbs or on the battles of the wets and drys had to share available news space with a story that was to go on producing major news until the start of World War II. On October 29, 1929, American stockholders dumped 16,400,000 shares on the market for any price they could get. The Great Depression settled in for a long stay. Before many months, The Courant, like other newspapers, began to reflect the depression in every department. Cheerless financial news haunted the front page; advertising income dropped off; editorials alternately faced the black reality and whistled in the dark. The Courant began to publish articles on "How to Feed Four on $9 a Week."

1929-1947
Depression and World War II

PUBLISHER Henry H. Conland's round, unlined face and big, round silver-rimmed glasses suggested little of the shrewd business sense in his head. Much sought after for his practical counsel, the publisher served on the boards of no fewer than ten insurance companies and manufacturing concerns. And increasingly, as he grew older, he was called upon to help direct important civic affairs. He served as Chairman of the Hartford Bridge Commission, Flood Control Commissioner, member of the Hartford Police Board, and member of the Special Water Advisory Committee. The Henry Conland Highway out of Hartford, named in 1945, remains a tribute to his public service as Bridge Commission Chairman. He served, too, on the board of the American Newspaper Publishers Association.

Publisher Conland guided The Courant through the shoals of the Great Depression and most of World War II. Back in 1904, at age 22, he had been hired as a reporter for The Courant by Managing Editor Clifton Sherman, a fellow native of Brattleboro, Vermont. Conland's father was a country doctor, the personal physician of Rudyard Kipling, who lived in Brattleboro for a few years. Conland, as a youngster, listened as Kipling and his father talked and as the famous story teller spun yarns about far places. Before coming to The Courant, the future publisher had spent his entire working career of three years on the Brattleboro *Reformer,* then a weekly paper, starting at $3 a week. Before he left the *Reformer,* he had learned something about reporting and knew how to operate the cylinder press and the hand folder. After he had been on The Courant for a few months, he was transferred to the business office, where he started as a general clerk at $8 a week.

Charles Hopkins Clark, with characteristic interest in an ambitious young man, encouraged Conland's promotion in the business office and saw to it that in 1911 he was permitted to become a stockholder. In January, 1913, Conland became a director of the company.

That was the year The Courant entered the Sunday field, and Conland was the major mover in this venture.

By the time he became President and Publisher in September,
1926, he had developed to a high degree the particular quality of
leadership that most impressed his colleagues—his willingness to
trust their competence. As Editor-in-Chief Maurice Sherman put it,
"He delegated responsibility to department heads and left them free
to work out their own problems." This ability to delegate had much
to do with shaping the character of The Courant over two decades.
It gave Sherman the scope an editor needs; it enabled City Editor
John Reitemeyer to shape up a well-trained newsgathering team;
and it allowed such veterans as Telegraph Editor Elijah T. Shurter
and State Editor R. Philip Rose to make the most of their obvious
skills.

The wide latitude the Publisher gave his department heads allowed Maurice Sherman to think out, in his own terms, the tremendous issues posed by America's plunge from prosperity to depression and by the onset of World War II. Sherman's editorials about
the depression show how a thinking man repeatedly adjusted his
ideas during the course of one of the great financial, social, and
moral crises of the nation.

When Sherman first used the word *depression* in his editorials,
he put it in quotation marks, as one would any outlandish term. By
1932 the quotation marks had long since disappeared. Presidential
candidate Franklin D. Roosevelt seemed to Sherman "a weak man
. . . vacillating, indecisive, and unreliable." Nevertheless, when
Roosevelt won, Sherman found that he had "surrounded himself
with men who promise well." During FDR's first days in the White
House the Editor called him "bold," "eminently sensible," declared
that he "understands the responsibilities of leadership," and—of all
things—remarked that his economies in government "have surpassed
all expectation."

Just the same, it was over the issue of economy that The Courant
began to drift away from Roosevelt. Sherman, reminding readers of
the Democratic platform pledge to preserve a sound currency at all
hazards, observed, "In all respects except his monetary plank Mr.
Roosevelt appears to have given force and effectiveness to the platform pronouncement." The Courant's slow drift from editorial
support of Roosevelt's program contrasts strongly with its highly
partisan editorial attacks on earlier presidents and their parties.

Part Three	**The Hartford Courant**	Feature Section

HARTFORD, CONNECTICUT, SUNDAY, OCTOBER 5, 1913.

Thomas Hooker: "*At Last, a Sunday 'Courant.' I Must Purchase and Peruse It.*"

HOW THE COURANT INTRODUCED SUNDAY PAPER TO
CONNECTICUT

HENRY H. CONLAND
"A good leader trusts colleagues"

MAURICE S. SHERMAN
"Readers have a right to be heard"

JOHN R. REITEMEYER
"A journal's prime asset: integrity"

Sherman counted Presidents Coolidge and Hoover among his personal friends. Coolidge liked to remind the editor, on his trips to the White House, that in the dark days of the Boston police strike Sherman, then on the Springfield *Union,* had strongly supported his handling of the "strike against the public safety." It was Coolidge's handling of this crisis that brought him national attention, possibly the Vice Presidential nomination. Hoover sent Sherman drafts of his proposed speeches, and Courant hands remember Sherman's calm editing of the manuscripts before returning them to the President. Sherman and Hoover enjoyed fishing trips together in the West, and in New York the two often visited at Hoover's quarters in the Waldorf Towers. Once, when Hoover visited Sherman in West Hartford during a speech-making trip, the local police went into a flurry trying to guard the house. As a crowning touch, the department installed a policeman in a dinner jacket to play the part of a butler in the Sherman home, to the great disgust of the editor.

The depression hit The Courant hard in every department—particularly in circulation and advertising. Daily circulation, well above 41,000 in 1930, dropped to 36,000 in four years. Sunday circulation fell about the same amount. Advertising dropped from a peak of 12.7 million lines in 1929 to a low of 7.0 million in 1933. Income from advertising fell even more sharply, taking a 50 per cent plunge to a low of $590,000 in 1933. The depression particularly hit income from financial advertising—that is, from brokerage houses, from notices of new issues of stocks, and the like— and from automobile advertising. Not for 17 years did the advertising income of The Courant return to 1929 levels.

Out in the city room it was John R. Reitemeyer, with a military bearing he had not lost since the First World War, who dominated the goings on. Exacting in his demands for thorough, accurate reporting and concisely tailored copy, he raged magnificently when he didn't get it. He loved a good joke, and his laugh pervaded the room—as did his occasional lacing-out of a hapless reporter.

There was always a contingent of bright young men fresh out of college who came to The Courant for solid basic training in journalism—and got it in full measure. They soaked up the discipline and the glamor in the old high-ceilinged city room. It was sound grass-roots training: years later William J. Clew was to move up to assistant managing editor and Charles A. Towne to city editor. Some of the others went on to larger metropolitan journals or to government posts.

The city room retained much of the flavor of the 1880's. Brown-varnished oak woodwork and drab painted walls were all the decor it needed to furnish a background appropriate to the age and prestige of The Courant. Scarred, varnished desks with their hefty typewriters stood empty until 1:30 p.m., when the city staff began to gather. On a warm afternoon, street noises from State House Square drifted in through open windows: the clang of streetcar bells, the squeal of their wheels on the curving tracks, traffic police whistles. And often, as presses turned out special sections of The Courant—or of the *Catholic Transcript,* which The Courant printed for years—the early afternoon quiet was disturbed by the rumble of heavy machinery in the remote intestines of the building.

At the front of the city room a door opened into the partitioned office of Managing Editor George B. Armstead, near the copy desk horseshoe where Edwin M. Allender, copy chief, sat in the "slot" as copy began to come through. Armstead was succeeded as Managing Editor by George E. Stansfield, who wrote poems that he ran on page one. Midway down the room sat City Editor Reitemeyer, and at right angles to him was the city desk manned by assistants Maurice R. Cronan and John F. Kelly. Against the opposite wall stood a bank of bound Courant volumes next to a row of telephone booths.

The constant clicking of the AP, UP, and INS wire machines played a staccato counterpoint to the clatter of typewriters, quickening the sense of urgency and excitement. Copy in a basket from the telegraph room whizzed with a metallic hiss along a high wire to the desk of Telegraph Editor Elijah Shurter. Another basket, worked by hand-pulley like a dumb waiter, lofted copy to the composing room above. Over all hung a blue haze of tobacco smoke. It was a masculine environment, although Mary Goodrich, The Courant's first woman reporter and Connecticut's first aviatrix, joined the city staff in the late '20's. Isabel Foster already was in the Sunday department, followed by Julia Older. Even in the '30's there were only two regular girl reporters, Melva Swartz and Betty Bradshaw. Not until the '40's might women smoke in this male precinct.

A fire bell on the wall, connected by wire to the main fire house, clanged furiously at irregular intervals as it does today. Reporters, familiar with the signals, stopped typing to count the gongs and locate the fire. The bell was the particular pride of Horace B. Clark, son of Charles Hopkins Clark and Secretary of The Hartford Courant Company. He had an alarm bell in his own home and often rode the hook and ladder in helmet and slicker. President of the Hartford

Board of Fire Commissioners, he made it his business to standard-
ize fire-fighting apparatus so that the fire fighters could come to the
help of neighboring towns when needed.

It was The Courant's policy, then as now, to cover Connecticut,
and the steady effort of State Editor Philip Rose over more than
three decades was largely responsible for the continuing success.
Correspondents in outlying cities and towns covered local news, as
exciting and important, locally, as any in the capital city. While the
immediate suburbs—West Hartford, East Hartford, Wethersfield—
were covered by the city staff, the surrounding towns had reporters,
some of them full-time, who placed their copy late at night on trolley or bus, to be picked up by runners at City Hall a few steps from
The Courant's front door. More remote rural correspondents phoned
in their copy, transcribed on typewriters as it was received by ear-
phoned state reporters.

Robert D. Byrnes, political editor, occupied a corner desk tucked
away near the switchboard, when he was not out after news on
Hartford's Capitol Hill. After Byrnes left to cover Washington news
for the newspaper, his successor on the State Capitol beat was a
lad who had been office boy—Jack Zaiman. Affectionately dubbed
"Grant" because of his admiration for sportswriter Grantland Rice,
Zaiman, still in knee pants, had landed a job from Reitemeyer.

Bert Keane presided over the sports desk. His dignity in a job
that brought him into contact with the hurly-burly of sports was a
reflection of The Courant's policy of picking for key posts men
whose bearing and character reflected well on the newspaper. With
him worked Bill Lee, who had joined the staff in 1925, and who became sports editor upon Keane's death in 1939. Lee's sports column,
"With Malice Toward None," is widely read throughout the state.

Across the hall Dorothy Sawyer and, later, Marjorie Heacox and
Helen Stafford, edited a society page that noted activities of Old
Hartford families. In the late '20's, The Courant published special
rotogravure sections running to nearly 30 pages of advertising in
which Junior Leaguers served as models. Advertising in the "Junior
League Gravure" sections helped pay for charities in which the society women were interested. Social coverage was increased as
women's activities expanded. The doings of ethnic groups such as
the Italian-American Junior League and the Polish Junior League
also appeared in the society pages, particularly on Sunday. Women's
clubs, too, proliferated and a special department for their coverage

was created. All this coverage suggests a view of women's interests far removed from the view expressed in a headline back in 1907:

IN HARTFORD SOCIETY.

CHRISTMAS WEEK SOCIALLY
AS DULL AS USUAL.

During the mid '30's the depression provided the big, running story. But there was other major news of special interest in Connecticut: the State's tercentenary celebration, its worst flood, and a devastating hurricane. As far back as 1929 The Courant had been urging a big celebration for Connecticut's 300th anniversary. It saw its dream come true on October 12, 1935: "400,000 PACK STREETS FOR PARADE OF FLOATS AND MARCHING LEGIONS."

After the 20,000 marchers and 105 floats had swept along the streets of Hartford, unrolling the panorama of the State's historic past that golden autumn morning, The Courant remarked: "It was worth waiting 300 years to see."

Another major story was the greatest flood in Hartford's long history. On Wednesday, March 11, 1936, warm rains forced the Park River out of its banks into Bushnell Park. Two days later, ice floating down the Connecticut River jammed at Bulkeley Bridge, forming a tremendous dam. As the rains continued, the Connecticut rose to 25, then to 30 feet. Water swept over the dikes in a 20-foot-high front, to put one-fifth of the city under water. At 5:30 p.m., Friday, March 20, a power failure made it impossible to set type or run the presses at The Courant. During the afternoon, the paper had given over the use of its facilities to print the already flooded Springfield *Union*. Now it was The Courant's turn to seek help. It accepted the hospitality of the New Britain *Herald*, where it continued to publish through Tuesday.

While the mechanical departments and the copy desk emigrated to New Britain, the reporters remained in Hartford. Couriers in automobiles plied between the two cities. Since telephone service had been knocked out, the city department maintained contact with some of its correspondents by short wave radio. Planes delivered The Courant to outlying districts. The newspaper had to be flown even to Hartford's immediate neighbor: East Hartford. East Hartford's bundles of The Courant were taken to the nearest usable fly-

ing field, which happened to be in Bristol— 16 miles to the west—
and then flown over to Rentschler Field in East Hartford. Later,
bundles of the paper bound for the same destination got there by a
roundabout route via Salem—a trip of more than 60 miles to a city
visible across the raging river from Hartford.

The scars of the great flood could still be seen in Hartford when,
two and a half years later, the waters of the Connecticut again began an ominous rise. This time The Courant was ready with plans
to cover the flood. Reporters were assigned to vital spots along the
city's threatened waterfront. The state desk notified correspondents
throughout Connecticut to stand by. Then, what came—entirely un-
expectedly—was a hurricane. In the early afternoon of September
21, 1938, "the staff working in The Courant office noted the howls
of the rising gale but paid no special attention at the time," one
staff writer has recalled. "Shortly after, when windows on the west
side began to give under the drive of the storm, and water was
forced in along the sills and frames, everyone was aware of the unusual. Then came a deluge of telephone reports of destruction . . ."

It took less than 15 minutes for the large Courant switchboard to
become choked with traffic. Thousands called from every part of the
city and state to tell of wreckage, homes gone, and widespread
havoc. Correspondents and reporters outside, newsmen on the inside, were all trying to establish contacts at once. Camera men and
newsgatherers pushed out into the teeth of the hurricane. In Bushnell Park a great elm crashed to the ground, killing a pedestrian before the eyes of a Courant photographer. Reporters driving their
cars found their way blocked in every direction by wind-strewn de-
bris or water. Big news was everywhere, but it was hard to get. Members of the advertising and accounting departments, distribution employees, and many others went out to help newsgathering.

A great swath through Connecticut and neighboring states had
been devastated. And the city of New London, isolated, its com-
munications lines down and its roads blocked, was reported in
flames. Byrnes, the political writer, and Charles H. Conland, of the
advertising department, set out by car at 7 p.m., when the first word
came, to reach the stricken city. Their ride through a darkened,
flooded, debris-strewn countryside seemed utterly hopeless to persons they met, who told them all roads were blocked. Not until 1:30
a.m. did they see the glow of the New London fire in the sky. The
story they reported was the first put through to any newspaper.

For the next four days, writers and photographers from The

Courant cut, hacked, and shoved their way to all parts of the state. But gathering the news was only part of the problem. The Courant had to be distributed. Thousands of people anxiously waited for details of what they already knew to be a major disaster. Thursday morning's was a near record press run. Trucks left the newspaper's loading platform much more heavily loaded than usual. By the time they had delivered Thursday morning's paper, they had run up six times their normal mileage. Before starting the drivers were briefed from route maps hastily sketched to show the least clogged roads. Each truck carried saws, axes, and rope. The experience of the driver starting for New London was typical. Within three minutes he made his first detour. And in less than ten minutes the tree chopping business began at Jordan Lane. The Courant reached New London at 11 a.m., some 10 hours for a trip of 40 miles.

On December 7, 1941, the attention of the Nation, long focused on the war in Europe, suddenly shifted to Pearl Harbor and the Pacific. At The Courant, even before America entered the war, staff members were leaving for active duty. In August, 1941, Captain Reitemeyer, City Editor since 1925, left for a long tour of duty, from which he emerged with the rank of Colonel. By February, 1942, the Courant's service flag showed 27 stars; by December, 72. In all, 130 members of The Courant staff served in the armed forces in World War II, two losing their lives: Donald T. O'Keefe and Harold R. Freckleton. As name after name lengthened the newspaper's Roll of Honor, women were hired to replace the departing males. The city room, once a masculine sanctuary, resounded to the click of high heels. As the war continued, even the women began to enlist, and City Editor Maurice Cronan, having resigned himself to seeing his masculine staff whittled away, now found himself bidding farewell to the ladies.

The newspaper streamlined itself for the long haul. In February, 1942, the Artgravure section, after a run of 22 years, was dropped, and the Hartford Courant Magazine begun in its place. This was The Courant's second magazine, the first having stopped in 1923. The Magazine was billed as "easier to read, more pleasing to the eye, and full of worthwhile articles, plentifully illustrated." It was edited, as it still is, by H. Viggo Andersen.

Newspapers were ordered by the Federal government to limit their consumption of paper. The Courant, in December, 1942, faced a War Production Board order to limit its newsprint for at least the first three months of 1943 to the tonnage it had used in the corresponding period in 1941, before America had entered the war. This order put the newspaper in a squeeze. Hartford was rapidly growing as war industries expanded. The Courant anticipated a ten per cent rise in circulation for the first quarter of 1943 over the first quarter of 1941, in addition to the ever-increasing demand for more news. Something had to give. On December 31, the paper announced that it would cut down on the size of each issue. From 'that date forward the problem was as easy to state as it was hard to solve: how to print much more news on much less paper.

Advertisers also felt the pinch. Depending on the amount of paper Treasurer John Sudarsky was able to obtain, John L. Coughlin set a monthly quota for each Sunday advertiser. He determined each advertiser's linage the previous year, and then cut all linage by as much as 20 per cent. Daily advertising quotas, also scaled to previous years' linage, were not cut back. One happy result of this arrangement was that a good many Sunday advertisers tried advertising in the daily, liked the results, and continued.

During the war and the immediate postwar period, The Courant's daily circulation rose slowly from about 45 thousand in 1941 to about 56 thousand in 1947. Sunday circulation rose faster, from 75 thousand to 97 thousand. Advertising, totaling 8.3 million lines in 1941, increased to 12.6 million in 1947.

On April 14, 1944, Publisher Henry H. Conland died, having devoted forty years to The Courant. Sherman said of him:

> There was never any question as to who was boss of the establishment, yet he had the faculty of treating everyone as his equal. He had only one policy for The Courant to pursue as a newspaper: That it report the news with all possible accuracy, keep speculation and opinion out of the news, have no friends to reward nor enemies to punish, be restricted in its editorial comment only by a fitting sense of the proprieties, and never to be afraid to take a position and defend it to the best of its ability.
>
> He paid particular attention to the typography of the paper and to seeing that the press work was well done. This diligence was rewarded by the recognition given the Courant in the annual competition among American newspapers for the Ayer award for typographical excellence . . .

Conland had taken great pride in the Ayer awards. The Courant, under his direction, had won the Ayer Cup in 1932—first place for typographical excellence among all American newspapers. By 1939 it had won two more first places, one second, and two thirds for newspapers in its circulation class.

Maurice Sherman became President and Publisher, still retaining the editorship. One would hardly guess, watching Sherman at his desk, that this calm, pipe-smoking gentleman in vest and shirtsleeves had the granite of New Hampshire in his character. If the Republican leaders of the state ever thought they had The Courant in their pocket, Sherman, a Republican himself, made it crystal clear that the newspaper he edited would serve as the organ of no party. Soon after the inauguration of Democratic Governor Wilbur "Uncle Toby" Cross, the Republican high command tried to get the legislature to pass a bill that would take away from the Governor the power to make major appointments. Sherman called this attempt "an astonishing piece of political stupidity." The bill died, largely, it was said, through the opposition of Sherman and of other editors who joined The Courant in its denunciation. Thereafter, Governor Cross called Sherman "my dearest enemy" and the two men, always in opposing political parties, remained close friends. Once, when Cross was reported to be dangerously ill, Sherman wrote his obituary. Cross recovered, and Sherman sent him what he had written. Cross replied that he was "delighted and flattered."

Sherman, a methodical, meticulous man, and an impeccable dresser—monogrammed shirts and handkerchiefs always matched—arrived at the office promptly at 10 a.m. and seldom left before 7 p.m. He frequently turned out as many as three editorials a day, always dictating to his secretary, Margaret A. Tormey, who typed them directly as he spoke. Sherman considered the taking of shorthand notes a wasteful step. When stirred by a cause he felt deeply, Sherman, usually a peaceable, quiet-mannered man, would stalk out into the newsroom and pound his fist on a desk as he let off steam by airing his views to anyone who would listen. At such times, the editor was quite a different man from the quiet trout fisherman his friends knew, or from the patient wood worker who turned out fine furniture in his own cellar.

It is not really a paradox that the idea of peace was always able to fill him with excitement. For many years he served as trustee of the Carnegie Endowment for International Peace, and was on its executive committee at the time of his death. In the late '20's he toured Europe with about 50 American newspaper editors studying problems of post-war Europe under the auspices of the Foundation. It is testimony to the esteem in which he and The Courant were held that Sherman went as chairman of the group.

After Sherman became publisher, Herbert Brucker was engaged as Associate Editor, to help him with his editorial work. Brucker, a professor at the Columbia Graduate School of Journalism before coming to The Courant, was the author of *The Changing American Newspaper,* was writing another book, *Freedom of Information,* and had traveled abroad under a Pulitzer scholarship.

Sherman, who lived only long enough to witness the end of the war and to feel some of the difficult problems of the post-war period, counted as one of his major accomplishments The Courant's editorial campaign to help Hartford modernize its government. When reform groups began to press for a council-manager charter for the city, Sherman backed the proposal with one of the biggest editorial campaigns in The Courant's history. Day after day he explained the advantages of council-manager government; and as the campaign entered its final weeks in November and December, 1946, he ran two-column editorials on the front page. On December 4 a jubilant front-page editorial announced "The Charter Triumph"—a 2-to-1 victory, despite what Sherman called "every obstacle that inertia, misunderstanding, and the combined efforts of the professionals of both parties could put in its way."

The biggest news story The Courant handled while Sherman was publisher was the grim news of Hartford's most spectacular fire, the 1944 Ringling Brothers Circus holocaust that took 168 lives. The Courant carried stories and pictures of the flaming tent, the panic and stampede of spectators, and the frantic search for loved ones, the identification of charred bodies, tales of heroism and heartbreak. The staff had covered fires before, but nothing to match this one.

Maurice Sherman died on June 27, 1947. Never one to try to impress others, he relegated his entire newspaper career of more than half a century to the single terse statment in *Who's Who*: "Formerly editor, *The Springfield Union;* editor and publisher, *The Courant,* Hartford, Connecticut." His death marked the end of an era for The Courant. The war was over, but spiraling costs, massive shifts in population, and The Courant's struggle with an inadequate plant nearly 70 years old posed tremendous problems for the man the Directors chose as his successor.

1947-1964
Yesterday; Today; Tomorrow

IF CONNECTICUT'S 50 per cent increase in population since World War II has properly been termed an "explosion," some stronger term is needed for The Courant's 120 per cent increase in circulation during the same period. The vital statistics since 1947 reveal an organization fairly bursting with energy. It took 183 years to build circulation to 55,900 in 1947: 13 years to double that figure. It took 182 years to build advertising to 10.9 million lines in 1946: 16 more years to double that. And while this growth has been going on, The Courant has moved to a new home, developed one of the most fully automated newspaper plants in the East, gone in for full process color, added 10 outlying news offices, and launched out in a dozen other directions.

The publisher under whom these galvanic developments have taken place is John R. Reitemeyer, who has found time in a strenuous career to serve as a director of the Associated Press, as President of the Inter American Press Association, as a colonel in World War II, and as a director or trustee of a long list of colleges, banks, insurance companies, charitable organizations, and a railroad. As his associates in these various fields—particularly The Courant—have found out, where Reitemeyer is, things start happening, and the things often bear the stamp of his personality. "No man has done more . . . for the strengthening and freedom of the press in the Americas," reads a citation awarded him in 1963 by the Inter American Press Association, when one speaker called him "Mr. IAPA himself."

Reitemeyer succeeded Maurice S. Sherman as President and Publisher of The Courant on July 16, 1947. Then 49, he had been on the staff since his undergraduate days at Trinity College in Hartford, when he covered Trinity for The Courant and worked occasional evenings in the City Room, sometimes lame and sore after a Saturday afternoon playing for the varsity football team. He landed a steady Courant assignment one night in 1917 when he covered one of the complicated meetings of the Hartford Board of Fire Commissioners, a task not relished by the other reporters. His story caught the eye of Horace B. Clark, Secretary of The Hartford Courant, son of Charles Hopkins Clark, and himself President of the Fire Board. Horace Clark made sure that The Courant did not lose its promising young reporter.

Reitemeyer advanced fast: Night City Editor in 1922, Sunday Editor in 1923, City Editor in 1925. He entered World War II in 1941 as a Captain in the Army, (he had interrupted his college career to serve in the Tank Corps in World War I), and emerged as Colonel with a Legion of Merit Award and two Army Commendation medals. In 1946 he was urged to return to The Courant as a future successor to Publisher Maurice Sherman. It is unusual for the city editor of a metropolitan American daily to become president and publisher of a newspaper without benefit of family connections or resources of very considerable personal wealth. The common path to the "front office" is through the business end of a newspaper or through stock control. Reitemeyer's career does not follow these patterns.

Before coming to work in the morning, the Publisher—tall, erect, his hair iron gray—takes his hunting dogs for a run near his home in Pleasant Valley, 24 miles from Hartford. His house, nearly as old as The Courant, stands within hearing distance of a splashing trout stream. Then he drives to work to begin a long day that is likely to last well into the night. He also takes his directorships and trusteeships seriously and works hard at them. When he was director of the Associated Press, he served the full three-term limit, part of it on the Executive Committee and chairman of the Finance Committee. When he became President of IAPA in 1963, he received the Association's Tom Wallace award (financed solely by the Latin American members) for his work "in behalf of greater inter-American friendship and understanding." With the accompanying honorarium he began a fund for awards for Latin American science reporting.

Reitemeyer's characteristic dynamic approach and often abrupt manner tend to awe some of his subordinates, although he still will come charging into the newsroom, enthusiastic as any cub reporter, with a tip on a major exclusive story. Sometimes his decisions have amusing repercussions. Once, while still City Editor, he read a satirical criticism of a local art show penned by staff member Albert W.

Coote and posted on the newsroom bulletin board. Reitemeyer shrewdly concluded that if Coote could write like that in jest, he could probably do even better in earnest, and promptly appointed him the newspaper's art critic over all Coote's objections. Not long thereafter, Mrs. Reitemeyer invited Mrs. Coote to lunch, but Mrs. Coote declined on the grounds that she had to accompany her husband to the opening of an art show to describe the colors to him. Her husband, she explained, was color blind. Reitemeyer grins when he recalls the incident. Coote was replaced by T. H. Parker, and Coote's obvious writing skill and critical judgment were transferred to the editorial page.

Reitemeyer is widely known in Connecticut. When a two-inch item appeared on an inside page saying he had been "slightly injured" when a car had bumped into his, his office was so deluged with solicitous phone calls and letters that Mrs. Ethel Jackson, his devoted and efficient secretary, hardly could get her work done. Reitemeyer averages five or six luncheons and banquets a week, where he is often a speaker. He is an old hand at speeches; as a colonel he wrote many for General Jonathan M. Wainright after that hero was returned to the U.S. from the Philippines, where he had been captured by the Japanese.

On quite unpredictable occasions Reitemeyer channels his energetic efforts into whimsy. Discovering in 1958 that the plans for Hartford's new police station did not include the traditional green lights out in front, he organized a Green Light Fund, and when the project was assured of success, was the moving force for a luncheon at which the Mayor threw a green light switch while the Chief of Police and dignitaries sipped green ice water and applauded. Reitemeyer's excuse was that as a "one-time police reporter" he was dismayed that the green lights did not figure in the original plans.

When Col. Reitemeyer returned to The Courant after World War II, Sherman immediately assigned him to a study of the Circulation Department, a continuing interest of Reitemeyer's ever since. The newspaper's remarkable surge in circulation dates from that point.

After World War II, the rapidly growing Courant was overflowing its office space. The old State Street building, which in 1880 had housed the newspaper force with rental space to spare, was now hopelessly inadequate. Foreseeing the need for larger quarters, Treasurer John Sudarsky urged the purchase of a new plant site. The Directors bought the Terminal Building on Broad Street in 1945. This property abutted the railroad, making it possible to deliver the heavy rolls of newsprint directly to the newspaper plant .The building was of factory construction, strong enough to support massive stereotype installations and linecasting machines weighing a good 3,700 pounds each.

It took five years and a lawsuit against the building's tenants, the State of Connecticut, to get the occupants out and the quarters prepared. But the big trick—if it could be done—would be to move an entire metropolitan newspaper, lock, stock and composing room, across the city without missing a story. First of all, a five unit Wood press was installed in the Broad Street building. This press began printing the Sunday Magazine and society section as early as May 30, 1950. By July 1 the Broad Street plant could handle The Courant's entire press run. Immediately, the composing room put on a 24-hour public performance as huge cranes lifted the massive, yet fragile, type-setting machines through a hole in the roof of the five-story-high State Street building and lowered them into trucks that rushed them to the Broad Street plant. There, crews moved the machines on rollers to their new spots, and Sunday evening, July 2, the composing room was in operation. One Courant worker, Arthur Randall, recalls, "The copy desk was a couple of turtles and a telephone; the proof room was a main thoroughfare in and out of the composing room; the machines were wired on a purely temporary basis and had to be watched closely for trouble. Forms that had to hold the pages for the paper were piled high with boxes; there were no stones for the make-up crew . . ."

Sunday morning, July 2, 1950, was the last issue published at State Street. Monday morning's paper came from Broad Street. But for months The Courant was written and edited at State Street, transmitted by courier, telephone, or teletype to Broad Street, there to be assembled and printed—an awkward process for the newsroom. The Courant held its formal opening on March 4, 1951. The affair was attended by Governor John Lodge and many state and city officials, by justices of the State Supreme Court, and by 13,000 other guests. To salute the occasion, The Courant got out a special 40-page section and a 16-page tabloid-size rotogravure section.

The visitor to The Courant today climbs a few stone steps above the Broad Street sidewalk, pushes through glass swinging doors, and enters a lobby lined with offices on one side and a long desk on the other, where girls take orders for classified advertising. Straight ahead are doors to the auditorium, a passage to the circulation department, and the elevator to the departments above. In one corner of the lobby stands the wooden press on which, it is believed, Thomas Green printed the first issue of the newspaper on October 29, 1764. Also in the lobby is a plaque presented to The Courant by the professional society of journalism, Sigma Delta Chi, which voted The Courant its Historic Site in Journalism Award in 1964. Nothing else in the clean, modern lines of the lobby hints at the antiquity of the Hartford Courant.

The visitor, in fact, is far more likely to be impressed by the bustling modernity of the newspaper than by its antiquity. Staff members he meets are much more likely to talk about the future than the past. One out of every three of them is a stockholder in the newspaper.

The corporation of which these employees are part-owners has, as directors, a blue-ribbon group of eleven leading Connecticut business and professional men, including some of the keenest investment minds in the state. The present board is made up of Mr. F. Russell Abell, Senior Vice President, Connecticut Bank and Trust Co.; Dr. F. J. Braceland, Psychiatrist-in-Chief, Institute for Living, Hartford; Lyman B. Brainerd, President, Hartford Steam Boiler Inspection & Insurance Company; H. Bissell Carey, Past President, The Collins Company and the Automatic Refrigerating Company, Hartford; Richard G. Croft, Chairman of the Board, Great Northern Paper Company, New York; Edmund W. Downes, Vice President and Treasurer, The Hartford Courant; Peter M. Fraser, Past President, Connecticut Mutual Life Insurance Company, Hartford; James Lee Loomis, Past President, Connecticut Mutual Life Insurance Company, Hartford; Mr. Reitemeyer; Olcott D. Smith, Chairman of the Board, Aetna Life Insurance Company, Hartford; and Michael Sudarsky, Attorney, Hartford.

The Courant sells its stock to its employees, offering them loans that are interest-free the first year and two percent a year for four years thereafter. One in six of the staff members has been with the newspaper 25 years or more—the personnel files contain records of many employees who have stayed with the newspaper 50 years or longer. Isadore Berkowitz, of the circulation department, saw 54 years of service before retiring in 1960. John Sudarsky, Vice President and Treasurer, was employed 56 years before his death; Jerome H. O'Callaghan, Executive Vice President and Secretary, served 53 years until he died in 1963; Jacob A. Turner, who died in 1924, spent nearly 70 of his 88 years with The Courant, and was voted a salary for life upon his "retirement" from the composing room in 1913 as "superintendent emeritus."

Most of the department heads have been on The Courant for more than 30 years: Mail Room Superintendent Andrew Patrizzi, 48 years; Advertising Director John L. Coughlin, 40 years; Classified Advertising Manager C. Kenneth Ward, 38 years; Production Manager Egbert E. Hunter and Circulation Manager Ray Schroll, 35 years; Personnel Director and Secretary of The Hartford Courant Company Thomas R. Barrett, 35 years; Managing Editor William J. Foote, 34 years.

The story is told of Frank M. "Cap" Jenks, for 63 years a Courant printer, who, on reaching the age of 85 in 1947, came into the office of Mr. O'Callaghan and said sadly, "Jerry, now that I'm 85, I suppose I have to retire." He knew The Courant was planning a luncheon to celebrate his birthday and years of service. "I don't know," said O'Callaghan, smiling at the spry, alert Jenks. He phoned Reitemeyer, then Executive Vice President. "You tell 'Cap'," said Reitemeyer jokingly, "that we won't allow him to retire until he is 90." O'Callaghan relayed the information straight-faced.

"Good," said "Cap," relieved, "that's fine with me." He died in 1961 at the age of 98. By that time The Courant had a strong, completely company-financed retirement plan, set up in 1956, which offers options on retirement age to employees but requires approval by the Board of Directors for any employees who wish to remain working after age 67. The Courant was a newspaper pioneer in group life insurance, setting up its plan more than 50 years ago when it became the first group client of the Connecticut General Life Insurance Company.

Under Reitemeyer The Courant has pushed vigorously into personnel policy improvement, hiring a former Hartford assistant superintendent of schools, Thomas F. Carberry, to take job applications and administer testing procedures. It sends department heads and employees to short courses and seminars, and pays for the tuition and books of employees wishing to continue higher education in any of Hartford's many colleges—although the employees must pass the courses to get the benefits. The Courant has also been interested in research. It was one of the relatively few newspapers that financially supported research into newspaper practices before the American Newspaper Publishers Association moved into that field.

The Courant sets perhaps twice as much type for news each day as do most newspapers. One reason is the relatively large percentage of space devoted to news, averaging 45 to 50 per cent. Another reason is that The Courant produces seven editions of each daily news-

THIS BUILDING SEEMED ROOMY WHEN COURANT MOVED INTO IT IN 1950

A large addition will be built in 1965

CHILDREN THRONG CAMP COURANT'S OLYMPIC-SIZE
SWIMMING POOL, LOWER RIGHT

*Camp's 45 acres include pavilion-classroom-kitchen (top), ball field (lower
left), much natural woodland and basketball court and play equipment*

paper, each edition carrying up to 22 columns of local news pertinent to the specific Connecticut area in which that edition circulates. The Courant's State Desk operation is the key to much of this local news. Each night the State Desk in the newsroom swirls into a small hurricane of activity to cover Connecticut, where the New England town meeting still reigns. By 7 p.m. the State Desk begins to feel the brunt of news pouring in from more than 100 correspondents and 19 staff men in 13 bureaus scattered throughout a state that measures little more than 100 miles at its widest.

By 10 p.m. the onrush of state news reaches its peak. Runners drop their dispatches and go out for more. Reporters, headphones clamped to their ears, sit at the desk flailing their typewriters as correspondents in the outlying towns telephone their news. Other correspondents, phoning in, cause little lights to blink on the small telephone switchboard at the center of the State Desk. Nearby, twelve teletype machines, linking the bureaus to the State Desk in direct two-way communication, reel off yards of copy. A reporter goes down the line of machines—labeled Bristol, New Britain, Manchester, New London, and so on—ripping off long ribbons of stories. By the time he has hustled these out to the State Editor, the teletypes have produced enough more copy to require a new harvesting. In the midst of all this activity, made possible by the latest electronic equipment, a dispatch is likely to arrive written in the clear, firm longhand of Mrs. W. Colton Bliss, a veteran correspondent in Somers, who turns in her copy in the manuscript form familiar to The Courant for 200 years.

The state staff produces on the average weekday a total of about 12 solid pages of local news and pictures for the first 5 of The Courant's daily editions—about 20 columns for each. The State Desk works closely with the Circulation Department—both being intensely interested in the town coverage in every edition. The Circulation Department has 15 branch offices throughout the state, sharing space with the State Desk's news bureaus in many cases.

Each of the seven daily editions carries the local news of the area in which it circulates. The sea is reflected in the first edition, which goes out to the coastal towns of Saybrook, New London, and Groton. In the second edition, the main news often concerns the industries of inland Torrington and Winsted and the bedroom suburbs of Avon, Simsbury, Farmington, and Canton. Into the third come the involved politics of Bristol and New Britain. The fourth and fifth editions often have a predominantly agricultural flavor. The sixth and seventh, whose news is channeled through the City Desk, go to Hartford and its immediate suburbs, reflecting the day-by-day history of the Capitol Area and Connecticut River Valley. Each edition carries, in addition to state, national, and world news, little

PAGE SIZES OVER THE YEARS
Shown: first issue, 1764; issue of 1964; blanket sheet of 1871

chroniclings of the area—deaths, births, school, court and police news, fires, politics—trivial matters, often, to those who live else-where but vital to the people affected by them.

The remarkably thorough coverage of state news and the highly developed organization of the Circulation Department go a long way toward explaining The Courant's rapid increase in circulation in the last two decades. The daily topped 130,000 late in 1963. The Sunday Courant, which has a larger Connecticut circulation than any other newspaper sold in the state, has nearly doubled its 1947 total of 96,800, despite going from 15 cents to 25 cents in price.

The feeling of proprietorship one senses in talking with members of The Courant's family owes something to the pride they share with the Publisher in the newspaper's record of growth. It also owes something to their knowledge that Reitemeyer has backed them up when the going has become rough. In 1953 a representative of the New Parsons Theater called on managing editor Foote and de-manded that theater critic T. H. Parker be taken off his beat. His reviews, they said, had been "savage." Foote let his visitors know that, if the play was to be reviewed in The Courant, it would be re-viewed by Parker. When Parker arrived at the box office, accom-panied by Foote, he offered tickets of his own, which had been bought in advance, but the theater managers refused to accept them. Flash bulbs began popping, and the next morning's front page carried a three-column picture and the headline: "COURANT'S DRAMA CRITIC BARRED FROM PARSONS."

The story prompted a blizzard of letters, telegrams, and phone calls. Clifford Odets, whose play, "The Country Girl," was showing, telegraphed "All my life I have been against such restrictions of opinions and free speech . . ." Brooks Atkinson, drama critic of The New York Times, termed Parker's exclusion "very poor judgment." The People's Forum in The Courant swelled to several columns as letters poured in. Publisher Reitemeyer backed Parker to the hilt. In a lead editorial, Editor Herbert Brucker demanded, "What is a critic for if not to hold standards high?" Reitemeyer took the posi-tion that the question was whether persons in Connecticut should be allowed to attend plays as long as they behaved. The Courant caused to be introduced into the Connecticut General Assembly, then in session, a bill to make it unlawful for theaters to ban well-behaved ticket holders. Governor John Lodge signed the bill into law on July 1, 1953. Reitemeyer then asserted that his newspaper would not use the new law to force its critic upon the theater.

In the fall of 1954 Parsons opened under new management. Parker received an invitation for the opening of Norman A. Brooks' *Fragile Fox* and, with his wife, made something of a triumphant entrance through the crowded lobby as friends and strangers came up to shake hands.

The proprietary interest felt by Courant employees owes a good deal, too, to their awareness that "the oldest newspaper of continuous publication in America" is constantly experimenting and planning for the future. The Courant is clearly more interested in the century ahead than in the two centuries behind. It was one of the first New England newspapers to install tape-operated typecasting. Some 90 per cent of its reading matter and close-set classified advertising is now set by tape-operated machines. Not only financial, but state and local news is fed into linecasting machines on tapes, as is much of the news from the Associated Press and United Press International wires. In the financial section, all the tables, both daily and Sunday, are set by tape.

This high degree of automation has been accomplished without firings and dismissals. Before the tape-fed type-setting machines went in, Reitemeyer met with each shift of compositors and gave them his personal assurance that the new devices would not cost anyone his job on the newspaper. Largely because employees feel confidence in the Publisher's reaffirmation of The Courant's tradition of job security, automation on The Courant has caused little uneasiness. It is worth noting, incidentally, that The Courant, though non-unionized, is the first newspaper ever to have one of its staff accorded a citation by the State Labor Council, AFL-CIO. Irving Kravsow's labor reporting won him a citation in 1963 from the officers of the Council.

Experiment and innovation also have characterized the women's pages of The Courant in recent years. The front page of the Sunday "World of Women" has been a proving-ground for full-process color pictures. The news columns of the section—once devoted almost exclusively to "social" news—have gone in for illustrated biographical sketches of prominent and interesting local women.

In 1959 The Courant added a color half deck to its Wood press —a far cry from the process used in its pioneering experiments with spot color in 1892. Advertisers, far more sophisticated than in earlier days when they would allow an ad to run unchanged for months, have shown an increasing interest in color. Reitemeyer encouraged the use of color years before The Courant was ready to come out with full process color. In 1951 spot color was used on the Sunday Magazine cover. Two colors appeared on the 4th of July, 1958—red and blue ink on white paper for a picture of the American flag. The first full process color picture in a Hartford newspaper appeared on the first page of the women's section on September 12, 1959. The Courant ran 217,000 lines of color advertising in that year, which was nearly tripled by the 598,000 line total in 1963.

As everyone on the newspaper knew early in the 1950's, Reitemeyer's ambition was to reach a daily circulation of 100,000 by 1960. By January, 1954, the Publisher announced with cautious optimism that "at the rate we are going now, we should reach this mark by 1960." Circulation was then comfortably above 80,000. "The Year" turned out to be 1955 as The Courant racked up an eight-percent increase and passed the 100,000 goal toward the end of the year. At a party to celebrate this occasion, the late George Clark, Circulation Manager, put on a frock coat and silk hat and cut the cake with a saber while guests cheered and flash bulbs blinked. The next year, 1956, the Sunday Courant topped 150,000. Soon the increasing daily circulation could no longer be printed on a single press. Starting September 17, 1956, both the Hoe and the Wood presses ran simultaneously to get out the daily. A year later a sixth Wood press unit had to be added.

This record of growth has been achieved despite competition. Connecticut, the third smallest state in area, has 26 daily newspapers, 8 Sunday newspapers, and 64 weeklies. New York and Boston papers, too, sell well in Connecticut. Hartford is one of the few remaining cities in the nation, and the only one in the state, where two newspapers under separate ownerships are published. Perhaps this helps to explain why both Hartford newspapers, on rare occasions, have devoted more than 30 per cent of their front pages to contests, announcements of coming features, tables of stories to be found on inside pages, and similar solipsistic material. Promotion is an important part of the Courant's operation. It is under the direction of Mrs. Paula Clark.

Under the stimulus of expanding circulation, the number of carrier-salesman routes has grown prodigiously—from 930 in 1952 to 2600 in 1963; an eleven-year increase of 1670. A century ago, news distributors picked up their copies of the paper at the newspaper office, folded each copy themselves, and personally delivered the paper to their customers. Today, a machine collates the various sections of The Courant, while tying machines automatically bundle them, and a roller belt conveyor delivers the bundles to trucks destined for distribution points throughout the state. In 1964 The Courant purchased a neighboring 45,000-square-foot property to the south, with an eye to future land needs. An addition to the north side of the present building will be constructed in 1965.

While expansion and plans for the future are conspicuously the order of the day at The Hartford Courant, the policies and traditions of the past still play an important role in the character of the newspaper. The Courant is still published in a medium-sized city sharing some of the points of view of its megalopolitan neighbors, New York and Boston, as well as some of the interests of Connecticut's small, traditionally agricultural towns. For years, this special blend of viewpoints has been discernible throughout the newpaper.

On most mornings, the topics covered in the editorial page range from the international to the local. To cover this spread, the editor of the editorial page, Herbert Brucker, has established a policy of running 6 to 8 editorials a day, or more than 40 a week. These are produced, after morning conferences, by a staff of four editorial writers headed by Brucker, who can count among his professional honors the presidency in 1963 of the American Society of Newspaper Editors. As in the past, some of The Courant's signed columns of opinion are produced by members of the newspaper staff: Jack Zaiman's observations on Connecticut politics in "The Needle's Eye"; T. H. Parker's critical views in "The Lively Arts"; and Thomas E. Murphy's comments on the passing scene in "Of Many Things." The Courant's syndicated columnists include Walter Lippmann, Joseph Alsop (a native of nearby Avon), Ralph McGill and David Lawrence.

Political news is important for a newspaper publishing in the state's capital city. The Courant's views on public affairs apparently have a strong impact in the Capitol; it is not uncommon to find a state legislator rising to read from The Courant to help make his point. The Courant takes a definite interest in Connecticut's political well-being. A case in point occurred after the U. S. Supreme Court's decision in February, 1964, that decreed the "one man, one vote" principle in the election of members of the U. S. House of Representatives. Connecticut had five representatives elected by districts of disparate populations, and one representative elected by the state at large. The Courant authorized political reporter Jack Zaiman to file suit in the U. S. District Court, requesting that the court order an election at large for all six representatives unless the General

PATHFINDER . . .

Start Every Day Right
Final Edition

The Hartford Courant

Weather Forecast
SCATTERED
SNOW FLURRIES

ESTABLISHED 1764, VOL. ( ) CCXVII NO. 51   HARTFORD 1, CONN.   THURSDAY MORNING, FEBRUARY 20, 1964—44 PAGES   7 CENTS

Unless General Assembly Acts:

Court Asked to Call At-Large Election

| NEWS in BRIEF | Stores Will Be Open Tonight Until 9 | 6 to 11 Inches Wind-Whipped Snow Slows Traffic; 2 Die | Publisher's Statement | Suit Filed By Zaiman Of Courant |

Danish Minister Pays Visit to Khrushchev

21 Rescued As Wild Sea Pounds Ship; 14 Missing

U.S. House Setup at Stake

'Arms to Ethiopia'

COURANT ATTACKS INEQUALITIES IN VOTING
Legislature made congressional districts more nearly equal

Assembly, before the next election, created new congressional districts. The Courant's suit and a front-page statement by Publisher Reitemeyer pointed out the "glaring inequality" in the number of voters in Connecticut's districts. The suit brought immediate response. A special session of the Assembly was called for April. The Assembly, acting speedily, in three days came up with an act that created six congressional districts of substantially equal population.

The Courant's interest in youth and the education of youth dates back at least as far as 1765, when a March issue carried the alphabet for readers and children. Today The Courant's Parade of Youth, running up to 12 pages in size as a special pull-out section in the Sunday Magazine, carries news of teen-age activities and sponsors a wide range of educational services. These include writing awards, a Junior Classical League, cash prizes and awards for the Connecticut Latin Contest, journalism awards, a Youth Forum, two music camp scholarships, and prizes to six top-ranking high school students excelling in college courses. The Junior Classical League has accomplished something unique among American newspapers: it has brought together a membership of more than 2,000 young people whose common bond is the study of classical Latin and Greek.

Also in line with its traditional concern for young people, the newspaper maintains Camp Courant, now in its 48th year of operation but dating back 70 years. The Courant founded this camp in the summer of 1916, but the newspaper's practice of helping children get away from hot summer streets goes back to July, 1894. The Courant then appealed to its readers to contribute toward a fund to give Hartford children a free excursion on the Connecticut River. Readers responded with $1,600. Year by year the outings increased both in frequency and numbers participating. In time, trolley rides to outlying parks took the place of river trips. In 1916 The Courant decided to open a day camp on a woodland tract in West Hartford. A dam across Trout Brook provided a swimming hole. The children got two meals a day. One they brought with them, milk being supplied at a penny a glass. The second meal was supplied to the children by the camp at a penny apiece. At the end of the first session, the newspaper had played host to 10,000 children, who were picked up by trolley cars, then by chartered buses.

More than twice that many children frolic at the present Camp Courant, which in 1963 moved to a new 50-acre woodland tract at Batterson Park, Farmington. Here some 1000 children a day can enjoy camp trails, arts and crafts instruction (many boys making portable shoe-shining stands to earn money with), picnicking, baseball, basketball, and swimming in a 100-foot pool. Swim suits are furnished by The Courant, laundered and dried daily. It costs about $1.50 a child a day to provide this kind of outing. The generous support of individuals and organizations contributing to a vigorous campaign makes Camp Courant possible.

Another long-standing characteristic of The Courant, its decided literary leaning, is evidenced today not only in the newspaper's special concern for young Greek and Latin scholars, but in its weekly book review section in the Sunday Magazine, and in the literary allusions and style on the editorial page. In 1962 The Courant distributed, at cost, some 50,000 modern language instruction records, more orders than any other newspaper in the country received in proportion to circulation. For ten years The Courant has sponsored a series of annual lectures on mental health by outstanding psychiatrists (attended in 1964 by 3,800 persons). Reprints are jointly distributed by The Courant and The Connecticut Mutual Life Insurance Co.

Undoubtedly most significant of all The Courant's long traditions has been its continuing emphasis on news as the chief reason for a newspaper's being. In spite of obvious special interests at various periods, the proprietors have always thought of their paper as a journal of news. The Courant has never become primarily an organ for temperance groups, abolitionist groups, or religious or political parties, as is quite evident when it is compared with the special-interest organs of any era. Even under its most militantly partisan conductors, The Courant has carried plenty of news that has had nothing to do with special interests. Reflecting on these matters, Editor Joseph R. Hawley wrote a policy statement in 1867 that has lost none of its force after nearly a century:

> The Courant is not only the oldest prominent journal in America, but there are in all the quarters of the globe less than half a dozen periodicals in the English language which go back to a more remote period. . . . It is now the determination of the proprietors to make it worthy of its venerable age . . . In the quaint language of the prospectus printed in our first issue of October 29, 1764, 'Great Care will be taken to collect from Time to Time all domestic Occurrences, that are worthy the Notice to the Publick.'
>
> [Hawley promised that The Courant would not become] a mere political sheet, after the manner of too much of our American journalism, but will strive to be a *news*paper in the broadest sense of the word. It will endeavor to keep its readers *au courant* of whatever happens in the world of science, of literature and of art, of the efforts of the human intellect in every department of knowledge, of affairs of foreign nations as well as those of our own.

Something of this generous conception of a newspaper's function has influenced The Courant from the beginning. In a report to stockholders in 1952, not long after the newspaper had moved into its new building and had bought new equipment, Publisher Reitemeyer said:

> A newspaper's greatest asset is not its building, its equipment, or the money in the bank or the bonds in its vault. A newspaper's greatest asset is public confidence, public belief in its fairness, in its honesty, in its integrity. Without this confidence, no newspaper can long survive.

If The Courant were a man, not a journal, he would be recognized in the community as a successful business man of long standing, a Republican, one who had often served his country and his community in peace and war. He would have fought in the great battles for freedom from political tyranny and from slavery, he would have been a personal friend of great men in politics and in literature.

Like other men, he would have had occasional backslidings, times when he seemed ready to settle for less than the best. Friends would point out his strong literary taste, his interest in children, and his many efforts in behalf of education. They would remember his success in weathering crises that had threatened to end his business career. He would today be a community leader, widely known, a daily visitor, as enterprising as men a fraction of his age, his business expanding, his opinions discussed in every part of the state, the senior member of his national fraternity.

Appendix A

Proprietors and Officers of The Courant:

1764-1964

PROPRIETORS: 1764—1890

Thomas Green (moved to New Haven in winter of 1767-1768)	Oct. 29, 1764—Dec., 1767
Thomas Green and Ebenezer Watson	Dec., 1767—Dec., 1770
Ebenezer Watson	Dec., 1770—Sept. 16, 1777
Hannah Bunce Watson	Sept. 16, 1777—Dec. 31, 1777
Hannah Bunce Watson and George Goodwin	Jan. 1, 1778—March, 1779
George Goodwin and Barzillai Hudson, husband of Hannah Watson, (Firm name: Hudson & Goodwin)	March, 1799—Nov. 15, 1815
George Goodwin & Sons (Richard, George, Jr., Henry)	Nov. 15, 1815—Nov., 1823
Goodwin & Co. (Charles and Edward, sons of George, Sr., join)	Nov. 1823—Sept. 12, 1836
John L. Boswell	Sept. 13, 1836—Dec. 31, 1849
John L. Boswell and William Faxon	Jan. 1, 1850—July 30, 1854
William Faxon	July 31, 1854—Dec. 31, 1854
Thomas M. Day	Jan. 1, 1855—Dec. 31, 1856
Thomas M. Day and Abel N. Clark (Firm name: Day & Clark)	Jan. 1, 1857—Dec. 30, 1864
Abel N. Clark (Day retains purely financial interest in paper thru Dec. 31, 1869. Firm name: A. N. Clark & Co.)	Dec. 31, 1864—Dec. 31, 1865
Abel N. Clark and William H. Goodrich	Jan. 1, 1866—Dec. 31, 1866
Abel N. Clark, Thomas M. Day, William H. Goodrich, Joseph R. Hawley, Charles D. Warner. (Firm name Hawley, Goodrich & Co.) A. N. Clark dies March, 1867, Stephen A. Hubbard buys his interest; Day withdraws, Dec. 31, 1869; Charles Hopkins Clark buys into company in 1880's.	Jan. 1, 1867—Dec. 2, 1890
Hartford Courant Co., Inc.	Dec. 3, 1890—

Officers of The Hartford Courant Company: 1890–1964

PRESIDENTS

Charles Dudley Warner	Dec. 3, 1890—Oct. 20, 1900
Joseph R. Hawley	Nov. 1, 1900—March 18, 1905
Charles Hopkins Clark	Jan. 15, 1906—Sept. 5, 1926
Henry H. Conland	Sept. 28, 1926—April 15, 1944
Maurice S. Sherman	April 25, 1944—June 27, 1947
John R. Reitemeyer	July 16, 1947—

VICE PRESIDENTS

Charles Hopkins Clark	Oct. 19, 1891—Jan. 15, 1906
	Jan. 15, 1906
	(No Vice President elected)
Frank S. Carey	May 9, 1911—Dec. 4, 1919
Henry K. W. Welch	Jan. 15, 1919—Jan. 30, 1946
Maurice S. Sherman	April 15, 1943—April 25, 1944
Charles H. Conland	Jan. 29, 1945—May 16, 1946
John R. Reitemeyer	Jan. 30, 1946—July 16, 1947
John Sudarsky	July 16, 1947—Oct. 1, 1959
Henry J. Conland	Jan. 26, 1956—June 1, 1961
Jerome H. O'Callaghan	Oct. 1, 1959—June 19, 1963
	(Exec. Vice President)
Edmund W. Downes	July 25, 1963—

SECRETARIES

Charles Hopkins Clark	Dec. 3, 1890—Jan. 14, 1893
Frank S. Carey	Jan. 16, 1893—May 9, 1911
Henry H. Conland	May 9, 1911—July 23, 1914
Horace B. Clark	July 23, 1914—Jan. 29, 1941
Jerome H. O'Callaghan	Jan. 29, 1941—June 19, 1963
Thomas R. Barrett	July 25, 1963—

ASSISTANT SECRETARIES

Walter St. George Harris	Jan. 15, 1919—Sept. 1, 1935
Henry J. Conland	Jan. 29, 1941—June 1, 1961

TREASURERS

William H. Goodrich	Dec. 3, 1890—Dec. 26, 1891
Arthur L. Goodrich	Dec. 26, 1891—April 16, 1911
Frank S. Carey	May 9, 1911—July 23, 1914
Henry H. Conland	July 23, 1914—May 8, 1929
John Sudarsky	May 8, 1929—Oct. 1, 1959
Edmund W. Downes	Oct. 1, 1959—

ASSISTANT TREASURERS

Edith E. Kibbe	May 9, 1911—Jan., 1921
John Sudarsky	Jan. 20, 1927—May 8, 1929
Jerome H. O'Callaghan	May 8, 1929—Sept. 16, 1948
Henry J. Conland	Sept. 16, 1948—Jan. 26, 1956
Edmund W. Downes	Jan. 26, 1956—Oct. 1, 1959

Appendix B

Circulation Volume and Rates
and Advertising Volume and Rates

I. CIRCULATION OF THE COURANT TO 1900

Reliable and comparable statistics for American newspapers before the founding of the Audit Bureau of Circulations in 1914 are hard to come by. In the following tabulation, circulation data for The Courant have been assembled from various sources. Examination shows that some of the figures deserve more credence than others.

Although The Courant published both a daily and a weekly from 1837 onward, early circulation claims seldom indicated whether figures for one or both were included.

Year	Circulation	Basis for Claim
1764	Unknown	Hartford's population was about 4,000.
1771-1772	–	*Courant* circulates as far as western Massachusetts and eastern New York. Published postrider routes, *Courant,* September 17, 1771; March 10, 1772.
1774	700	Watson's appeal to subscribers to pay up. *Courant,* November 21.
1776-1777	–	*Courant* has circulation "equal to if not greater than, any other paper then printed on the continent." Isaiah Thomas, *History of Printing in America,* 1810, Vol. II, 278.
1778	8,000	Ledyard and Watson petition to Connecticut General Assembly after paper mill fire. *Connecticut Archives, Industry.* (First Series), II, 59.
1795	3,500	*Courant* claim, January 12, a letter of Jeremiah Wadsworth to Alexander Hamilton, conjecturally dated 1795, and now in the Library of Congress, says *The Courant* published "more than five thousand papers."
1799	ca. 5,000	*Courant* claim, January 7.

Year	Circulation	Basis for Claim
1804	–	*Courant* claims largest circulation in the country, July 18.
1808	4,600	*Courant* claim, October 12.
1823	–	Larger than any other Connecticut paper. Claim made in George Goodwin and Sons, *Letter Books,* Vol. IV, December 19. In Connecticut Historical Society.
1837	200 (daily)	*Courant* claim made October 17, 1846. Weekly figure not given.
1846	5,544	*Courant* claim October 17. A notarized claim of 720 for the daily and 4,824 for the weekly.
1861	17,000-26,000	*Courant* claim that circulation rose from 17,000 to 26,000 after the firing on Fort Sumter. Claim made May 11, 1861.
1861-1863	–	*Courant* claims largest circulation in the state, May 11, 1861, and November 30, 1863.
1864	–	*Courant* claims that subscribers have trebled since 1855, and that circulation has never been so great before, October 29.
1868	over 9,000	*Courant* claim, January 30. "Rapidly approaching a circulation of 10,000."
1871	–	*Courant* claim that only one or two New England newspapers outside Boston reach so many readers, December 25.
1886	6,000 (daily)	*Courant* claim, November 4. Morning after election.
1888	–	Goes to more Hartford homes than any other paper. *Courant* claim, January 2.
1890	4,800	*Courant* claim, October 29, 1939, *Courant Magazine,* p. 5. Evidently applies to daily circulation.
1895	60-70,000	*Courant* claim, July 13, for this one edition only. A special promotional effort, featuring a story "Inside a Modern Newspaper Office." The edition is said to be "the largest edition of any paper ever printed in this State."

Year	Circulation	Basis for Claim
1900	9,500	*Courant* claim, October 29, 1939, *Magazine,* p. 5. Evidently applies to daily circulation.
1900-04	—	Figures not available for this period. The claim of 9,500 for 1900 and the figure of 11,101 from the press-run book for 1905 (see next table) indicates a slow but steady growth for the 1900-04 period.

II. CIRCULATION AND SUBSCRIPTION RATES OF THE COURANT: 1905 – 1964

Year	Circulation		Subscription Rates *
	Daily	Sunday	
1905	11,101a		3¢ daily
1906	11,800		
1907	12,800		
1908	12,800		
1909	13,800		
1910	14,900		
1911	15,000		
1912	15,600		
1913	15,694b	23,800b	5¢ Sunday
1914	16,892	16,660	
1915	16,859	19,159	
1916	17,261	18,675	
1917	19,766	21,885	6¢ Sunday
1918	23,702	25,919	
1919	24,497c	28,796c	7¢ Sunday
1920	25,410	33,873	10¢ Sunday
1921	28,599	39,265	
1922	30,194	43,708	
1923	29,010d	48,231d	
1924	35,958	50,041	
1925	34,289	52,854	
1926	34,390	56,909	
1927	33,736	58,460	
1928	36,742	59,888	
1929	39,373	61,012	
1930	41,563	63,317	
1931	39,922	63,468	

| Year | Circulation | | Subscription Rates * |
	Daily	Sunday	
1932	38,627	61,689	
1933	35,845	57,131	
1934	36,088	58,845	
1935	37,471	60,560	
1936	38,501	64,892	
1937	43,115	65,740	
1938	42,691	67,334	4¢ daily
1939	41,950	70,478	
1940	41,358	72,365	
1941	44,607	74,724	
1942	48,185	79,437	
1943	48,178	81,423	12¢ Sunday
1944	45,825	81,022	
1945	48,666	85,108	
1946	51,560	91,463	⎰ 5¢ daily
1947	55,854	96,798	⎱ 15¢ Sunday
1948	56,903	98,272	
1949	61,222	102,932	
1950	64,442	110,372	
1951	68,899	112,628	20¢ Sunday
1952	73,427	117,192	
1953	78,440	123,292	
1954	85,411	130,672	
1955	92,264e	135,650	
1956	98,513f	143,226f	
1957	102,731	145,951	25¢ Sunday
1958	104,260	146,544	
1959	107,843	149,658	
1960	112,212	153,363	7¢ daily
1961	112,643	156,183	
1962	117,520	161,017	
1963	124,058	171,332	
1964	130,261g	176,246g	

* For subscription rates of earlier period, see next table.

a. Figures for 1905 through 1912 from Courant's press-run books kept by Fred Salzer. Nearest date to April 1.

b. Figures for 1913 through 1918 from Courant's Day Book. Nearest date to April 1. Sunday circulation for 1913 is for October 5.

c. Figures for 1919 through 1922 from ABC "Total Distribution."

d. Figures for 1923 through 1955 from ABC "Total Net Paid Circulation."

e. Circulation reaches 100,000 in spurt toward end of this year.

f. Figures for 1956 through 1963 from ABC "Total Paid Circulation."

g. Nine-month average, from October 1, 1963, to June 30, 1964.

III. Advertising Volume and Rates and Subscription Rates of The Courant to 1900

The following table shows advertising volume and rates, and subscription rates of The Courant at regular 5-year intervals before 1900, as well as for miscellaneous years of special interest.

In the earlier years, rates—especially advertising rates—were seldom quoted. Evidence from various sources shows that both advertising and subscription rates were often individually adjusted for various reasons, as the entries in the table for 1778 and 1795 suggest.

Year	Whole Paper		Advertising			Subscription Rates (b)	Comment
	Total Pages (a)	Total Cols. (a)	Cols. (a)	% of Total (a)	Rates		
1764	4	8	$\frac{1}{13}$	1	—	6 shillings probably	2 ads. totaling 9 lines in 1st issue. 6s. a common subscription rate at that time.
1765	4	8	$2\frac{1}{2}$	31	—	—	
1768	—	—	—	—	3 shillings for 10 lines for 3 weeks, then 6 pence each.	6s. yr.	8s. by special post rider.
1770	4	12	$3\frac{1}{4}$	27	—	—	
1771	—	—	—	—	—	7s. yr.	9s. by special post rider.
1775	4	12	$5\frac{3}{4}$	48	—	—	
1778	—	—	—	—	—	18s. yr.	After Oct. 6; 1 bu. and 3 pks. wheat, rye, flour, wood, or cash.
1779	—	—	—	—	—	30s. yr.	
1780	4	12	$4\frac{1}{2}$	38	—	10s. in silver yr.	No front page ads.
1784	—	—	—	—	—	7s. probably	"at the same price it was before the war" Courant, Dec. 30, 1783.
1785	4	12	$5\frac{1}{2}$	42	—	—	
1790	4	12	$5\frac{3}{4}$	48	—	—	
1795	4	16	$5\frac{3}{4}$	36	—	9s. yr.	"to those who pay not, the price will be raised considerable." i.e. price of ads. No. adv. prices quoted Courant, Jan. 5.

Year	Whole Paper		Advertising			Subscription Rates (b)	Comment
	Total Pages (a)	Total Cols. (a)	Cols. (a)	% of Total (a)	Rates		
1800	4	20	10	50	—	—	
1803	—	—	—	—	—	$1.50 yr.	Evidently the approximate equivalent of 9s.
1805	4	20	6¼	31	—	—	Subscription $1.75 in early Dec.
1810	4	20	9¾	49	—	$1.75 yr.	Payable in advance.
1813	—	—	—	—	—	$2.00 yr.	$1.25 in quantities.
1815	4	20	9½	48	60¢ single ☐; $1.00, 3☐'s; then 20¢ ea.	$2.00 yr.	Payable in advance. A ☐ was 12 to 14 lines.
1820	4	24	12	50	—	—	
1825	4	24	13½	56	—	—	
1830	4	24	11¼	47	—	—	
1835	4	24	14¼	59	No change since 1815.	No change since 1815.	

Daily Paper

Year	Whole Paper		Advertising			Subscription Rates (b)	Comment
1837	—	—	—	—	$10.00 per ☐ to end of yr.	$2.00 to end of yr.	Squares "changeable at pleasure."
1838	—	—	—	—	$25.00 per ☐ per yr., or $20 without the paper.	$5.00 yr.	
1840	4	20	12	60	$1.00, 3 ☐'s (i.e. 3 days).	$5.00 yr., or $4.50 in advance.	Weekly subscription: $2 yr.

Year	Whole Paper		Advertising			Subscription Rates (b)	Comment
	Total Pages (a)	Total Cols. (a)	Cols. (a)	% of Total (a)	Rates		
1841	–	–	–	–	–	–	Tri-weekly: $3.00 yr.
1845	4	20	11	55	$15.00 per □ per year.	$4.00 yr.	No per diem adv. rate quoted.
1850	4	24	16½	69	Per □, no change of ad.: 1 day, 60¢, 3 days, $1; 1 week, $1.50; 1 yr., $10. Per □, with changes: 3 mo., $7; 6 mo., $12; 1 yr., $20.	$5.00 yr.	Subscription rate $4.50 if paid in advance. Ads run exclusively on inside pages cost 50% more.
1851	–	–	–	–	–	–	Daily mailed as far as 50 mi. from Hartford for extra $1. Weekly sent free of extra charge in Hartford County.
1855	4	28	22⅓	80	60¢ a □ then 20¢ ea.	–	
1860	4	28	21	75	–	–	
1864	–	–	–	–	$35.00 per □ per yr.	$8.00 yr.	$1.00 per □ in weekly. Weekly subscription $2.00 yr.
1865	4	28	21½	77	75¢ a □	–	
1870	4	36	23	64	–	–	
1875	4	36	21½	60	–	–	
1880	4	36	23	64	–	4¢ a copy	
1885	4	36	24	67	–	–	
1887	–	–	–	–	–	3¢ a copy	

Year	Whole Paper		Advertising			Subscription Rates (b)	Comment
	Total Pages (a)	Total Cols. (a)	Cols. (a)	% of Total (a)	Rates		
1890	8	56	39	70	—	—	
1895	12	84	51	61	Classified, 3 days, 25¢; 12 days, $1.		
1900	16	112	66	59	—	—	

a. In first issue of the year.

b. For subscription rates after 1900, see preceding table.

IV. ADVERTISING LINAGE OF THE COURANT
1913–1964*

Year	Advertising Linage		
	Daily	Sunday	Total
1913	7,965,468a	395,794a	8,361,262a
1914	6,844,180	1,509,246	8,353,426
1915	6,156,696	1,575,280	7,731,976
1916	6,730,598	2,086,448	8,817,046
1917	6,744,346	2,306,694	9,051,040
1918	6,055,476	2,018,398	8,073,874
1919	7,954,800	3,119,100	11,076,900
1920	8,521,200	3,410,100	11,931,300
1921	7,378,600	3,102,000	10,480,600
1922	7,451,400	3,537,300	10,988,700
1923	7,609,500	4,198,500	11,808,000
1924	7,066,500	4,341,300	11,407,800
1925	7,135,200	4,556,700	11,691,900
1926	7,175,100	4,786,500	11,961,600
1927	6,950,100	4,764,300	11,714,406
1928	7,282,200	5,089,600	12,371,800
1929	7,642,875b	5,068,004b	12,710,879b
1930	6,645,801	4,389,212	11,035,013
1931	5,867,088	3,701,844	9,568,932
1932	4,462,769	2,843,819	7,306,588
1933	4,245,110	2,708,893	6,954,003
1934	4,358,926	3,134,389	7,493,315
1935	4,456,918	3,552,595	8,009,513
1936	4,582,209	3,504,152	8,086,361
1937	4,534,035	3,551,717	8,085,752
1938	3,885,739	3,232,330	7,118,069
1939	3,971,554	3,446,679	7,418,233
1940	4,298,972	3,742,600	8,041,572
1941	4,532,821	3,768,241	8,301,062
1942	4,628,123	3,301,265	7,929,388
1943	5,274,370	3,659,143	8,933,513
1944	6,211,931	4,236,186	10,448,117
1945	6,197,626	3,838,859	10,036,485
1946	6,531,007	4,350,021	10,881,028
1947	7,640,171	4,975,400	12,615,571

Year	Advertising Linage		
	Daily	Sunday	Total
1948	7,974,307	6,305,558	14,279,865
1949	7,364,788	6,382,694	13,747,482
1950	7,193,964	6,607,752	13,801,716
1951	7,624,389	6,714,519	14,338,908
1952	8,476,737	7,189,522	15,666,259
1953	9,429,215	7,990,019	17,419,234
1954	8,758,041	7,641,688	16,399,729
1955	10,467,976	7,948,461	18,416,437
1956	11,532,236	8,286,124	19,818,360
1957	11,968,972	8,428,449	20,397,421
1958	10,865,769	7,934,104	18,799,873
1959	11,520,336	8,556,494	20,076,830
1960	12,372,871	8,569,499	20,942,370
1961	11,745,675	7,928,937	19,674,612
1962	12,859,190	8,604,483	21,463,673
1963	12,949,349	8,791,150	21,740,544
1964	6,604,045c	4,481,666c	11,085,711c

* There is a 12-year gap between the count of advertising volume in this and the preceding table. Because of increased seasonal fluctuation in advertising after the turn of the century, the basis for counting used in the preceding table does not provide a reliable indicator after 1900. The Courant's records of advertising volume start in 1913.

a. Figures for 1913 through 1928 from Courant's records.

b. Figures for 1929 through 1964 from Media records.

c. Six months.

Index